A Cultural Perspective on a Historic Chinese City

People of Nanjing

YE ZHAOYAN
Translated by David Charles East

Bridge21 Publications | Alhambra, CA

People of Nanjing: A Cultural Perspective on a Historic Chinese City
by YE Zhaoyan
Copyright ©2021 YE Zhaoyan

Published by Bridge21 Publications, LLC
Distributed by Casemate Group
Casemate Academic: USA and North America
Oxbow Books: UK, Europe, and the Rest of the World

Originally published in Chinese in 2016 as 南京人 by Nanjing University Press.
English language rights are licensed to Bridge21 Publications, LLC.
All rights reserved.
No reproduction and distribution without permission.

Published in the United States of America
ISBN 978-1-62643-064-8 Hardcover
ISBN 978-1-62643-076-1 ePub | ebook pdf | Kindle

Contents

The Nostalgia Complex	7
The History of Nanjing	13
The Regal Aura of the Golden Hill	21
The Sound of a Vanquished Nation	29
Opportunities for the City	37
A Strategic Town in the Southeast	45
A Picture of Migration	53
The Figures of the Six Dynasties and Nanjing Radishes	61
South Nanjing	71
North Nanjing	77
Eating in Nanjing	85
Drinking in Nanjing (Part I)	93
Drinking in Nanjing (Part II)	101
Leisure in Nanjing	109
The Seasons of Nanjing	119
Nanjingers	127
The Outsiders of Nanjing	135
Nanjing's Authors	141
The Salaried Classes of Nanjing	149
The Men of Nanjing	155
The Women of Nanjing (Part I)	163
The Women of Nanjing (Part II)	171

Nanjing, 100 Years Ago	179
Nanjing, History, and Culture	189
On the Qinhuai River	199
Tianxia Wenshu ("The Literary Center of All-Under-Heaven")	205
Excursions on Donkeyback	214
The Streets that Lu Xun Walked	217
Zhu Xie	219
Remembering Tiger Bridge Prison	221
The Ballad of Nanjing	223
Remembering the Dead	226
Old Buildings Lost	228
The Season for Love Songs	233
Remembering the Willow	239
Seeing the Willow Through the Mists	241
The 480 Temples of the Southern Dynasties	244
Autumn Cool and Summer Heat	247
Cycling in Nanjing	250
A Gathering at Anleyuan	252
Nanjing in Culture	255
Nanjing's Character and its Authors	259
Drinking Tea at the Vanguard Bookstore	265
Repairing the City Walls	267
Inscriptions on the Bricks of the City Wall	269
The Ineffable Xuanwu Lake	271
Nanjing, Nanjing	273
Nanjing in the Xinhai Revolution	287

The Nostalgia Complex

One

Nanjing has no use for nostalgia. A place of beauty which is located south of the Yangtze, it was once Jinling, the Seat of Kings. For ten dynasties, it stood as the capital; it has seen the rise and fall of a hundred generations. Many years ago, Nanjing's rivers and mountains granted it a position of strength, attracting countless heroes and warriors who fought for sovereignty, for a place to establish their great capital and to bear witness to their deeds. It is a place of stories, a place of interest. A land that has inspired impassioned sighs and lines upon lines of literature, both good and bad.

The rarer a thing is, the greater its value. Many cities will shout themselves hoarse to protect their historic monuments, the dwellings of their famous figures, and their crumbling buildings. In Nanjing, such places are of little import. They are in great supply, and it is no great tragedy if such a place should crumble to dust.

Perhaps the sites and relics of history do not necessarily require our protection to survive. Many of Nanjing's great places have vanished without trace, but perhaps it is precisely because they no longer exist that they are remembered all the more. Nostalgia is a psychological complex; it is an innate thing. Sometimes those historical sites which only exist in our imaginations hold more interest and provoke more thought than the overprotected relics of our modern day.

For example, Fenghuang Mountain rose greatly in reputation and value after Li Bai wrote his poem about it:

Through Sanshan's mists I catch a glimpse of blue sky
The water split in two by an island of white herons

Li Bai's poem has been passed down through the ages. Whether Fenghuang Mountain actually exists is of no real consequence. Historical records suggest that Fenghuang Mountain was of little importance. The river waters have changed their course, and we shall never see Fenghuang's majesty again. The incorporeal will triumph again and again over the tangible. Falsehood may defeat truth. The spiritual will vanquish the material. It is impossible to imagine that a pseudo-classical building made of reinforced concrete has any need to exist. Thus, anyone who wished to restore Fenghuang Mountain to its former glory would be committing complete folly. Returning to the old ways usually destroys the old. This lesson is only too common.

Two

Once, as I passed over the ancient ferry crossing at Guazhou, a signboard suddenly caught my eye. It was particularly noticeable. At the top was clearly written: "HERE, DU SHINIANG SUBMERGED THE TREASURE CHEST IN ANGER". I was rather surprised. How could one say such a thing so resolutely? On what grounds could one make such an arbitrary assertion? How could one act so unilaterally?

In such a vast body of water, the river rolls along, its turbid waves dashing skyward. How could one say that this was the place where Du Shiniang cast off the treasure chest? That which a novelist writes as amusement may come to be taken as truth, and it is rather amusing to spoil their fun. On many occasions, I have heard people criticize Nanjingers. Both outsiders and Nanjingers themselves will earnestly denounce the people of Nanjing for their inability to preserve historical relics and their lack of awareness regarding the ways of conservation. The subtext to such criticism is that Nanjingers are stupid, that they lack knowledge and that they do not understand their own history when there are so many things that they might flaunt.

You might well say that Nanjingers are simple-minded. But you cannot say that they have no knowledge of historical preservation. Historical sites always take on the flavor of human affairs. If there is heart, then that will show. If there is no heart, then there is no use in trying to make things better. History cannot be repaired. It is not just Fenghuang Mountain. It is the place where the Jin dynasty's General Zhou Chu studied, and the place of Qing poet Yuan Mei's private Suiyuan garden at Xiaocangshan; to rebuild such places would be to gild the lily. To expend so much in human and physical resources would not be as beneficial as promoting the reading of books, thus both saving money and accruing knowledge.

History is created. It cannot be produced through preservation. History is history. If all of Nanjing's bright future is only for the sake of protecting a few historical sites and restoring a few cultural relics, that is an alarming prospect.

In the ancient capital of Nanjing, bustling with people and prosperity, historical sites and cultural relics can absolutely withstand being trampled on. In all of the nation's former capitals, it is possible that none have endured anything that can be compared to Nanjing's misfortunes. And no city has endured the trouble that Nanjing has. Nanjing's pain surpasses its splendor. Without destruction, there can be no construction. So much of Nanjing's landscape is famous. So, it may pass on its song for all eternity, while destruction may have its greatest effect. Destruction cannot eradicate history altogether. Heroes often create history; likewise, losers will leave their own mark upon it.

Three

History is everywhere in Nanjing. It permeates the air. There are plenty of places in Nanjing where one may remember things past.

The history of Nanjing is right beside us. One may summon up examples of its history from anywhere. When I was young, I lived close to Hubu Street. During the Southern Tang dynasty, this was the location of the Eastern Palace, the residence of the crown prince.

How many sorrows do you have?
They flow eastward like the river in spring.

The Southern Tang ruler poet Li Houzhu, who wrote this verse, grew up in this area.

It is not the case that the last traces of the Southern Tang have vanished from our sight. They are our ancestors, and with the help of historical records, we may guess at their historic locations. "The most ruthless of all are the willows of Taicheng", but the Taicheng we see today is fundamentally different from the one that was written by the Tang poets. Yet, the false Taicheng left to us by the people of the Ming dynasty is enough to satisfy our nostalgia.

Nanjingers do not make a great show of their genealogical records. Stelae throughout the city explain and comment upon historical method. It is true that good intentions lie behind the preservation of historical sites and relics, but it is difficult to avoid the ambition to exploit tourist dollars. Antiquity is an inexhaustible resource. There are countless places in Nanjing where one may erect signage, and justifiably so. Every street has a story, and every old building has something to say. Nanjing is a natural historical museum.

But now we must speak of events that transpired less than a century ago. For example, my office was located for many years at the provincial military compound at Number 10 Hunan Road. Opening the window, one could see a building that looked rather like a western-style palace, then catch sight of two armed guards standing outside the gate. No one could imagine that inside the tall, yellowing clock tower, beneath that precipitously slanted roof, a world-shaking incident had occurred not even a hundred years prior. Many people are unaware that this was once the location of the Jiangsu Provincial Assembly, or the seat of command of General Zhang Xun. When the Xinhai Revolution erupted in 1911, Zhang Xun escaped without trace. Here, representatives of the 17 rebel provinces of the nation met and declared the establishment of the Republic of China. They elected Sun Yat-sen as interim president. In other words, this is the delivery room where the Republic of China was born. It became the provisional location for the Senate of the Republic of China. It is worth remembering that this senate was the first constitutional institution established not only in the history of the republic, but in the history of China itself.

It was here that Wang Jingwei was attacked in an assassination attempt. Because this place was designated by the Kuomindang (i.e., the Nationalist Party) as their party headquarters after Nanjing was declared to be the capital, it is said that an assassin wanted to assassinate Chiang Kai-shek, but because Chiang did not appear, Wang Jingwei became the assassin's target instead. The attempt on Wang Jingwei's life illustrates the determination of the Chinese people during the war of resistance.

Four

Nanjing truly has no need for nostalgia. It is a city that can never escape the history that lingers in its air. Wherever you go, you walk in the shadow of the past. History has bestowed a rich and fertile inheritance upon Nanjing, but not all of it is necessarily good.

In Nanjing, one's mood can find itself easily intertwined with the nostalgia complex. One may tumble deep into the annals of history and never climb out. Just as one may learn from the past in order not to make the same mistakes, one may find oneself caught deep within the trap of history. If they did not regard the ancient city of Nanjing while still being mindful of the need to break new ground, then the people of Nanjing would be left blinded, bound hand and foot, and immobilized by the burden of history.

If a city relies on nostalgia to survive, then it has no future. Nanjing is not the only ancient capital city of China. But few cities have undergone such great, intense changes as Nanjing; few are as worthy of the nostalgia of later generations. It is of no matter whether you seek to understand it or not. The people of Nanjing cannot escape the nostalgia complex. For those of us au fait with culture, the city of Nanjing is a window through which we may look back on history.

The History of Nanjing

One

Nanjing's history can be traced back to around 300,000 years ago. In a karst cave in the Tangshan hills, a place known as Hulu Cave, the fossilized skull and teeth of the "Nanjing Man" were recently discovered. This was perhaps the primogenitor of the people of Nanjing. I once had a badge that featured a reconstruction of the skull. It had a benign face, with large ears and square cheeks. It looked quite adorable.

Around 6000-4000 BCE, within the confines of the modern city, around the area of the Drum Tower and the Qinhuai River, the first tribe of Nanjing's residents emerged. Later on, during the period of the legendary Five Emperors, Nanjing was part of ancient Yangzhou. The scribe of the Wenxian Tongkao chronicles the history of ancient Yangzhou: "Shun established 12 fiefdoms, one of which was Yangzhou." The Erya also gives this explanation: "South of the Yangtze is the area known as Yangzhou." Thus, we learn that ancient Yangzhou and modern-day Yangzhou signify two different regions.

The boundaries of Nanjing were not clear-cut. During the Zhou dynasty, it belonged to the State of Wu. From a geographical perspective, the State of Chu was extremely close by, and as a result of their proximity, the two states went to war at that time. At one time, Wu made great accomplishments. However, by the end of the Spring and Autumn period, the long-suffering and vengeful King Goujian of Yue exterminated Wu and made Nanjing the border of the State of Yue. Sixty years later, the State of Chu eliminated the State of Yue, and bestowed upon Nanjing the name Jinling. Then, 90 years after that, Qin Shi Huang wiped out the State of Chu, united China, and divided it into 36 prefectures. Jinling was renamed Moling. It was first administered by Zhang Prefecture, and then by Kuaiji Prefecture.

Two

In the 400 years covering the Qin and Han dynasties, Nanjing was a small, unremarkable city. That was the case until 229 CE, when Sun Quan, the King of Wu, renamed Moling to call it Jianye. It was here that he declared himself emperor. From that point forth, Nanjing truly began to grow in renown. This was the beginning of Nanjing's reputation as the capital city of six different dynasties. It became the first great capital of the southeast.

From its beginnings, Nanjing has been a place of short-lived dynasties. After Sun Quan's death, Sun Hao, another emperor of the Kingdom of Wu, had only been on the throne for 16 years when the Jin dynasty's armies forced their way through the city's stone walls. Sun Hao surrendered, and Wu was abolished.

Thirty-seven years later, the Western Jin fell, and the Eastern Jin declared Nanjing their capital. It remained so for a full century. The Eastern Jin general Liu Yu broke away from the dynasty and marched northward, capturing Chang'an, the capital city of the Later Qin of the Sixteen Kingdoms. Taking advantage of the situation, he wiped out the Eastern Jin dynasty and declared himself emperor. Liu Yu named his own nation "Song", but this was not the same as the Song dynasty that came in between the Tang and Yuan dynasties, instead coming over 500 years prior. Thus, it is called the Liu Song dynasty.

After the Liu Song came the Qi dynasty; after the Qi, the Liang dynasty; and after that the Chen dynasty. Eastern Wu and Eastern Jin, combined with Song, Qi, Liang, and Chen, together formed the Six Dynasties. Song, Qi, Liang, and Chen ruled for over 100 years altogether. Of these, Qi's reign was the shortest at only 23 years.

The end of the Six Dynasties, from a Chinese historical perspective, was a good thing. It meant the end of the historical period of China's separation between the Northern and Southern dynasties. The conflict between north and south eventually came to a close. The south lost and capitulated to the north. The Chen dynasty, the last of the Six Dynasties, was wiped out, and this meant that Nanjing went from splendor to ruin. Because the Sui dynasty that had wiped out the Liang dynasty came from the north, the people worried that the south's power might rise once more. Emperor Wen of Sui chose a particularly violent method to prevent this: razing Nanjing to the ground. Nanjing suffered terrible damage and would only recover its strength many years later.

Three

During the Tang, Song, and Yuan dynasties, Nanjing held an important economic position. It was a strategic town administered by the centralized northern state, a stronghold of governance over the south. The regional governors dispatched from the north kept a close eye on the south's power from this important watch post. The populous and affluent area south of the Yangtze provided a material safeguard for the bustling city of Nanjing. In the short period between the fall of the Tang and the rise of the Song dynasty, Nanjing was home to the court of Tang of the Five Southern Dynasties; this was merely a brief interlude in history.

The most enthusiastically discussed product of this interlude was Li Houzhu, who wrote of sorrows that "flow eastward like the river in spring".

When Zhu Yuanzhang founded the Ming dynasty in Nanjing, declaring himself Emperor Hongwu, Nanjing would once again catch the eye of the nation. Nanjing had finally reached a level of development like never before. The basic structure of modern-day Nanjing was laid down in the early years of the Ming dynasty. The Ming dynasty lasted nearly 300 years, though Nanjing's days as its capital were not long, lasting only around 50 years altogether.

The Ming dynasty court moved to Beijing, and Nanjing was officially given its name of Nanjing, the "Southern Capital". In China's history, at least seven cities have been dubbed the southern capital. For example, Chengdu in Sichuan Province. Emperor Xuanzong of Tang, escaping the An-Shi Rebellion, fled to Chengdu and dubbed it the southern capital. And, having conquered the Song dynasty capital of Kaifeng, the Liao and Jin dynasties named it the southern capital. The Song dynasty also gave the title of southern capital to the city of Shangqiu in Henan Province. Most interestingly, our modern-day capital of Beijing was also once named the southern capital. At that point, it was under the control of the Later Jin of the Five Dynasties.

From the Ming dynasty onward, Nanjing held the monopoly on the title "Southern Capital". Nanjing held a great many different names throughout history. Apart from Jinling, and Moling under Qin Shi Huang, it was also named Jianye, with the "ye" being represented by two different characters at different points, both pronounced ye. After the War of the Three Kingdoms, Nanjing was briefly called Jiangning. Ning meant a place of peace and security. In the last years of the Western Jin, because Emperor Min's personal name was Sima Ye, its name was changed from Jianye to Jiankang in order to avoid breaking naming taboos (the ye in Jianye being the same as the emperor's personal name).

During the Yuan dynasty, Nanjing became the Jiankang Road, and then the Jiqing Road. This was the name given to Nanjing by the swift, fierce, horse-riding Mongols. Nanjing has two connections to the Yuan dynasty. The first is that the Mongol armies attacked and entered the walls of Nanjing from the direction of the Yuhuatai district. The

Japanese army attacked the city from the same position 662 years later. The second is that the Mongol nobles particularly liked the silk produced south of the Yangtze River. Thus, a great weaving industry developed, becoming the foundation for the establishment of the silk-weaving industries of the Ming and Qing dynasties.

By the Qing dynasty, the official name of Nanjing's administrative subdivision was Jiangning. Nanjing was the seat of the Viceroy of Liangjiang, but the scope of its jurisdiction was rather scattered. During the reign of Emperor Shunzhi of Qing, Nanjing was conquered, and the small court of the short-lived Southern Ming dynasty collapsed. Nanjing became part of Jiangnan Province, and Yingtian Province became Jiangning Province. The viceroy had administration over Jiangnan, Jiangxi, and Henan. After that, the scope of its jurisdiction changed constantly. It was more or less responsible for the provinces of Jiangsu, Anhui, and Jiangxi.

When the Taiping Heavenly Kingdom was established, Nanjing became its capital, its name changing to Tianjing ("Heavenly Capital").

Four

Jinling, Moling, Jiangning, Jianye, Jiankang—all of these were names bestowed upon Nanjing by the various edicts of kings and emperors. Nanjing has many other names, beloved by the poets of nostalgia. In ancient poetry, it was often seen as the "White Gate of the Willow", and spoken of regularly—for instance, "The willow by the white gate hides many crows" and "the hills surround the walls beneath white". Even today, a district of Nanjing is called Baixia, "Beneath White".

Song dynasty writer Zhang Dunyi's *Compilation of Deeds of the Six Dynasties* records that an emperor disliked the superstitious story of the "White Gate". It is quite a story. This emperor saw white as an inauspicious and taboo color. Once, an official carelessly referred to the "White Gate". As a result, the emperor was enraged, and scolded him shrewishly: "May the gate of your own house be white!"

The words are vivid, and I investigated the story further. Emperor Ming of Liu Song was the one who uttered these harsh words. He reigned for around eight years.

Nanjing also has a host of other names which are almost completely forgotten by many, such names including Jiangcheng, Hushu, Danyang, Laizhu, Pingling, and Guihua. One could write an entire essay on each name. But I am in no mood to do so. Such an essay would rely entirely on guesswork. I believe that Hushu has a connection to the pressed duck that Nanjing is known for producing today, much like how Danyang can be connected to "Little Danyang" on the east side of the city.

The section "Records of Geography" in the History of the Jin Dynasty explains the origin of "Danyang": the name is due to the red willows on the nearby mountainside. "Dan" refers to the color red while "yang" refers to the willows. "Danyang" (with the character yang referring instead to the sun) is no more than an error that has survived through the years.

Five

Nanjing was the capital city of the Republic of China. After the National Revolutionary Army was victorious in their Northern Expedition, Beijing's name was changed to Beiping. Ping in this instance referred to an auspicious sign of peace, just as Nanjing's name was changed to Jiangning ("Peaceful River"). There was a hidden agenda behind the change. After Nanjing became the capital, it was classified as a directly governed city by the Executive Yuan of the Nationalist government. The government of Jiangsu Province moved to Zhenjiang. This remained the case until Chiang Kai-shek fell from power in 1949. Nanjing's first mayor was Liu Jiwen. The most notable of his achievements in office was the opening of Nanjing's roads. Nanjing's Zhongshan East Road, Zhongshan North Road, Zhongshan Road, and Zhongshan South Road were all opened under his administration. After 1949, Nanjing became the seat of the regional government. The renowned Marshal Liu Bocheng was the first mayor of this new Nanjing.

The Regal Aura of the Golden Hill

One

Visitors coming from elsewhere who have read a number of books on Nanjing will tour the city and find themselves sighing with emotion at the regal air of its forbidding terrain.

So much has been said about its aura of imperial grandeur, and its symbolism of the fate of monarchs, that one could write a series of essays on the matter. Nanjing is a place that either creates emperors or plays host to them. For better or worse, Nanjing has been the ancient capital of ten different dynasties, and so this point comes as no surprise.

The Illustrated Classic of Jinling explains why Nanjing was once named Jinling: "Long ago, when King Wei of Chu saw its regal splendor, he buried his gold here to safeguard it, and thus it was named Jinling [Golden Hill]." Another, more specific explanation suggests that King Wei of Chu buried a small golden statuette here, but this statuette has never been uncovered.

It is also said that when Emperor Qin Shi Huang toured the south, Nanjing's regal air worried him greatly. So that his descendants would not be disturbed by it, he ordered a canal cut into the Qinhuai River in order to drain it of its royal aura. The Chinese expression "where dragons coil and tigers crouch" refers to a strategically significant place. It is an abbreviation of "The dragons of Zhongshan coil and stone tigers crouch"—an expression uttered by Zhuge Liang, the famous military leader of the Three Kingdoms period. By this, he meant that the Purple Mountain coiled itself around the capital like a dragon, and the city's walls guarded it with the might of a tiger.

To this day, there is no definite evidence to corroborate these stories involving King Wei of Chu and Qin Shi Huang. Zhuge Liang's words are not completely reliable either because investigation has shown that he never visited Nanjing. Perhaps these are merely tales, stories woven by later generations. These tales, though, have hoodwinked many; even the Tang dynasty poet Li Bai believed them without doubt. He wrote of Nanjing: "This place is a residence of emperors, and in its mountains dragons and tigers crouch." Successive generations of poetry have praised Nanjing, and Li Bai's words are resolute.

The first emperor to declare Nanjing as his capital city was Sun Quan of the Three Kingdoms period. Talk of Jinling's regal aura quite possibly arose from this time. This story repeats itself throughout history. When a new political order is about to be born, there are always a number of advisors willing to offer their advice, finding reasons to establish capital cities in specific locations. Sun Quan's establishment of Nanjing as the capital of the state of Eastern Wu has had a definite effect on the city's history. In fact, for Sun Quan, who had taken control of the lower reaches of the Yangtze that year, there was quite a degree of hesitancy when it came to choosing a capital. His first choice for his capital city had not been Nanjing, but rather Wuchang.

In 211 CE, Sun Quan moved his political center from Jingkou (modern-day Zhenjiang) to Nanjing. The state-building ideal for the Eastern Wu was to expand the limits of their power westward. Moving west from Jingkou to Nanjing was not enough. By 221 CE, Sun Quan decided to make Exian his capital, changing its name to Wuchang, and in 229 CE, he took the throne as emperor in Wuchang. This Wuchang is not the same as the Wuchang district of the city of Wuhan. The Wuchang where Sun Quan founded his capital is the modern-day city of Ezhou in Hubei Province. Because Wuchang was located upstream from Nanjing, the clans east of the river who formed the backbone of the Eastern Wu regime's power did not wish to move too far away from their own spheres of power. Thus, one by one, they agitated for the title of capital city to return to Nanjing. A folk song of the time spoke of it:

I would rather drink the waters of Jianye [Nanjing] than eat the fish of Wuchang
I would rather die in Jianye than live in Wuchang

Sun Quan had no other option. In the same year that he took the throne, 229 CE, he returned the title of capital to Nanjing. Mentions of Jinling's regal air were also quite possibly a part of the folk ballads of the time. Later generations have become accustomed to using the mountains that surround Nanjing as an explanation for its royal aura. In fact, Nanjing is not unique in its topography along the banks of the Yangtze. It is a matter of human effort; Nanjing's mountain topography is important, and its water features are equally important. The Eastern Wu navy was fierce, indeed. Cao Cao's later defeat at the Battle of Red Cliffs was reliant on naval force. At that time, the Qinhuai River was vast, and there were many lakes surrounding Nanjing in which navies could run drills. The famous stone-walled city was the navy's base of operations at that time. As a result, Sun Quan ultimately established his capital in Nanjing after weighing all kinds of advantages and disadvantages and giving sufficient consideration to geographical and social conditions as well as timing for war.

Later on, another Emperor of Wu, Sun Hao, carried out almost the exact same course of action. In a huge waste of manpower and resources, he moved his capital to Wuchang, wasting at least a year there before the capital moved back to Nanjing once more.

 Two

Jinling's royal air can be seen from two different perspectives.

From one perspective, it offered a pretext of boldness and confidence to those men who wished to reign as emperor in Nanjing. The subtext of its royal aura is that the Emperor, the Son of Heaven, receives the Mandate of Heaven, and so the fact that this place has such regal splendor is the so-called Will of Heaven. It is not that I am so bold as to revolt against the Emperor, but that the Mandate of Heaven may not be disobeyed. This so-called regal aura serves as an overt act of division.

During the Three Kingdoms era, Sun Quan was slow to adopt the title of emperor. An important reason for this was that he felt that it was being illegitimately conferred. He waited patiently until Cao Cao and Liu Bei both declared themselves emperors. Only when the time was right did he uneasily establish Eastern Wu and claim the title of emperor. Eastern Wu was the first dynasty to name Nanjing as its capital. One could say that this is when Nanjing's regal aura first arose, seemingly lacking in confidence.

Seen from another angle, the possibility of rebellion exists in Nanjing. In all of China's history prior to the Yuan dynasty, capitals were usually founded near the Yellow River. The Han, Tang, and Song dynasties, not to mention the Shang and the Zhou—all influential dynasties—almost always situated their capitals upon the Yellow River. The Yangtze River Basin was always subordinate to the Yellow River Basin. When attempting to seize the throne, this was a fact which was almost impossible to ignore. Whoever controlled the Central Plain would be Emperor of China. It was the established practice that orders coming from the Yellow River Basin had to be obeyed. Thus, much of Nanjing's regal aura signifies this action of prizing the Yangtze River as paramount over the Yellow River. To the northern political order which centered itself around the Yellow River, its royal air was a reminder, and also a warning. A hidden factor of instability.

In truth, it had few opportunities to pose a threat to the north. In a crude comparison of semantics, we can see that, when the south confronted the north, the north occupied a position of complete superiority. Many years ago, we became accustomed to saying "to go down south"—the Chinese expression suggests a downhill journey. It was simple for the northern powers to invade the south, akin to playing a game or taking a leisurely trip. And when it came to southern resistance to the north—"going up north" in Chinese suggests climbing upward—these moving and tragic northern expeditions were succeed-or-die-trying affairs.

Northern expeditions were not easy undertakings. To rally one's troops for the journey northward would be a spectacular sight, indeed. It was a serious affair, travelling against the desolate winds and cold waters, with soldiers uncertain of their return. There are two northern expeditions remembered in history as the most successful. The first is that of Zhu Yuanzhang, Emperor Hongwu of Ming, when he overthrew the Yuan dynasty and returned the rule of China to the Han people. The second is the Northern Expedition of the National Revolutionary Army in 1926. The National Revolutionary Government began its Northern Expedition in Guangzhou. After assaulting Wuchang, the Revolutionary Government—in accordance with the wishes of the late premier Sun Yat-sen—established its capital in Nanjing in April of 1927. Nanjing's significance as a capital lay in its legitimization of the Northern Expedition armies as the troops of the ruler. The year after the National Revolutionary Government declared Nanjing its capital, its troops entered Beijing and brought the era of the Northern Warlords to an end.

Three

Anyone who has read *A New Account of the Tales of the World* will likely remember "Weeping at the New Pavilion". In 316 CE, Liu Yao took Chang'an, ending the Western Jin dynasty. The next year, the emperor founded the capital of the Eastern Jin dynasty in Nanjing. At the time, the vast areas surrounding the Yellow River had all been invaded by foreign ethnic groups. Many scholar-officials escaped to

Nanjing, and it became a gathering place for the cultural elite of the Central Plain.

Whenever the weather was good, these literati would invite each other to the New Pavilion, sitting on the grass to eat, drink, and be merry. In the face of this beautiful scenery, an old bureaucrat named Zhou gave a genteel sigh. "The landscape remains the same, but its ruler has changed!" His words reached the ears of the others who sat nearby, and who looked at each other and wept. Only the Prime Minister Wang Dao, who was there at the time, became angry. "We must unite our strength, swear devotion to our emperor, and recover our motherland. How can you weep like a slave whose homeland is no more?"

The people of the Eastern Jin never did recover their motherland, but the story of weeping at the New Pavilion has left two echoes in Nanjing. The first is that of pitiful lamentation. The second of heroic exhortations to recover lost territory. These entirely different sounds have reverberated throughout Nanjing for many years. Unfortunately, the former is a musical theme, a chorus, while the latter is rarely heard, and is little more than a lone shout.

Nanjing's status as an ancient capital was mostly a result of groups being forced to relinquish territory elsewhere. As a capital city, Nanjing could make edicts upon the whole nation. Its power as a center of government seems limited to the early Ming dynasty and the short years when China was united under the government of the Republic of China. In many more instances, Nanjing was merely the seat of governments-in-exile. When the Western Jin was no more, Nanjing played host to the Eastern Jin as it tried to retain its remaining territory; when the Ming dynasty fell, Nanjing did the same for the Southern Ming dynasty.

Nanjing has always been a place where governments attempt to hold on to power. The Eastern Jin did so for 100 years, unlike the Southern Ming, which lasted less than a year under the onslaught of the Qing armies. Nanjing's rulers seem destined to rule over only half of their own countries. If their territories are not delineated by the

Yangtze, then they end at the Huai River. The valiant north has always held a position of superiority, and the weak south has always been in a position of defense.

The Eastern Jin and the Southern Ming both chose Nanjing as their capital, and when China suffered invasions by foreign races, it became an outpost for the preservation of the culture of the Han people. In such crucial moments, the city's royal air did not serve as a means of division, but as a way of recovering lost territory, of restoring China to the Han people. The cultural confrontation between the Yellow River and the Yangtze River is no more. The two cultures have been forced to integrate. "Regal Jinling" is an epithet of the united Han people.

When foreign tribes invaded, the tyrannical landowners of the north became stray dogs, anxious and desperate. As buildings fell, darkness descended, and food stocks dwindled, the northern landowners fled like rats on a sinking ship, bringing their official titles, their linguistic habits, their families, their servants, and their ill-gotten gains to Nanjing.

An emaciated camel is still larger than a horse; the vanquished north was still greater than the south. Nanjing had no choice but to accept these defeated northerners. In Nanjing, northerners went from being guests to being rulers. The fallen generals were still heroes, and Nanjing could only continue to accept these bedraggled remnants of the north as their superiors. There was nothing the city could do except accept the leadership of the routed north. Unfortunately, the regal aura of Jinling, in most cases, became a grand pretext for the defeated north to remain in the city, a reason for them to carry on enjoying themselves and ride roughshod over others.

Its royal air became a shot in the arm for the decaying north, which had lost its territory and had no home to return to. Talk of reclamation of lost territory became specious and quixotic—little more than empty words. At times, no one even wanted to speak such empty words out loud. The northern political powers that fled to Nanjing very rarely undertook the great work of re-uniting the country once more. As a result, the regal aura of Nanjing is no more than an illusion.

The Sound of a Vanquished Nation

One

There is no ancient city more befitting of being considered a place to listen to the sound of a vanquished nation than Nanjing. Jinling has had its regal aura since antiquity, but rather than bold, visionary words, it is a sigh of those who cannot bear to recall the past.

That the Southern Song did not establish a capital in Nanjing is an exception that historians have commented upon. The Jurchen Jin armies were ruthless, and they broke through the Yellow River region, crossing the Huai River and even crossing over the Yangtze. Emperor Gaozong of Song made his escape and did not stop for breath until he reached Hangzhou. Many Southern Song patriots such as Li Gang, Yue Fei, and the poets Xin Qiji and Lu You urged the emperor to move his capital from Hangzhou to Nanjing. This was because establishing a capital in Nanjing would be a greater show of strength in reclaiming lost territory than doing so in Hangzhou. The concept of Nanjing's regal aura was deeply imprinted upon the minds of the people of the Southern Song. It could be said that moving the capital was an inescapable dream for Lu You. He wrote poetry on the matter: "In my dreams, I forget the difficulties of the evening's journey / I write in cursive script on moving the capital city." He even angered the emperor with his insistence, but his determination did not waver. In *Notes from an Old Scholar's Hut*, he wrote: "The walls of Jiankang

[Nanjing] were built by Li Jing [Emperor of Southern Tang]. They are three zhang [~10m] high, and because of the rugged and solid landscape, they can only be assaulted from the east and the north. With the moat surrounding them, they will hold fast."

The Southern Song court considered moving the capital to Nanjing on a number of occasions. Emperor Gaozong of the Song dynasty once declared Nanjing to be his eastern capital and ordered that the palace and the city be renovated. Yue Fei defeated Jin Wuzhu on Nanjing's Niushou Mountain. After forcing the powerful Jin armies across the Yangtze, Gaozong even made his residence in Nanjing for nearly a year. Perhaps it was the excessive heat of the Nanjing summer at a time without air conditioning. Perhaps it was the fear that the Jin armies would cross the river once more, leaving them without enough time to escape from the area surrounding the riverbank. Thus, on the pretext of "cultivating morality and virtue and not staying in a chosen strategic location," they slipped away once more to Hangzhou. Hangzhou was naturally a fine place, and was unlike Nanjing, where they carried the banner of "Regal Jinling"—endlessly dreaming of reclaiming their lost territory and, as a result, spending every moment on the front line feeling apprehensive. Recovering lost territory was easier said than done. Emperor Gaozong seemed to feel that speaking such fine-sounding and yet empty words was thoroughly tiring. "The warm breeze brings a fragrance that intoxicates the travelers, simply turning Hangzhou into Bianzhou [Kaifeng, the former Song dynasty capital]." The Song dynasty's court at Hangzhou indulged in pleasures and forgot their homeland and their duty, staying in Nanjing for 150 years, longer than any other dynasty in history.

Two

As it happened, Emperor Gaozong mentioned a key point. Perhaps cultivating virtue and morality really was more practical than remaining in a strategic location. The Southern Song made no use of Nanjing's forbidding territory, and indeed only held on to half the country. Whether its prosperity and decline were a result of human endeavor or the terrain, whether or not Emperor Gaozong feared the Jin, and whether or not he was on the route to surrender, at least one thing is clear: the power of Nanjing's terrain could not save a defeated nation from its fate. Gaozong understood this about the royal aura of Nanjing. Sun Quan of the Eastern Wu repaired the city's stone walls. Li Jing of the Southern Tang repaired the three-zhang high walls of Jiankang. Emperor Taizu of Ming is said to have built the world's longest walls. All of these efforts were of no use. Whether it was the Eastern Wu, the Southern Tang, or the illustrious Ming dynasty, in their second generations, the problem re-surfaced. Ever since Emperor Sun Hao of Eastern Wu "dropped his banners and came forth from the stone walls in surrender," being the first emperor of a defeated nation in Nanjing's history, the city has been the graveyard of one state after another.

No other ancient city is like Nanjing in having had so many noted "last emperors"—the last remaining monarchs of dynasties—worthy of discussion. Dynasties have ended in other places, but Nanjing is the resting place of the most historically significant dynasties. Other places have stories of defeated nations, but their tales are nowhere near as moving as Nanjing's. It is puzzling that Nanjing's royal air would seem to be no less ephemeral than a soap bubble, and that its forbidding territory seemed to be of little aid. In all of the battles fought to protect Nanjing throughout history, none has ended in victory. Those who arrive at its gates are seldom good-intentioned; when great armies amass on its borders, Nanjing is always predestined to fall. When Sun Hao installed an iron chain across the Yangtze, he wished to obstruct the Western Jin fleet. It was a romantic notion and could only end in ridicule.

There is no harm in looking on these last dynasts of shattered empires with pity. When Sun Hao, the last Emperor of the Eastern Wu, surrendered, his hands were bound, and he was carried to the gate of the Western Jin army camp. When the last Emperor of Chen of the Southern dynasties found himself with soldiers of the Sui armies at the walls, he panicked and hid with his favored concubine in a dried-up well. He was discovered by Sui troops, who spent most of the day trying to get him out of the well. Li Houzhu, the last emperor of the Southern Tang, took his wife Queen Zhou the Younger to Henan and surrendered. All day, as he said, he "washed his face solely with tears." The beautiful Queen Zhou the Younger was even raped by Emperor Taizong of Song. It is said that Li Houzhu died by taking poison that had been given to him, made from the strychnine tree. The poison makes one convulse and curl up in a miserable death.

My state lasted forty years and stretched over three thousand *li* [1500 kilometers].

My Phoenix Pavilion and Dragon Tower touched the heavens, with jade trees and jasper branches a net of mist, and I never once took up a spear.

Suddenly, I was a slave, my waist frail and my temples grey as I ground away.

Finally came the day that I said a panicked farewell at the ancestral temple, the court musicians playing songs of parting.

Gazing at the court maidens, I shed tears.

Li Houzhu was a fine poet. Unfortunately, he was not cut out to be an emperor. He lost his country, weeping not for his ancestral shrine but for his women. He would perhaps have been more suited to being a secretary of culture.

Three

For many years, more than one person has harbored a degree of skepticism regarding Nanjing's royal aura. "Three hundred years have passed, disappearing like a dream at daybreak. Where are the coiling dragons of Zhongshan?" The Late Tang poet Li Shangyin accompanied his father to Nanjing before the age of ten, then living in the city for six or seven years. Later, when he became an official responsible for taxes on iron and salt, he travelled again to the area south of the Yangtze. In Nanjing, he wrote a series of poems, including a poem that ended with these two lines. With a questioning tone, he expresses his disbelief over Nanjing's majesty.

    Another Late Tang poet, Du Mu, also seemed not to believe in Nanjing's royal eminence. In his famous work *Red Cliffs*, he reaches a stunning conclusion: "If the east wind had not aided [Eastern Wu General] Zhou Yu [in his fight against Cao Cao], the Qiao sisters [Sun Ce and Zhou Yu's wives] would be captured and sent away to Tongque [Cao Cao's palace]." It was not the crouching tigers and coiling dragons of Nanjing's landscape that saved it from being overrun by Cao Cao, but the naturally occurring eastern wind. This timely east wind saved Eastern Wu from its demise, and thus Zhou Yu could "fan himself in his casual clothing, laughing and chatting as Cao Cao's navy was scattered."

Later generations would take exception to the statement that "The Qiao sisters would be taken to Tongque," believing it to be the joke of a frivolous youth, another example of weeping for women rather than for the ancestral temple. Without this eastern wind, not only would the Qiaos have been captured, but the war would have concluded with the ruination of the country and the starvation of its people. The trifling young women were nothing in comparison to the great cause of the nation; how could these two things be juxtaposed?

This juxtaposition is rather amusing. In fact, the State of Wu cannot be separated from the Qiao sisters. Da Qiao was the sister-in-law of Sun Quan and Xiao Qiao was the wife of Zhou Yu. Cao Cao wanted to capture two women; how could Eastern Wu escape defeat? Historically, the eastern wind blowing across the Red Cliffs, far from Nanjing, allowed the city to escape the nation's downfall just once. National subjugation was not a rare occurrence in Nanjing. It was simply a symbol of the city. The music of Nanjing is the sound of a vanquished nation. It reverberates through the air, lingering as a warning to future generations. It seems that the role that history has bestowed upon Nanjing is twofold: unceasing splendor, then unending ruin. During the Six Dynasties, it flourished and became a beautiful scene upon the Qinhuai River. Since the downfall of the nation was inevitable, living out one's days in a drunken haze in Nanjing became the best option. This drunken haze was the reason behind the nation's downfall, and also a result of it.

It is perhaps more accurate to say that Nanjing's air is not one of royalty, but of ruin.

Four

Zhu Yuanzhang, Emperor Hongwu of Ming, the first of his dynasty, was a powerful ruler. He built high walls in Nanjing, accumulated vast stores of grain, and established the illustrious Ming dynasty. After his death, his title passed to his heir and grandson, the Jianwen Emperor. Jianwen was a pitiful ruler. Before the former emperor's body was cold, his uncle Zhu Di, Prince of Yan, who was the fourth son of Zhu Yuanzhang, mounted a rebellion. Four years later, Zhu Di brought his armies to Nanjing and wrestled the title of emperor from his nephew's hands, crowning himself as the Yongle Emperor. Jianwen's ultimate fate is uncertain. One story suggests that he disguised himself and lived as a monk.

Under the Ming dynasty, the country finally escaped the clutches of a foreign power. Many people see Zhu Di's decision to move the capital as his own personal decision. It seems that his headquarters were in Beijing, and since he was emperor, he should indeed have moved the capital from Nanjing to his center of power. But this was not the case because what is often overlooked is that his decision to move the capital did not come immediately after he took the throne, but nearly two decades after he became emperor. Zhu Di had reigned in Nanjing for 18 years by that point, and his position was unassailable.

He had long ceased to be the rebellious Prince of Yan and had become the illustrious Yongle Emperor. In ruling the country, he was by no means inferior to his father Zhu Yuanzhang. His decision to move the capital had an extremely important effect on the Ming dynasty's almost-300-year rule.

The Yongle Emperor did not care for Nanjing's majesty. Although he had renovated its city walls, making them the country's finest, and built the grandest palace in history as well as the Ming tombs, he still firmly decided to leave Nanjing. It was a wise decision.

In fact, if his father Zhu Yuanzhang had not become feeble in his old age, he would likely have done the same. In Zhu Yuanzhang's later work, *On Sacrifices to the Kitchen God*, he laments that he is not strong enough to move the capital city despite his will to do so, and that he has no option but to resign himself to the Will of Heaven.

There were a number of reasons why Zhu Yuanzhang chose Nanjing. Primarily, it was because most of the territory of the north was still yet to come under his control. He chose Nanjing as his base because he had no alternative but to do so as a stopgap measure in order to unite the territories in the southeast and the middle stretches of the Yangtze. Zhu Yuanzhang accepted his advisors' suggestion to "take time in claiming the throne." He made full use of Nanjing's regal aura and did not dare to act ostentatiously, all in order to avoid the attacks of heroes from all sides. While he was quietly unifying the lands south of the Yangtze, the Red Turban Rebellion in the north, led by Han Lin'er and Liu Futong, was mounting its decisive battle against the Yuan dynasty, becoming a natural barrier to Zhu Yuanzhang's great cause of unification. In the south, Zhu Yuanzhang put an end to Chen Youliang, Zhang Shicheng, and Fang Guozhen. These men were the same as he was: all leaders of peasant rebellions, all ambitious about crowning themselves emperor. Zhu Yuanzhang was a calculating man. He spent as much as 12 years in Nanjing, and only after armies led by Xu Da attacked the Yuan capital of Dadu (Beijing) did he formally declare himself emperor.

Those who are familiar with the history of the Ming Dynasty

will know that Nanjing and Beijing were not the only capitals of the Ming dynasty; there was also the "Middle Capital" of Fengyang. Archeologists have discovered that plans for Fengyang could easily be considered a match for the palaces of Nanjing and Beijing. Fengyang was the former home of Zhu Yuanzhang. After he became ruler, he wanted to build a capital city in his former hometown and he officially initiated work on it.

The fundamental reason behind these plans was Zhu Yuanzhang's resourcefulness. He had heard the sound of national defeat that reverberated throughout Nanjing. Water may keep a boat afloat, but it may also sink it. The city of Nanjing could accomplish great things, but it could also destroy them. Nanjing was the best fortification for resisting the power of the north, but it was still unsuitable as a seat of national political power. In establishing Nanjing as a capital, there has always been a suspicion that one is being forced to relinquish the middle ground.

The Yongle Emperor followed the final wishes of his father, whose body lay in the Ming tombs of Nanjing. He knew full well that the Ming dynasty's true adversary would be the invasion of ethnic groups from the north, as well as the entrancing and decadent atmosphere of the south. If he had not relinquished his plans to move away, then the farce of the nation's downfall during the splendor of the Six Dynasties period would have repeated itself once more. The Yongle Emperor deserves to be called a hero of his age. He overcame hardship and chose the north. He died, and even had his tomb built in the north of Beijing, leaving behind another problem for his descendants: if they wanted to give up the country, it would mean relinquishing the tomb of their ancestor.

Opportunities for the City

One

Being designated as a capital will bring prosperity to any city. People will always build capitals up to be beautiful because a capital city is the face of a nation. Nanjing is the ancient capital of ten dynasties, located in the populous and affluent area south of the Yangtze. Throughout history, it has been bathed in splendor. Seventeen-hundred years ago, Zuo Si's bestselling work *Rhapsody of the Three Capitals* described it very well:

> The palace and the royal court stand, the roads flat as whetstone,
> The green scholar trees extending all the way to the crystal-clear waters.

People often describe the Nanjing of the Six Dynasties era as the center of a golden age. There is an abundance of historical material regarding Nanjing's splendor at the time. The Zizhi Tongjian records: "During the time that it was the capital of the Liang dynasty, it held 280,000 households." This is quite an astounding number. If we assume five members per household, then the population would have been 1.4 million. The Liang dynasty was 1500 years ago and was only a minor part of the Six Dynasties. On April 29th of 1937, a population survey of Nanjing lasting over three months calculated an accurate population figure of 945,544 residents. At that time, it was the capital of the Republic of China and the largest city in the country. In comparison to the Liang dynasty, it was quite a bit smaller. From this detail, we can see just how astounding Nanjing was 1,500 years ago.

Being designated as capital gave Nanjing a fantastic opportunity to build. Historically, the city's greatest periods of opportunity were during the Eastern Wu and the Ming dynasties, and also during the era of the Republic. Sun Quan of the Eastern Wu established Nanjing as his capital, and from that moment on, Nanjing's assets grew significantly. Without the Eastern Wu, the golden age of the Six Dynasties would never have occurred. Zhu Yuanzhang of the Ming dynasty built his high walls—the largest in history. The Republican government undertook modernization efforts within the ancient city. Because the Republican era was closest to the modern day, its influence upon the city was also the greatest.

The foundations for many things which are in the city today were laid during the Republican era. In my recently completed novel, *Nanjing 1937: A Love Story*, I wrote this about Nanjing:

In establishing Nanjing as the capital of the Republic of China, the Republican government gave the city an extremely rare opportunity. But at the beginning, no one could have imagined that this opportunity arose from the soul of the late Premier Sun Yat-sen. On April 1st of 1912, a year after the Xinhai Revolution, and a day after Yuan Shikai had forced Provisional President Sun Yat-sen to resign, Sun had gone hunting in the Purple Mountain region of Nanjing. He was thoroughly moved by the scenery, and for the first time, he revealed his wish to be buried there after his death. By 1925, Sun had fallen gravely ill in Beijing, and he resolutely demanded to be buried in Nanjing. Just why exactly Sun fell in love with Nanjing's beautiful landscape has been the subject of all kinds of conjecture and dramatization. However, his final wishes were faithfully carried out by the Kuomindang once they had accomplished their project of unification. On June 1st of 1929, his burial ceremony became the city's greatest event. In order for Sun's coffin to disembark at the railway station, make its way through the packed city streets, and proceed to his mausoleum in a solemn and stately manner, the city government resolutely seized the opportunity to completely transform Nanjing's transport network. Swathes of old housing were demolished, and the long Zhongshan Road was specially designed to usher in his coffin. The vast, imposing construction project completely transformed the appearance of the ancient city. Nanjing immediately took on the might of a great capital city. Decades later, Zhongshan Road is still Nanjing's most important thoroughfare.

To be designated a capital city is an extremely important opportunity for any city. All Nanjing had to show off was its ancient culture. Thankfully, "Regal Jinling" helped them in their mission. Nanjing had flourished in olden days, so it could rank among the best of all of the prosperous southeastern provinces. It was in a position of leadership, and it could not be separated from its status as a former capital.

Nanjing was granted a particular status after the Ming Yongle Emperor designated it as his capital. Despite it no longer being a capital city in actuality, due to the Yongle's decision to do so, and his burial there, it still retained its aura as a capital, benefiting from its proximity to such a grand historical figure, and thus it was no surprise that it became an important strategic city in the southeast.

Nanjing's many opportunities seemed only natural.

Two

These past few years, "seize the opportunity" has become a popular catchphrase. Opportunity is indeed important. If it had not been the ancient capital of ten dynasties, Nanjing would not exist today. Nanjing has been bathed in the light of history.

Opportunity can also be seen from another angle. Just as Nanjing has seen the splendor of a capital city, it has seen the tragedy of national defeat. For later generations, the splendor of the Six Dynasties is little more than a historical record. The city's parks and pavilions once reached the peak of extravagance, but unfortunately, when the armies of the Sui dynasty swarmed Nanjing, they were destroyed. Emperor Wen of Sui is said to have been much like King Wei of Chu and Qin Shi Huang, developing a sudden fear of Nanjing's regal aura. He worried that its royal splendor would cause people to raise their banners in revolt, and thus he gave the absurd order that Nanjing and its palaces be razed to the ground and turned into arable land.

Thus, the splendor of the Six Dynasties was burnt to ash, and the city of Nanjing almost completely destroyed. Its status took a devastating fall. All that was left of the city which had once stood so magnificently were the stone city walls which proved impossible to burn, then forming the walls of what was called "Jiangzhou". I know of no other city in Chinese history that has suffered such an awful blow. Emperor Wen's order reduced a city to farmland in the blink of an eye.

The Sui dynasty was very quickly toppled, and the proceeding Tang dynasty inherited the style of their predecessors, still maintaining proper vigilance in regard to Nanjing. In the early Tang, the military governorate of Yang Province moved to Jiangdu. From then on, the southern capital was no longer in Yang Province, and Jiangdu became another name for modern-day Yangzhou. Historically, Yangzhou was the Chinese name for Yang Province, a region somewhat equivalent to today's PLA military region. It was an important part of the "Nine Provinces" of ancient China. Nanjing's rise and fall in status brought with it a series of understandable difficulties. It is no wonder that future generations would read this Tang poem: "With ten thousand strings of cash around one's waist, one rides a crane to Yangzhou." In this instance, there is ongoing debate over whether Yangzhou refers to Nanjing or to Jiangdu; both sides claim to be correct.

For Nanjing, every national defeat is a disaster, a painful

experience. The downfall of nations forces the flourishing city to retreat. Because of Nanjing's particular geographic position, its status as a cornerstone of politics and culture for over 300 years during the Six Dynasties cannot be expected to be snuffed out in a short space of time on the basis of one political order. There is no way to prevent future generations from looking back with nostalgia. With such a disastrous backdrop, the pens of Tang dynasty poets would produce no end of nostalgic verse on Jinling.

By the time of the Song and Yuan dynasties, the rippling blue waters of Xuanwu Lake that we see today could not be seen. They had been a sacrifice of Wang Anshi's reforms. Wang Anshi, who was a government official in Nanjing, felt that Xuanwu Lake was merely a "place of recreation for previous generations which is now left unused and of no importance for preservation"—and thus its waters were drained, forming 1,300 hectares of land. The facts would prove the unsuitability of this action. During the centuries that followed, the supply and drainage of water in the north of Nanjing continued to be a problem, and eventually there was no alternative but to restore it. It is worth pointing out that the Xuanwu Lake that we see today is merely a third of its original size. One does not imagine that such a prominent figure as Wang Anshi could make such a mistake.

The city of Nanjing was no longer the capital, so it could be defiled as was seen fit. Those who fall from grace are more wretched than those who never ascended, and it is difficult to find a city that has undergone such tribulations as Nanjing. Nanjing's rise and fall have always formed a clear distinction: one moment, splendor; the next, ruin. Like a malaria sufferer tossing and turning, the people cannot be at peace. And we are still yet to reach the Taiping Rebellion. When the Taiping army entered Nanjing, the common people suffered for their crimes; when the Taiping army fell, they suffered once more. It is barely an exaggeration to call it urbicide. The victors entered the city, and for three days their swords remained unsheathed. Such was the usual practice. In modern-day Nanjing, the memory of 60 years ago, when Japanese invaders carried out a bloody massacre that lasted over six weeks, still remains strong.

Three

In Nanjing's historical development, there has always been a particular element of passivity. History has brought about in the people of Nanjing a sense of idleness in submitting to the Will of Heaven. The Will of Heaven cannot be disobeyed, thus blaming the gods and accusing others becomes an excuse. The people of Nanjing hope that their own city will be like others that have experienced rapid development, and thus they are unsure what to do. Opportunity seems to always be far away from the Nankinese.

It is extremely important to seize opportunity. When Zhongshan Road was being built, because it passed through the middle of the city, many of the common people's houses and stores were demolished, and a large number of people were opposed to it. Those in opposition took up the flag of the Three Principles of the People and believed that if Sun Yat-sen were still alive, he absolutely would not have approved of such an assault on working people's livelihoods simply in order to transport his coffin. But the city government firmly withstood pressure from all sides, and regardless of the consequences, they demolished vast swathes of buildings, changing the face of the ancient city.

Nanjing's first mayor was Liu Jiwen. He only had 3,000 yuan of silver to hand in order to start the project, and he resolutely seized the opportunity. As the road was being built, there were not just financial pressures, but obstacles in all aspects. For example, as work began on Zhongshan South Road, the general headquarters was located on Sanyuan Alley, and this was an intractable issue. In order to ensure the smooth construction of the road, Liu Jiwen decided to tackle the general headquarters first. Once the general headquarters made way for the road, the other obstacles naturally would be a cinch. Once the road was finally built, Liu Jiwen's boldness won him the respect of the people of Nanjing.

The 1995 National Intercity Games were likewise an opportunity, and in the wake of the games, Nanjing undertook a large-scale transformation of its transportation infrastructure. Before the opening of the Intercity Games, the people of Nanjing suffered the labor pains of this transformation, with their roads dug up and their trees mercilessly felled. Seizing opportunity means paying a price. Many years before, Nanjing had seemed to fall into silence, waiting bitterly for the next opportunity to develop. If it had not emerged from that silence, then it would have died there. It had already waited for too long. Opportunity leaves as quickly as it comes; if it is not seized, then it will disappear in the blink of an eye. Nanjing should not make a fuss of its ancient capital pedigree, and it should not live in the image of a decaying city.

After reform and opening up, Shenzhen seized the first opportunity. In the past few years, Shanghai has done the same. It is undeniable that the cities which grow quickest are those that seize opportunity where it lies, such as those smaller cities in the south of Jiangsu like Zhangjiagang and Jiangyin.

A Strategic Town in the Southeast

One

Nanjingers have never been greatly accepting of the Shanghainese. Particularly when traveling, when they have no choice but to change planes or trains in Shanghai, they feel a sudden unease. When compared to the vastness of Shanghai, the ancient city of Nanjing becomes a mere village in the wilds. One is required to spend a night in Shanghai, to bother one's Shanghainese friends to buy train or plane tickets in advance on one's behalf. Nanjing also has an airport and a train station, but it turns out that there are a great many destinations which one cannot reach directly from Nanjing.

Time changes all, and things now are very different from how they once were. You might feel that Shanghai, 300 kilometers away from Nanjing, is something of a parvenu of a city. You simply cannot comprehend how Shanghai could become so rich. Over 100 years ago, Shanghai was a small county town, a little bit larger than the average fishing village. Compared to Nanjing, it was a subordinate of a subordinate of a subordinate. If the official responsible for Shanghai wanted to pay a formal visit to the one responsible for Nanjing, he would have to jump through quite a few hoops. But things change, and today, Shanghai's haughtiness is such that it barely deigns to recognize outsiders.

Compared to Shanghai, modern-day Nanjing is something of a

poor cousin. In times past, there is no doubt that Nanjing would have been considered a city of strategic importance within the southeast. Put aside its status as ancient capital of ten dynasties and the military governorate of Yang Province. During the Qing dynasty, nearly 300 years ago, the highest commander responsible for military affairs in the southeast would conduct all of his affairs in Nanjing. Nanjing was not only a seat of provincial government. There were a number of provinces under the scope of its jurisdiction. Nowadays, the military region is still named for Nanjing, and the military affairs of the six provinces and one municipality of the southeast remain under its administration, but these are times of peace, and the economic, political, and cultural center of the southeast is clearly not located in Nanjing.

Nanjing, of course, is not content with this state of affairs. Of course, its discontent is of no use. There is little to be done to stop Nanjing's decline. In years past, Nanjing was indeed extravagant. The distant past aside, there is still the Qing era of 200-300 years ago. Three great works of the era are connected to Nanjing: Kong Shangren's *The Peach Blossom Fan*, Wu Jingzi's *The Scholars*, and last but by absolutely no means least, Cao Xueqin's *Dream of the Red Chamber*. There is no place more suited to being the cradle of great writers than Nanjing. By chance, these three authors all happened to make records of Nanjing's splendor during the Qing dynasty. We need only consult this passage from *The Scholars* for an example:

This Nanjing was still the site where the Emperor Hongwu of Ming founded his capital. Thirteen inner city gates and 18 outer city gates, with a diameter of 40 li (~20km) and over 120 li (~60km) in circumference. There were a dozen major roads in the city, and hundreds of smaller alleyways, all packed with the hustle and bustle of human activity and lined with splendid houses and pavilions. Within the city stood a river, its waters flowing west to east, ten li (~5km) long; this was the Qinhuai River. When its waters ran high, barges would sail upon it, with the sound of the pan pipe and the drum heard night and day. Inside and outside the city stood gloriously decorated temples and sanctuaries, beautiful and pleasing to the eye. At the time of the Six Dynasties, there were 484 temples; now, there stood 4,800! In the vast avenues and small alleyways, there stood six or seven hundred taverns, and over a thousand teahouses. No matter which secluded alleyway you strolled through, there would always be a place lit by hanging lanterns, decorated with fresh flowers, boiling top-quality rainwater to sell tea. The teahouses would be full of people drinking tea. When evening came, the taverns would light the lanterns on their upper floors, and every street would be filled with thousands of lamps, shining bright as daylight. Those walking past would have no need of their own lanterns. When the moonlight hit the Qinhuai River, later on in the night, the barges would float along with the sound of pipes and singing, somber and soft, in a breathtaking scene. Wearing soft silks, their hair pinned up with jasmine flowers, the young women who resided on either side of the river would roll up their hanging screens and lean on their parapets, listening quietly. So, when the drums sounded upon the lantern boats, the scrolls would be rolled up on either side of the river. The thick aroma of burning ambergris would fill the air, and rays of moonlight would drift upon the water; looking upon such a sight, one would be put in mind of the beautiful paradise of the Daoist immortals. There were also sixteen official brothel-houses, with women adorned in makeup and splendid costumes, receiving all comers. Truly, "Every morning was the Qingming festival, and every night was the Lantern festival."

This was a description of Nanjing at the time. These words once stirred the hearts of many an outsider who came to stroll Nanjing's streets and take in its wonders, walking along the banks of the Qinhuai River. Clearly, Nanjing's important position among the cities of China was not solely a result of its status as a capital of ten dynasties and the regal aura of Jinling. Regardless of which era is examined, Nanjing's importance lay in its position as a leading strategic town and an image of splendor. Even though Emperor Wen of Sui ordered the city burned to Nanjing, were busy with civil war and had no energy to rebuild the city. Not long after this point, the Guomindang fled to Taiwan, Beijing became the capital of the new China, and the ruined city fell into disrepair. Nanjing missed out on the post-war development opportunities seen by Tokyo, Rome, and London. These capital cities had all suffered huge damage during the war; yet, they were all political, economic, and culture centers. They all arose from the ashes. And Nanjing seemed all but forgotten.

In past years, Nanjing has struggled to keep its position as a strategic town in the southeast. For this ancient city, this position was most suitable. Nanjing was not the appropriate place for the capital of a vast and united nation. The scope of its authority was more appropriate for governing the provinces of the southeast. With the passing of time, its position has not recovered, and now Shanghai has undeniably taken its place as the most important city in the southeast.

In fact, 100 years ago, Shanghai had already emerged as a contender for Nanjing's throne. During the Republican era, although Nanjing was the capital, nearby Shanghai was prosperous to an almost equal degree. Shanghai's rise was nearly unpreventable. Whether Nanjing accepted it or not, in short, it had to relinquish its throne. Nanjing's atrophy was unavoidable. It had forfeited its superior position in the southeastern provinces. Nanjing, a city that had demanded so much, had ceased to have any significance.

Three

For Nanjingers, something that had to be quickly revised was their traditionally idealistic attitude. The possibility of returning to its past glory perhaps no longer existed. What's past is past, and the opportunities that history has given Nanjing will not return. Nanjingers must understand that merely waiting for opportunity to arise is not enough. They must rely on themselves in order to seize the day.

It is not right to stake one's hopes on the outmoded and the outworn. Nor is it realistic to assume that Nanjing will be built up into an internationalized metropolis. On this great, national chessboard, Nanjing is destined to play the part of Shanghai's pawn. There is no need for that many international cities in the Yangtze River Delta. In other words, Nanjing's last hope cannot be to become an international metropolis. Nanjing's true place should be that of an ever-developing city of culture. It should develop vigorously in a way that the new-built city of Shanghai could never maintain.

Nanjing should become a warm and comforting city; it should make improving the lives of its citizens its top priority. Historically, the importance of Nanjing's prosperity has not lain it its status as an ancient capital, nor in its leading position among strategic towns of the southeast. The most important point is that this was a place where its people lived well, in abundance, and with rich spiritual lives. To live in peace and work happily is heaven for the common people. This would be the best direction for Nanjing's development.

Not everyone wishes to advance the ideal of the international megalopolis. Bigger does not necessarily mean better. Size brings with it the trouble of redundant overgrowth. Internationalization is not a synonym for living well. A poor person living in an internationalized metropolis will not find that their personal worth increases like a bullish stock market just because they are living there.

One year, I went to Chengdu, and a friend there spoke to me candidly... Chengdu was such a great place to live, so how did I feel about Nanjing? I was stumped, and for a moment, I did not know how to respond.

A Picture of Migration

One

The source of Nanjing's population is an interesting topic. First, let us explore those Nanjingers who were forced to relocate.

After Zhu Yuanzhang, the first Ming emperor, established Nanjing as his capital, in order to purify the city's population, he ordered that Yuan dynasty citizens left behind within the city be exiled to Yunnan. For the incoming political order, the leftovers of the previous dynasty were not to be trusted, so they could take a hike. This kind of large-scale mass migration somewhat resembled the "Down to the Countryside" movement of the Cultural Revolution. It is said that, in a number of places in Yunnan, to this day, you can still find villagers who speak with a Nanjing accent, who can perform the songs passed down to them by their ancestors. It is not easy for one to retain one's native accent and remember the ancient melodies when 600 years have passed.

Another category of Nanjingers forced to move were those affected by disaster. Not long ago, the Nanjing newspapers reported that, somewhere in Jinhua, Zhejiang Province, there was a village that spoke in the Nanjing dialect. The village was big, with a large population. Their local customs were particularly simple and unostentatious, and yet they maintained the traditions of Nanjing. Upon closer inspection, it turned out that the founders of this village were those who had fled from bloodshed years before. But exactly when they had done so was unclear. Chaos has fallen all too frequently upon Nanjing throughout history. In any case, anyone who could pay such a high price, fleeing so far away with a wife and child in tow, was definitely from a rich family.

There is much to say about the inward flow of migration into Nanjing's population. In every dynasty, there has been large-scale immigration into Nanjing, and there are all sorts of reasons for this. For example, when the northern government was forced into exile in Nanjing, it inevitably brought a large northern population with it. Historically, the ancestors of the most prominent clans would undoubtedly be people of the Central Plain. Otherwise, there would not be stories of those who crossed the river, such as "Weeping at the New Pavilion". Naturally, the exiled government brought the milieu of the northern bureaucratic classes to Nanjing with them. Because the northerners continued to occupy their superior positions after coming to Nanjing, their customs and language soon caught on among the common people of the city. This is why a large number of northern features can be spotted in the language and culture of Nanjingers.

In the last years of the Western Jin, war in the north meant an increase in population as a result of Han people crossing over the river, and to a larger extent than the migration of the northern bureaucrats. There were far more poor people than rich people, and they followed the officials in setting to work. They greatly increased Nanjing's productivity and had a great effect on the economic development of the south. The large scale of migration even became a serious societal concern for a time. As a result, the exiled government had no choice but to examine the boundaries of Nanjing, building the so-called "migrated commanderies" for northerners to live in. The northern exiles settled in the "migrated commanderies," and these commanderies were named after commanderies and counties in the north. Thus, when reading old texts, one can find names such as "South Xuzhou", "South Donghai", and "South Lanling" within Nanjing's jurisdiction.

Because they could not confuse these with their namesakes in the commanderies and cantons of the north, when writing essays, authors would often intentionally or unintentionally omit the character meaning "south". Time passed, and as a result, there are many boring written polemics left behind. For example, *The Plum in the Golden Vase* was written by the pseudonymous "Scoffing Scholar of Lanling". No one can say for sure which Lanling this referred to. One can imagine, however, that 1,600 years ago, Nanjing was no longer an authentically southern city. The city was filled with northern refugees, and these refugees immediately went from being their guests to being their masters. They became the principal characters upon Nanjing's stage and brought about the fashions of the era. This pattern repeated itself throughout history, and objectively speaking, after a period of time, they would intermingle with the city's population. This integration raised the innate quality of the city's population. In this exchange, southern culture and northern culture collided and gave off dazzling sparks.

History always repeats itself. The northern ethnic groups appeared again and again, chasing away the Han people, who fled southward.

Two

There are historical records of a large influx of migrants into Nanjing in the early years of the Ming dynasty. Zhu Yuanzhang, the Hongwu Emperor, drove out the majority of the remaining Yuan dynasty inhabitants, and a new population flooded the city, coming from all across the country. Among this new population, most people were the families of laborers and artisans. Historical records show that such households numbered 45,000, and with an average of five members per household, 200,000 people belonged to this population category alone. The motives for this migration of skilled workmen to Nanjing was very simple: to allow them to quickly build up the city into prosperity. At the time, there were only 200,000 of these households across the entire nation. For the sake of Nanjing's prosperity, Zhu Yuanzhang moved a fifth of the personnel of the nation's construction industry.

With laborers employed, it was still necessary to invite rich families to the capital city. Zhu Yuanzhang, who had arisen out of leading a peasant revolt, personally summoned rich families from all over the nation to Nanjing. Since he was emperor, the rich could not dare disobey. Around 15,000 rich households were compelled to enter the city, coming from provinces such as Jiangsu, Zhejiang, Jiangxi, Huguang, Fujian, and Sichuan.

Among these rich families, the most famous of men was Shen Wansan, who came from Zhouzhuang, a town in Kunshan County near Suzhou, Jiangsu Province. There are many tales about him. This rich merchant bankrolled much of Nanjing's construction, including several of the city gates. One story noted that one-third of the money used to finance the building of the city was his own. Although Shen Wansan spent plenty of money, Zhu Yuanzhang was not enamored of him. Shen Wansan's ostentatious achievements were a threat, as was his spending. He was ultimately found to be at fault by Zhu Yuanzhang and was exiled to the far border where he died.

Population mobility is the most important factor in the formation of a city. Nanjing's population mobility seems to have been higher than that of any other city. We can imagine that, in the early years of the Ming, Nanjing felt a lot like the recently arisen city of Shenzhen in the 1980s, having a truly spectacular scene of prosperity. The skilled laborers and artisans coming from outside got straight to work, building tall buildings and walls, and at their diligent hands, Nanjing's beautiful pavilions and towers were constructed. Likewise, the rich merchant outsiders could do nothing else but become the city's typical consumer class, and they spent their days drinking and making merry.

Jinling, with its ancient history, was caught up in an explosion of new expansion, with scenes of prosperity visible everywhere. The population of Nanjing experienced one upheaval after another, and this complete upheaval, in a sense, became characteristic of the city.

Nanjing was a city in constant flux. Endless change became a part of the city's long-standing traditions.

Three

In the past, people have debated who truly constitutes an "old Nanjinger". People have also made a habit of going to the banks of the Qinhuai River south of the city and trying to find traces of old Nanjing.

Many people who are considered to be old Nanjingers, or who consider themselves to be such persons, will peruse the records of their ancestors and soon discover that their antecedents' history in Nanjing does not stretch so far back as they expected. In this ever-shifting city, seemingly predestined for frequent meetings with disaster, it is difficult to stay for generation after generation.

I have come across an interesting phenomenon. In Nanjing, the oldest families are not of the Han majority, but of the Hui, a Chinese Muslim ethnic group. I have a number of Hui friends, and they are indeed true old Nanjingers. When I bring up the subject of their ancestry with them, there are many who have nothing to say in response. Their ethnic group has lived in this city for many years—so long that even their grandparents cannot answer these sorts of questions.

For the Hui of Nanjing, discussions of their ancestry are filled with vague conjecture of years past. What they know is only what has been passed down to them through oral tradition by their ancestors. In the past, I always presumed that the Hui of Nanjing were made up of two categories: the first being those who had travelled across the Silk Road by land from Persia and Arabia into northern China, then migrated southward to Nanjing; the second being those who had come by the Maritime Silk Road, setting off from the Mediterranean Sea and travelling to Nanjing from the coast of Fujian Province in the southeast. Evidence has shown my understanding of Nanjing's history to be thoroughly incomplete.

Many of Nanjing's Hui people came, in fact, from Yunnan. For example, two friends of mine who are surnamed Su can trace their ancestry back to the renowned minister Ajall Shams al-Din Omar—a provincial governor of the border region during the Yuan dynasty. His eldest son was named Nasulading (Nasr Al-din), and future generations sinicized their surname, dismantling the four characters that made up his name to do so. Of these four characters, ding was very common. The others were rather options that were strange to take as surnames.

I do not know whether my friends surnamed Su are aware of their distant relation to Zheng He, the famous eunuch admiral and explorer of the Ming dynasty. Zheng He's surname was originally Ma; Ajall Shams al-Din Omar was also his ancestor. When he was still a young child, he was kidnapped by the armies of Zhu Yuanzhang, brought to Nanjing, and castrated. He became a servant boy to Zhu Di, Prince of Yan, who would later become the Yongle Emperor. Due to his astounding intelligence, at the age of 28, he won the favor of Zhu Di for his advice in battle during the Jingnan Campaign. Zhu Di became the Yongle Emperor and, accordingly, Zheng He was given the surname "Zheng" for his "valiant efforts in Zhengzhou."

Zheng He's former residence is on Mafu Street. In my childhood, I would often play in Taiping Park, now named Zheng He Park, which was made up of the private gardens of his family. Before the Taiping army entered Nanjing, the descendants of the Zheng clan lived mainly on Mafu Street. Afterward, they gradually spread out, taking on the names of the places where they lived for ease of appellation. For example, the Zheng clan who lived in Dazhongqiao became the Dazhongqiao Zheng; those who lived in Zhimaying became the Zhimaying Zheng; others included the Zheng of Xiafuqiao, Xiajiekou, and Zhangfuyuan.

The Hui of Nanjing who are surnamed Zheng are not necessarily descendants of Zheng He. Generally, only those who moved from

Mafu Street can be considered to be authentic descendants of Zheng He. Because Zheng He was a eunuch, how exactly he came to have descendants is not made clear in historical records. Perhaps they were adopted from a close branch of the family. In any case, the Hui of Nanjing with the surname Zheng can be divided into three branches: one branch are the descendants of the illustrious Zheng He, the so-called Mafu Zheng; one branch are the Taoyuan Zheng; and one are the Xiangfang Zheng. The ancestors of the Taoyuan Zheng planted peach gardens (taoyuan) for the emperor in the early years of the Ming dynasty. The Xiangfang Zheng raised elephants for the emperor, and it is from this act that they derived their name.

It is rather interesting to think about. In over 600 years of upheaval, Nanjing's population has seen countless changes. Some people came in a hurry, and even more left in a hurry. But, incredibly, the Hui, who came to the city by chance, managed to stay. In times of danger, they did not flee. Their descendants were born here and grew up here in an unbroken line. Like duckweed, they drifted on the waters until they reached Nanjing with no home to return to; they endured, and Nanjing became their home instead. The rootless became rooted, and thus they became the true old families of Nanjing.

The Hui of Nanjing are not many in number. But if one wishes to understand Nanjing, if one wishes to grasp its charms, then one cannot overlook the city's Hui families. In terms of food culture alone, so many of Nanjing's famous restaurants were opened by Hui people. Halal restaurants have never limited themselves to only serving the Hui, however. In fact, going to a halal restaurant to eat heartily has become a beloved pastime of the people of Nanjing. When we go to enjoy the delights of restaurants such as Maxiangxing, Qifangge, Jiangyouji, or Anleyuan, we rarely think of the differences between China's ethnic groups. We do not often think about how this restaurant was opened by members of a different ethnic group, and we do not even think of how their religion differs from our own, even now. We are all Nanjingers. From a certain perspective, the Hui of Nanjing are more authentically Nankinese than we who are not.

The Figures of the Six Dynasties and Nanjing Radishes

One

There is no one way for a city to become suitable for its inhabitants. By most standards, low prices, a good atmosphere, and simple social relationships and customs will be enough. In the past, there was a saying: "Above, there is Heaven; below, Suzhou and Hangzhou." In fact, this came about because it rhymed and rolled off the tongue (shang you tiantang, xia you sukang), and su and kang did not necessarily refer to Suzhou and Hangzhou. Suzhou and Hangzhou together formed a clear conceptualization; they represented the populous and affluent area south of the Yangtze, and today this area is called the Jiang-Zhe-Hu (Jiangsu-Zhejiang-Shanghai) Delta. Historically, Nanjing has evidently been a very inhabitable city. Yuan Mei, the Qing poet who hailed from the Qiantang River in Zhejiang Province, settled in Nanjing. His reason for doing so was simple: "I wish to live in Jinling of the Six Dynasties." He personally designed the Sui Garden, and wrote poetry which built upon the garden's history, characteristics, and reputation:

> *I bought a patch of land in the mountain of Xiaocang,*
> *which stood between a hill and a ravine.*

> *The plum blossoms coil around the house in an ocean of fragrance,*
> *the long thin bamboo hangs upon the walls, covered in cloud-like patches of green.*
> *Glass is embedded upon the walls, displayed for the world to see,*
> *The lamplight of a canopy of stars falls upon the pond.*
> *My lord, you have heard late that these are fine gardens,*
> *Come, paint the hut, the geese, and the old study.*

Yuan Mei was a great talent; a successful graduate of the imperial exams, he was a magistrate in a number of counties. At the age of 33, he became suddenly weary of officialdom and withdrew, buying a patch of land in Xiaocangshan in Nanjing, where he built the Sui Garden. There, he lived simply as a scholar among the common people. Yuan Mei said of himself: "I am no official. I am not destined for greatness, but simply for idleness. It is difficult to become a Buddha when one loves writing and flowers." He was an old-style scholar who loved life's pleasures. *On Nanjing* describes the Sui Garden in this way: "Outside the gate stands an enchanting bamboo-lined path with a wooden fence. It is surrounded by hills and water. There are a number of different buildings, and wonderful drawings abound. Of the famous gardens of the city, this is the finest."

The Sui Garden was famous, indeed. As a result, when the Qianlong Emperor came to the region south of the Yangtze, he sent men to paint pictures of it, so that they could refer to it when renovating the imperial garden. At the time, there were many beautiful private gardens in Nanjing, and the Sui Garden was well-known among them.

Yuan Mei was not a figure of the Six Dynasties, and yet he wanted to live a life akin to that era. The Six Dynasties era and the late Tang dynasty make up a period on which the Chinese literati hung many of their hopes. Yuan Mei lived in the golden age of the Qing dynasty, and yet he enjoyed the carefree pleasures of an era of decline. As a youth, he accomplished his ambitions; in middle age, he resigned his position in order to concentrate on his literary work. His poetry made him a leader of the literary world of the time, and his essays and collected writings—such as "The Xiaocangshan Anthology", "Sayings from the Sui Garden", and "What the Master Would Not Discuss"—saw substantial success. The most hotly-discussed aspect of Yuan Mei's life, save for his host of concubines, was the clique of female poets who studied under him. These "three thousand goddesses, with the spring wind in their laughter" had quite an imposing manner.

As an old man of 80, Yuan Mei still wanted governors to prohibit prostitution on the banks of the Qinhuai, and he fought for justice. He wrote poetry which one cannot help but find amusing:

Embroidered banners and halberds decorate the governor's office.
His might is such that the eight counties call him "the father of the people".
How can one help to ensure the safety of the people?
Simply by cultivating flowers on the riverside.

A distinguished old man of letters, he seemed to see through the games of the bureaucrats, and by prohibiting prostitution, he wanted to use the money officials spent on prostitutes—so-called *maixiaojin*, "money to buy laughter"—for other means. The literary inquisitions of the Qing dynasty were frightening, indeed. Luckily, as long as one did not offend one's superiors or oppose the emperor, there was no problem with scolding officials. Yuan Mei was a prominent writer, and as such, he knew how to write an appropriate rebuke. Sure enough, writing poetry such as this did not lead to any trouble for him.

Two

In the history of Nanjing, authors like Yuan Mei are far from a unique phenomenon. As an inhabitable city, Nanjing's advantage lies in its ability to retain and appropriate such fine writers. Nanjing is an ideal place to grow old. There are countless predecessors who one may imitate; here, both the upper crust and the common people may live happily. After all, the Chinese people will always long for home. But, in fact, those who came from peasant villages to become officials did not return to their hometowns in order to live out their sunset years. Many people choose Nanjing as a place to care for their ailing parents. It is a city filled with an air of debility. The nostalgic atmosphere is quite a comfort to the elderly.

Wang Anshi chose Nanjing as the place to spend his final years, and there are many similar examples. Wang Anshi chose to live in seclusion in a place named "Banshanyuan" ("Halfway Hill Garden"), and the Qing dynasty painter Gong Xian's residence was named "Banmuyuan" ("Half Field Garden"). The area south of the Yangtze has produced gifted scholars since antiquity, and these scholars have mostly preferred Nanjing as the site of their activities. The Six Dynasties were not rich and powerful in national terms, but when it comes to culture, the figures of the Six Dynasties have always been an example to follow. Chen Sanli, one of the four great poets of the late Qing, who was also the father of the noted scholar Chen Yinke, was dismissed permanently for his participation in the Hundred Days Reform. He spent his later years in Nanjing, planning to live there in a house he had built and named the Sanyuan Retreat. Chen Sanli's poetry is intricate and unorthodox, and he was considered a leading light of the Tongguang School of the time. When he settled in Nanjing, a countless stream of younger poets attempted to seek his guidance.

Unlike other cities, Nanjing has never bathed in the glory of its indigenous poets. It is hard to find a city as large as Nanjing that does not favor its own. The characters of the Six Dynasties did not signify one particular native place, but represented a kind of spirit, a sort of literary acknowledgement. Not corrupted by wealth or honors, not shaken by poverty, with a might that could not be cowed, the figures of the Six Dynasties were a kind of spiritual aristocracy. Many may be aware of Nanjing's Lin Sanzhi, a celebrated calligrapher of the modern age, but fewer are aware of Lin's good friend, Shao Zitui. Shao Zitui was from the village of Wujiang in He County, Anhui Province. If you look at a map, you will note that although He County is in Anhui, it is in fact quite close to Nanjing. Historically, Wujiang came under Nanjing's jurisdiction, and its people's customs and speech were very close to those of the Nankinese. Shao Zitui was born in the late Qing/early Republican era. He did not sit through the imperial examinations, and nor did he attend a contemporarily styled college, but thanks to his family's riches, he was well-schooled, having relied entirely on private tutoring and self-study. He studied ancient poetry meticulously and was particularly interested in calligraphy. As a result, he became a close friend of Lin Sanzhi. After Shao Zitui passed away, Lin Sanzhi immediately wrote *Mourning Zitui*: "From now on, I shall write no poetry to be seen by others. The wind and rain bring my old friend back to me, and I close my book and let out a long sigh." Lin Sanzhi was famous for his calligraphy, but he prized poetry even more. Like Qi Baishi, he felt that his poetry was better than his writing. His old friend had passed on, and Lin Sanzhi vowed not to write any more poetry, as well as to have nothing to do with calligraphy for an entire winter. He once even said to someone who asked him to write: "If you can bring Shao Zitui back to life, then I will write!" The two men's friendship was clear. Shao Zitui was briefly a teacher at a primary school in Wujiang. The school asked him to fill out a resume, to which Shao indignantly sighed and responded: "I am a scholar of the common people, and I shall write nothing!" In fact, Shao Zitui made friends with the best and the brightest.

With his experience, whether in commerce or in politics, he could have had a bright future ahead of him, but he became the era's answer to Tao Yuanming. Unwilling to be a teacher, in accordance with the wishes of his ancestors, he worked as both a farmer and a writer, finding his own amusement. Chatting with old friends, writing poetry for older women, not considering himself a scholar and thinking it beneath him to have dealings with petty officials, he spent his life among the common people, his tastes unchanging.

The first time I came across writing of Shao Zitui, it felt like I had read some old myths. Shao passed in 1984. When I read his poetry and looked upon his paintings and calligraphy, as well as his commentary upon Lin Sanzhi's calligraphy, I was surprised to an unimaginable degree. As I saw it, the figures of the Six Dynasties were in the past and had become inimitable history. But Shao Zitui's story seemed to show that, even today, so long as we cultivate ourselves mentally and spiritually, the past can still be tracked down, and the flow of time can still be reversed. If we look carefully, the figures of the Six Dynasties can not only be looked for in the suburbs but can be discovered in even the bustling city itself.

Three

After victory in the war of resistance, a number of public figures were gathered to decide upon the flower that would represent Nanjing. Everyone gave their own opinion. Some suggested the plum blossom, some the Chinese flowering apple, and some suggested the cherry blossom. There was no agreement, and participants in the debate attacked each other—particularly those who had suggested the cherry blossom, who were attacked most fiercely. The cherry blossom is the national flower of Japan, and the enmity between the two nations was still extremely fresh; how could they choose the cherry blossom to represent the city? Ultimately, they came to no conclusion. One person interrupted, saying that Nanjing should not be represented by a flower at all, but by the radish.

When people talk about the stupidity of Nanjingers, they will shake their heads and call Nanjingers "radishes". A Nanjing radish is indifferent to praise and censure; he just records the facts. Describing the people of Nanjing as radishes is very fitting. The people of Nanjing have never been seen as particularly shrewd. It's not clear where this story comes from. Although people have historically investigated whether Nanjing really did produce radishes, from a culinary perspective, whether past or present, Nanjingers have always loved eating radishes. "Nanjing radish" is a sort of kind-hearted teasing. The Jinling Evening News and Southeast University worked together to send out 180 surveys, and they received 171 completed surveys. For the phrase "Nanjing radish", the three most common associations were "unsophisticated", "passionate", and "conservative". From three different perspectives, these associations all confirm that the "Nanjing radish" is an honest, straight-talking person. The conclusion of this survey provides food for thought. Those surveyed were Nanjingers, and their evaluation of Nanjing is perhaps not so highly valued as the opinions of those who are not from Nanjing. That is to say that the image of the Nanjing radish, in the eyes of outsiders, is perhaps more loveable than the fashion in which Nanjingers themselves see it. Beauty is in the eye of the beholder, and Nanjingers do not see beauty in their fellow denizens.

In a sense, the Nanjing radish is a remnant of the folk spirit of the Six Dynasties era. In The Scholars, it is written that "The waiters and bartenders have the vapor of the Six Dynasties"—easy-going, and neither tense nor lethargic in their doings; this relaxed attitude was handed down by ancestors. Sometimes, the slightest change in wording can represent a difference in culture. For example, the golden age of the Six Dynasties is referred to as liu chao jin fen, "Six Dynasties gold powder". The so-called "gold powder" in fact refers to cosmetics, but the saying is not "Six Dynasties makeup"—Nanjing has never been an effeminate city. Likewise, for "vapor of the Six Dynasties", there is essentially little difference between vapor and smoke, but vapor is used to signify a refined air, and smoke is used to signify crudeness.

Of the largest cities, Nanjing is one which does not look down upon farmers. But farmers have a deep understanding of the flow of migrant labor into the city. This is another loveable thing about the Nanjing radish. When I was in middle school, Nanjingers liked to use the term er ge, "second brother", to describe people from the countryside. This phrase has its origins in gongren lao dage, "big brother worker"; naturally, farm workers were reluctantly put in second place. For a time, "second brother" was a synonym for a fool, a country bumpkin. Nanjingers did not use this phrase to insult farmers, but in a self-effacing way, mocking themselves and those around them. A Nanjing radish does not feel much in the way of urban superiority.

It is not easy to see traces of the people of the Six Dynasties in today's Nanjingers. It has all already faded. A report suggested that although the monthly salaries are high, Nanjingers snub jobs in the hospitality and leisure sector. In the winter, the newspaper went to all kinds of public baths, where business was booming. Following the sudden increase in bathers, a few bathhouses and even hotels placed adverts for pedicurists, masseurs, and ear cleaners. Although some adverts promised an income of 3,000-4,000 yuan a month, these well-paid offers only attracted temporary workers from outside the city; very few of those who enquired were Nanjingers themselves. One hotel advertised for a careful female earwax cleaner; as a result, those who responded to the advert were young female migrant workers. Another bathhouse worked to recruit a back masseur; originally, they were optimistic that they could find a talkative local in the prime of his life, but ultimately there was not a single Nanjinger who responded.

Recruitment specialists believe that employment prospects in Nanjing are rather grim; those laid off say that as long as the money's right, there's little they won't do. But with the opportunity right in front of them in these cases, they still recoiled from it. It seems that Nanjingers must rethink their outlook on employment.

Simply explaining such an outlook as a fear of drudgery does not offer the whole picture. In every city, there are few who enjoy tedious or unpleasant work; Nanjingers are not unique in this. Just as it can seem to become a common belief that it is better to abandon one's scruples than succumb to poverty, Nanjingers appear to have a sense of apprehension when it comes to hospitality work. The majority of the service workers in Nanjing's bathhouses are from Yangzhou in northern Jiangsu. Almost all of the attendants in bathhouses are from Yangzhou, and to be frank, many Nanjingers feel that they should not take other people's jobs.

It cannot even be said that Nanjingers disdain such work. Are the aristocracy born to be innately as they are? Nanjingers just instinctively believe that they are cut out for one particular type of work and not another. They don't put much thought into why. Nanjing is a conventional consumer city. In this city, it would appear that many do not have particularly noble jobs. There will always be those who are willing to be waiters, barmen, or tea-servants, and Nanjingers will do such work without complaint. Thus, there is no need to describe Nanjingers as "aloof" and "haughty". It is no great offense to wait upon others; there is nothing wrong with making a living in this way.

Nanjingers can be somewhat sluggish regarding a number of things. A monthly income of 3,000-4,000 yuan is enticing; this salary is almost ten times more than what can be found for a factory job which brings little benefit. One cannot say that Nanjingers are indifferent to money; no one can hate having cash. We can only say that Nanjing is a city whose people are unskilled in taking advantage of opportunity. In this city, many people are not particularly adept at seizing the day.

South Nanjing

One

The south of the city is emblematic of old Nanjing.

As for many cities, the south of Nanjing has been the commercial and cultural center of this ancient city for a long time. For all that time, it has been the busiest place in Nanjing.

Representative of the south of the city, the Confucius Temple stands on the banks of the Qinhuai River. Compared with Beijing's Tianqiao, and Shanghai's City God Temple, it clearly has its own unique character. With the sound of oars and the display of lights along the Qinhuai River, south Nanjing has an advantage over the busy spaces of many other cities. The barges along the Qinhuai River are world-class. People travel along this river, its banks filled with historical sites, scenic spots, taverns, and inns; they might moor at a restaurant or give a farewell dinner by the waterside, and each and every place one might go has its own air of poetic character and historical interest. Historically, Nanjing's splendor has always been the splendor of the Qinhuai River. Whether we speak of emperors or governors, the first thing that has come to mind for Nanjing's rulers when they have considered the wellbeing of the people is how to return the Qinhuai River to its former glory. If the Qinhuai is brought to life, then so is the city. If the Qinhuai is bustling, then so is Nanjing.

The Qinhuai is the cradle of Nanjing. During the Six Dynasties, the river was very broad, and one would see countless boats moored upon its surface. At that point, international trade was already thoroughly developed, and traders coming from foreign countries included people from Lâm Ấp (modern-day Vietnam) and Funan (modern-day Cambodia), as well as Persians, Indians, Sri Lankans, Japanese, Koreans, and ancient Romans from the Mediterranean Sea. With his order to "flatten Jiankang's [Nanjing's] palaces and buildings and turn it to farmland," Emperor Wen of Sui put a stop to all of that. Nothing but grass and sky were left of the Six Dynasties' prosperity; The Flowers of the Jade Tree Hall [an air composed by the final emperor of the Chen dynasty] could be heard no more. Eight hundred years later, Zhu Yuanzhang named Nanjing his capital. The Qinhuai finally came to life once more, and this would be the foundation stone of the city's future. The Qinhuai River that we see today is broadly similar to how it was back then. Eight hundred years previously, the river had been silted up and the waters narrowed, looking much like Xiaoqiao does today. The Qinhuai was dredged, the buildings on its banks left to rot and then repaired, and so the cycle began again.

The Qinhuai's splendor comes from two things. One is the Confucius Temple; the other is its location as a place for finding courtesans. The first was a cause, the second a result. During the Ming and Qing dynasties, exam candidates from the southeast provinces would gather at the temple to take part in the imperial exams in the examination hall. Since this was a major event for the scholar classes, all sorts of industries would spring up to serve them, including bookstores, stationary stores, fortune tellers, taverns, tearooms, restaurants, and brothels. Everyone rose to the occasion. In modern terms, south Nanjing's prosperity was a result of the equivalent of the gaokao exams.

The exams made the Confucius Temple into a place of leisure. As the day approached, exam candidates coming from all over Jiangsu and Anhui would find places to live near the Qinhuai River. As they were characters much like those in *The Scholars*, it was only natural that they would get up to similar things as those characters did.

Because only a very small number would pass the imperial exams, the overwhelming majority of candidates would indulge in serious hedonism, gambling and whoring as they pleased along the Qinhuai River. Confucius would no doubt turn in his grave. These were all moneyed scholars; if they failed, then they could come back and try again. The purpose of trying again was not necessarily in order to succeed—it could just as well have been to make another courtesan's acquaintance.

There were some who, having arrived, thought that they might as well stay, ostensibly in order to prepare for the next exam, but in reality, to spend their money on prostitutes.

Everything in the south of the city seemed to have been, at least initially, among these kinds of complementary service industries. Seemingly in response to the exams, the Qinhuai riverbanks became well-known as a romantic location—as did their dancing girls. People on the Qinhuai riverbanks were all caught up in this cycle of service industries. All demands would be catered to, and since people came to spend large amounts of money, the inhabitants had no choice but to consider how they could get them to part with it.

Two

When old Nanjingers bring up Shiba Street, or Diaoyu Alley on the banks of the Qinhuai River, they know these are not good places. Many years ago, along the banks of the river between Wuding Bridge an Dongguantou, there stood one brothel after another. After the Republican government named Nanjing its capital, prostitution was forbidden. On the long screen wall that stretched around Yueya Pond, one could see the pronouncement: "Put New Life into Practice; Smoking, Gambling, and Prostitution is Forbidden." From this, we can see that, at the time, the Qinhuai River had a reputation as a hive of villainy.

It was only after the Communist Revolution that prostitution was finally truly prohibited along the banks of the Qinhuai. I know a woman who worked as a nanny, but who before the revolution was an underage prostitute. She had a similar experience to what is depicted in Su Tong's novel, *Blush*: married off to a transit worker, she worked at a sewing factory, and when the factory closed down, she had no choice but to become a nanny. I still remember what she looked like. She had delicate, pretty features, big eyes, and a startlingly loud voice. When I was young, I stayed at her home for a few days. She had a pretty young daughter and would always tell me that if I did what I was told, then she would let her daughter marry me.

I once worked at a factory outside Wudingmen for three years. I heard an unschooled worker talk about the Confucius Temple. He began to denounce the old society, and after he said his piece, I couldn't stop myself from discussing it enthusiastically. In banning prostitution and changing the lives of prostitutes, they had brought about a series of changes. There were no more prostitutes and no more clients. Rather than working as merchants and hawkers in complementary service industries, many people had to find other work. Many of the madams and pimps had been taken to court, and the worst of them had been executed by firing squad. The prostitutes were sent into rehabilitation, and they became factory workers and got married.

The brothels that had been filled with music and merriment until dawn were left deserted. The buildings with their decorations and carved railings were confiscated and transformed into various housing units to be rented out to those without proper housing. Post-revolutionary Nanjing had a period of population growth. Many of those who had fled the chaos came back again, and much of the population moved into these renovated and transformed buildings. Soon after, there was a great increase in birth rates, as people gave birth to and raised children in these crowded buildings. After the revolution, there were great changes in southern Nanjing. A large population of workers settled in the area around the Confucius

Temple. The Confucius Temple that towered over the transient population slowly became a building that towered over the permanent population, and finally became a residential area.

In the days when I was a worker, I used to have to pass along Shiba Street and by the Confucius Temple every day. It left an impression on me. The street was very narrow and very old and filled with chamber pots from the houses along the alley, left outside in the sun. As I walked along, young children would be playing, the girls jumping rope and the boys playing with milk caps. Most of the streets and alleyways in south Nanjing were like this; this part of Nanjing became the domain of the workers. I know a lot of people who live in south Nanjing. Their houses are narrow, with multiple families sharing a single water faucet and a single power meter. Because there are no sanitation facilities, going to a public toilet requires a journey by bicycle.

The population density of south Nanjing is much higher than that of the north side of the city. South Nanjingers seem to be more representative of the city. They speak the authentic Nanjing dialect and retain many of the customs of old Nanjing. In Nanjing, in the days before the Gang of Four was crushed, the majority of Nanjing's population was crowded into the south side of the city. The new population coming from outside seemed to have no choice but to squeeze in. When you bring up south Nanjing, people think of old Nanjing; they also think of the overcrowding.

After the Qinhuai River area was transformed, a lot of inhabitants took the opportunity to leave the south, moving into new public housing. Although the Confucius Temple area is bustling—indeed, it is jam-packed with those living in its old houses without sanitation facilities, shooing their family members out when they bathe in the summer and asking guests to use a chamber pot—the whole situation is rather unpleasant, all in all. For a number of denizens, being able to leave would be cause to rejoice even though the area is close to the bustling business district. The old houses of south Nanjing are suitable for nostalgia, and suitable for those tourists who wish to understand how the common people live, but unsuitable for habitation.

Three

The people of south Nanjing were once very simple people. I remember back to when I was a workman in the period after the Cultural Revolution. During the summer, I took the night shift. I got off work just as the sun was rising and walked past the Confucius Temple. All throughout the city, a cool breeze was blowing. People were sleeping in open spaces, their arms and legs stretched out as they lay down face-up, men and women alike, without the slightest apprehension. Nanjing in summertime has always been called a furnace. Due to the city's dense population, everyone was crowded into narrow spaces. At the time, there was no air conditioning or even electric fans, and everyone was suffering from the heat, with no choice but to sleep outside their houses. At the time, all along the Qinhuai River, once the sun set over the hills, doors and shutters would open, and the empty space outside people's doors would be splashed with cold water to cool it down. Then people would eat dinner outside, chatting and cooling off in the shade, talking until late into the night. The whole family, old and young, would sleep outside their doorways, and those who couldn't lie down would bring out chairs and iron bedframes.

No one could imagine a scene like this nowadays, where no one locked their doors on summer nights. In those days, there wasn't anything inside worth stealing. Neither did we hear anything of perverts, because there was nowhere near as much sex crime as there is now. There weren't even as many mosquitos in those days, and the ones that did exist weren't so drug-resistant, either.

I can still remember such scenes. Cycling along streets and alleys, with the doorways packed with people, required a significant amount of skill. In the early hours of the morning in summer, the torrid heat was no longer so devastating. South Nanjing was fast asleep, and I rode my bike gently past the borders of their dreamland. It was a wonderful feeling. Streets lined with sleeping people were a customary sight in old Nanjing, and it is a sight that we shall not see again.

North Nanjing

One

There are many differences between the south and the north of the city. Historically, south Nanjing has always been bustling while north Nanjing has been desolated. Looking at a map of Nanjing, we see that two rivers pass through the city. One is the great Qinhuai River, and the other is the Jinchuan River. The Qinhuai flows through south Nanjing, and during the golden era of the Six Dynasties, there were countless stories about its beautiful scenery. The Jinchuan winds its way through north Nanjing, so unremarked upon that even Nanjingers do not understand the rise and fall of its terrain.

For Nanjingers, the south side of the city is clearly set in place: it is always wound around the Qinhuai River, particularly in the bustling area around the Confucius Temple. North Nanjing, however, is not so well-defined, constantly shifting northward—at least conceptually.

In any case, the Gulou area can be considered to be in north Nanjing. Over 60 years ago, Jiang Biwei, the wife of painter Xu Beihong, built a new residence with great fanfare, buying an unused plot of land in the Fuhougang area and announcing in the newspapers that burial plot owners were to move their plots within a limited time frame; after that, unclaimed graves would be dealt with. These sorts of advertisements were seen over and over again in Nanjing's newspapers during the era of large-scale construction projects in the 1920s and

1930s. From this development, we can tell that the Gulou area was expanding northward at the time, and into a thoroughly desolate area. Not only did Gulou expand northward, but it also expanded southward in the same fashion. Nanjing University's historical records indicate that many of the areas now belonging to the school were once desolate gravesites.

Over the decades, north Nanjing finally became a prosperous area. Of course, this was first and foremost a result of the Republican government's designation of Nanjing as its capital. Once the capital label had been declared, development was inevitable. Nanjing was densely populated and wanted to develop northward. Before this, the north had always provided services to the south; it was an area of vegetable farmers and fishmongers. After the capital was established, many new offices were built in the north of the city, with a whole host of them on Zhongshan North Road alone. Institutions such as the Ministry of Foreign Affairs, the Ministry of Railways, the Ministry of Agriculture, the Supreme Court, and the Admiralty all stood on the same road. Embassies of all nations were also built in the north of the city. The Japanese embassy was built in Gulou on what is now the site of a fire station; the French embassy was built in Gaoyunling, only around 30 meters from my current residence; the American embassy was on Xikang Road, which is now the site of a provincial Party hotel.

The most magnificent sights were the personal residences of bureaucrats. Because the south of the city was already saturated, Republican officials wanted to build their houses with everything they could wish for, and they could only do so in the north of the city. At the time, the area around Shanxi Road and Yihe Road was called the New Residential Area, with countless new and unique foreign-style buildings cropping up on every street. These beautiful buildings were a harmonious combination of East and West, built by architects who had studied abroad and returned home, designing buildings in both the American style and the Japanese style. In this American-European milieu, there were distinctions made between Northern and Western European design. The blocks of foreign-style buildings made for a complicated, crisscrossing maze of roads in the area. Even today, people get lost navigating it. The motorcar had become the main mode of transport for the city's bourgeoisie, and they feared that if they had to walk on foot, they would have no idea how to find their own front doors when travelling even a short distance.

The great and the good set about beautifying their residences. The most notable feature of the Republican bureaucrats' residential area was the fact that one would find it nearly impossible to catch sight of two identical houses. These houses were not only a symbol of class stratification, but because they had been built with private money, the higher your rank was, the more unique your house was likely to look. Some preferred luxury, some coziness, and some minimalism. From one look, one could gain insight into a particular homeowner's frame of mind.

For example, the official residence of Yan Xishan was of a luxury one would expect from a rich provincial type. It looked more like an office, and was built in a thoroughly imposing, nouveau-riche style. The nearby former residence of Wang Jingwei was quite inferior. It was clearly secluded, with curving, shady footpaths and a literary character. Yu Youren's old residence was also close by, this being a foreign-style building made with grey brick and glazed roof tiles, surrounded by bamboo and flowers. It is worth pointing out that the houses of Wang Jingwei and Yu Youren were not paid for by the men themselves. Wang Jingwei's residence was given to him by his brother-in-law Chu Minyi, and Yu's rent was paid for by the public purse. The true owner of the house was probably Feng Yunting. Feng Yunting was originally a military officer under Feng Yuxiang. On the eve of the beginning of the Warlord Era, he left the military and came to Nanjing in order to set up a real estate business, through which he made a great deal of money. His willingness to rent a house to Yu Youren could be considered a mark of public praise, which allowed Yu to not only become a major public official, but also write poetry and literature which garnered him a reputation as a contemporary sage of cursive script calligraphy.

Two

The important difference between south and north Nanjing is that south Nanjing is busy while the north is quiet. South Nanjing is filled with the common people while the north is filled with bureaucrats. The south is popular, and the north is elitist. The bureaucrats of north Nanjing could take a car to the south of the city to enjoy its sights and its drinking establishments, but the commoners of south Nanjing could only argue among themselves as to what the northern bureaucrats were like.

This set-up changed little after the Guomindang fled to Taiwan. The differences were that the south's drinking establishments did not re-open, and the officials from the Communist Party were much less corruptible. Clearly, the residences of the city's great and good in days past could not simply be turned into living spaces for the common people just because of the huge changes that had gone on. The common people lived where they still do today. Some of the opulent mansions became enemy property, confiscated by the People's Government, and were then turned into new residential complexes. Those who were allowed to live there were cadres—and higher-up ones, at that. Some of the buildings were too large, with no way to turn them into appropriate living spaces, and so they became offices for government institutions. Some of the houses were targets for consolidation, kept in good condition due to the status of their former owners.

Unlike the profane atmosphere of south Nanjing, in the years after the Communist revolution, north Nanjing had an unreal feeling about it. There were slums in the north of the city, and the population was by no means small, but they were divided into different areas. They no longer lived by the riverside, but in Xiaguan. As a result, no atmosphere could develop. The atmosphere was that of the party cadres and their children. In south Nanjing, the people spoke the authentic Nanjing dialect. In north Nanjing, the children of party cadres spoke perfunctory Mandarin. The children of the cadres in the north and of the commoners in the south may have been born in the same city, but they had little to do with each other. They did not exactly see each other as enemies, but they were by no means friendly. These children were two different kinds of Nanjingers.

The offices of provincial government organizations were in the north of the city, and the provincial and municipal leaders mostly lived in the area around Shanxi Road and Yihe Road. As well as the provincial and municipal officials, a number of senior army officials also lived in North Nanjing. Army children were an additional feature of north Nanjing. When I was in middle school, the People's Liberation Army was highly respected by everyone, and every boy longed for an authentic soldier's cap of his very own. At the time, among all the squabbling, fighting boys of Nanjing, the "cleaver squad" was said to be the fiercest and most daring. It was said that the "cleaver squad" members were all army children. They spoke nonstandard Mandarin and wore civilian clothes for shirts, along with a pair of their fathers' old brown army pants and military sneakers. On their backs, they had green military satchels, inside of which they kept shiny kitchen cleavers.

In the eyes of children from south Nanjing, the cadres' children of the north were a mystery. The children of south Nanjing were always a target of the cadres' children's disdain. At the same time, the cadres' children also influenced the poor children of north Nanjing. And so, the poor children of the north, the descendants of those vegetable farmers and fishmongers, would also sometimes look down on the south Nanjing kids. They thought their speech was too rough and their behavior too common.

Three

The impasse between north and south is gradually thawing, but this is happening over a matter of decades. Nanjing has expanded greatly, and its original structures have naturally been demolished. Change is everywhere, and Nanjing cannot resist it. Looking at it from above, north Nanjing and south Nanjing still exist, but what were originally the north and south are now called the city center.

The glum desolation of north Nanjing has begun to disappear. Bustling commercial districts are not seen only in the south. North Nanjing's narrow Hunan Road was widened, becoming one of Nanjing's busiest streets. Before, Zhongshan North Road was empty, lined with lush trees and the long perimeter walls of government office compounds. Now there are shops everywhere. Empty spaces are immediately occupied by tall buildings. In 1983, when I moved to Zhongying Road in north Nanjing, what is now the Xuanwu Hotel was still a row of short houses. I went there every day to boil water on a large, old-style kitchen stove. Opposite the Xuanwu Hotel, the Jiangsu Exhibition Hall now stands on what was then still farmland.

Many south Nanjingers moved to the north side of the city. There are still provincial government offices on the north side as well as a number of technical training colleges. By comparison, north Nanjing is still unlike south Nanjing. The Nanjing accent is heard everywhere, and everywhere belongs to the common people. On the north side, one often hears accents from different places. Countless outsiders come to Nanjing, attend the university, and then become staff in government offices, toiling away unremarkably, looking forward to the day where they might receive an official appointment. North Nanjing is still steeped in an air of bureaucracy. Its offices remain the cradles of the managerial class; the people are prudent, but their ambition is vigorous. In north Nanjing, the top-class officials have long awaited their moments, and their loneliness is inescapable.

When it comes to their children's education, north and south Nanjing are also different. In the north and the south, parents will hire private tutors for their children from elementary school onwards. In the south, it is because their children's grades are poor and parents fear that they will be unable to graduate; in the north, parents hope that their children will get into Nanjing's best foreign-language schools. Education in north Nanjing is clearly better than in the south—this much is obvious from annual test scores.

Eating in Nanjing

One

There are a great many people around me who have settled in Nanjing, but who did not grow up here. Because of their maturity and abilities, they have come from all over the country, particularly from other places in Jiangsu, to settle in Nanjing, becoming honorary citizens of the city. When I talk with them about food, and particularly the food of Nanjing, each of them is filled with righteous indignation, turning up their noses. As outsiders see it, Nanjing food is terrible.

As a born-and-bred Nanjinger, I feel ashamed. I am not a particularly eloquent debater, and practically speaking, Nanjing's food nowadays is not particularly amazing. Facts will always win over rhetoric, and there is no need for me to defend the honor of Nanjing food to the death. Whether one admits it or not, in any case, Nanjing's food has never been worse, more expensive, or more unremarkable than it is now. The food that I remember was never like this.

This year, in late spring, I had the opportunity to go to Gaoyou in northern Jiangsu. Naturally, I wanted to sample the local delicacies. Eight years ago, Wang Zengqi's work, in which he explores the food of his hometown of Gaoyou, left a deep impression upon me. Before this, the food of Yangzhou had left a similar impression. The impression I had at the time was that the people of Yangzhou ate better than the Nankinese, and that the people of Gaoyou ate even better than the people of Yangzhou. To this day, this viewpoint has not changed. But I feel a certain regret over the fact that, compared to years before, in such a short space of time, culinary standards have dropped in Gaoyou, and Yangzhou has become even worse.

Gaoyou is merely a small county town which is a subsidiary of Yangzhou. Yangzhou seems to have returned to Nanjing's jurisdiction, and thus the simplest conclusion is that the further away one goes from the large cities, the more attention is paid to cuisine. In other words, the smaller the place is, the better its food and the greater possibility one has of enjoying its delights. This simplified conclusion will no doubt draw criticism from urban chauvinists. Firstly, Nanjingers themselves will disagree, and cities larger than Nanjing will not even bother to respond. Beijingers will not accept it, even though Beijing's food is even worse than Nanjing's. When Nanjingers treat their Beijinger friends to a meal in a restaurant, they will rarely be fussy about Nanjing's dishes, but pointing fingers at Beijingers and telling them that they know nothing about food will only vex them. People from Shanghai and Guangzhou eat better than modern-day Nanjingers and advancing this sort of argument with them is simply asking for trouble.

Let us approach cuisine from another perspective. The larger a city is, the easier it is for it to lose its finest culinary conventions. Cuisine should be a convention in the first place. Without such convention, we have no way of discussing food and we have no way of assessing its quality. We do not eat simply to taste; we also experience nostalgia through food. People from Guangzhou and Shanghai have no need to argue with Nanjingers over who pays more attention to cuisine or who truly appreciates it. They should compare themselves to the Guangzhou and Shanghai of the past. Even though there are more and more restaurants of higher and higher quality, we have no choice but to concede that the standards regarding our food have gotten worse. We face an issue of widespread degeneration when it comes to cuisine standards.

Historically, Nanjing cuisine was by no means inferior to that of Yangzhou, and likewise, Yangzhou's was not inferior to that of Gaoyou. The important factor in these falling standards has been these large cities' excessively rapid pace of development, their anxious restlessness causing them to lose their finest culinary conventions. The smaller towns cannot expect to escape this, either—it will not be long until it is difficult to find good food there, too.

Two

To say that Nanjingers know nothing of food is an unjust accusation. A pair of couplets once hung on the walls of a teahouse by the Confucius Temple:

Enter the Master's residence, eat naught but finely ground grain and finely chopped meat,
On the bank of the Qinhuai, grow fine as a flower, and round as the moon.

This couplet is a vivid depiction of the relaxed attitude of Nanjingers and paints an image of the origins of their maturity. Traditionally, Nanjingers have always known how to enjoy life's pleasures. This bon vivant custom contributed to the golden age of the Six Dynasties, advanced the cultural splendor of the Qinhuai River, and naturally brought about the downfall of nations. After "mooring near a Qinhuai tavern in the evening", Tang dynasty poet Du Mu could only then feel that the singing-girls "still sang Flowers of the Jade Tree Hall by the river." The Scholars records that taverns along the Qinhuai would operate day and night. "Each day at the fifth watch [3 a.m.] they would open, carrying on until the third watch [11 p.m.]." From this description, we can see that as long as there was no war, and people had money in their pockets, the Nankinese were committed gourmands and drinkers. In those days of peace and prosperity,

Nanjing had a great many taverns and restaurants lined up next to one another in a true glutton's paradise. No wonder Qing dynasty poet Yuan Mei could earnestly write his work *Recipes from the Sui Garden*.

Historically, Nanjingers have been obsessed with food. Eating in the capital of the Six Dynasties was always a feast and a pleasure. Gourmands and tales of gluttony abounded. This connoisseurial tradition still clung on even after the communist revolution. Hu Xiaoshi, the famous scholar of Chinese at Nanjing University, was a well-known gourmand, and, many years ago, the restaurants Dasanyuan and Liuhuachun both had signs written in his calligraphy. Hu was a famous academic, but because of his reputation as a gourmand, the proprietors of those restaurants went to extremes to get his sign of approval for their dishes.

In the past, famous people were proud of their knowledge of cuisine. For example, "Mr. Hu's tofu", said to be beloved by Hu, became a specialty that attracted customers to restaurants. The culinary traditions of Nanjing were all-embracing, tending toward innovation rather than conservatism, appreciating both novelty and nostalgia. People could sample fine delicacies from all over the country, losing themselves in pleasure. As a result, Nanjing became a place of wide-ranging and profound epicurism. The Nankinese were not as stubborn as the Sichuanese or the Hunanese, who would only eat spicy food, and nor were they like the people of south Jiangsu, who would refuse to eat anything spicy. The Nanjingers followed a path between the two, and when they appreciated food, they did so without any sense of regional prejudice.

Nanjingers have always been very open-minded as eaters, conscientiously mulling over every dish's real meaning. If they are to eat, they want something more than meets the eye, something of high quality. Nanjingers are unavoidably tarred with the brush of snobbishness, being too fond of fine food and eating new and famous dishes. In short, Nanjingers are absolute gluttons. Nanjing was once a diner's paradise, filled with gourmands seeking to eat their fill. When Tan Yankai (a Hunanese) was Chairman of the National Government in Nanjing, he once spent 120 yuan on a Cantonese banquet in honor of Li Ruiqing. He had an ulterior motive in doing so. The attendees were all famous poets as well as gourmands, and so the climax of the occasion was not the sacrifice in honor of Li, but the banquet afterward. At the time, a shi [roughly 60 kilos] of rice would cost eight yuan. One hundred and twenty yuan for a banquet was an exceptional figure! This feast of gourmands was no doubt an extraordinary sight. Li Ruiqing was Hu Xiaoshi's former teacher. At the end of the Qing and beginning of the Republic, everyone in the academic world would have known of him. His calligraphy was known both at home and abroad. Interestingly, Li Ruiqing was not only an erudite scholar, but also a gourmand and a skilled cook himself. Because of this, his students all became scholars with great appetites, such as Hu Xiaoshi. I was born too late. Although I spent seven years of study in Hu's Chinese department, I did not have the chance to see the man himself. But I did once dine with Hu's student, Wu Bo. Wu was not only an accomplished scholar in the field of Chinese opera, but also an established gourmand who I had the fortune of meeting.

Historically, in Nanjing one could find plenty of banquets akin to the one held in honor of Li Ruiqing. It was not a shameful thing to eat one's fill; on the contrary, not eating properly made one seem tasteless. It is said that Chiang Kai-shek was not much of a gourmand. An old man who once worked as a servant for him once told me that, because of his poor teeth, Chiang would only eat soft foods, such as yellow croaker in soup, a dish from Ningbo. Compared to Chiang, Wang Jingwei took more pleasure in eating. For example, Maxiangxing Restaurant's famous meiren gan ("beautiful liver") was one of Wang's most beloved dishes. While he was leading the treacherous puppet regime in Nanjing, he would often write letters on stationery from the famous Rongbaozhai store in the dead of night, saying "Ordering dishes on behalf of the Wang residence, all army and police are to allow to pass without exception," and dispatching a car to pick up meiren gan so he could eat heartily.

Meiren gan is not a particularly amazing dish—it is simply duck pancreas, which in Nanjing dialect is referred to as yizi bai (white pancreas). In traditional halal food, this ingredient is not used, but Maxiangxing Restaurant made it into something wonderful, employing extraordinary skill to make it into one of its specialty dishes. Of course, meiren gan is not an easy thing to make. Leaving aside the fact that each duck only has one pancreas, and making the dish requires 40 to 50 ducks, the control of heat needed to cook the dish properly must be gotten right the first time. If the heat is too high, then the dish will be soft rather than crisp, and if it is too low, then the dish will be leathery rather than tender. Cooking it well is impossible for all but the greatest of kitchens and chefs.

Three

Historically, it would be a mistake to presume that cuisine in Nanjing was the preserve of celebrities. Great men can often only fan the flames; it is the people who are the true driving force of history. Nanjing's food is noteworthy not for the presence of a few celebrity gourmands, but because of its wide-ranging, popular basis in the city. The people prized food above all else. Culinary culture can only be elevated from a popular foundation. It can only be developed with the active participation of the masses. The historical splendor of Nanjing cuisine is a result of the fact that it can be earnestly made and earnestly eaten.

In most people's imaginations, eating is best done in the city center. In fact, this is a great misunderstanding. The food available in the city center today is a shadow of its former self. Eating is not done simply for the sake of eating; it is not the primary reason that people come to the city center. Eating has become more and more adulterated. This is an important reason for the decline in food standards. In the busy city center, when people are already exhausted from shopping, the most ideal food is simple fast food. As a result, a fast-food culture has quickly arisen.

Adulterated eating also appears in many invitations to meals. Whether it is a dinner paid for with public money or private money, eating takes second place. The various reasons why one might invite guests to a meal have taken the delight of appreciating food away from the practice of dining at restaurants. Eating has become a method of communication, with the ulterior motives of investment and reciprocation, and, as a result, it has become utterly debased. This adulterated eating has created a series of vicious circles. Consumers do not spend money in order to eat; managers do not need to spend effort on food, and thus they can only think about how to earn money.

After 1958, Maxiangxing moved from its remote location outside the Gate of China to its current location in the central Gulou district. Its golden age appears to have disappeared forever. People are unconvinced that it can recapture its former glory after moving to the city center. Maxiangxing is now rarely a topic of discussion. There are so many people who walk past it each day without giving it so much as a second glance. When comparing these two eras, the hypocrisy can feel unbearable.

When one remembers Maxiangxing, it is as a thoroughly fine restaurant; there was no advertising or embellishment, and yet business was booming. The great and the good of the city were not the only ones who came to enjoy it. The common people also sat at its tables, drinking tea and wine alongside the celebrities. People came from far and wide with pure intentions: they wanted to eat, and they loved eating. They came to Maxiangxing to eat its steamed egg dumplings, phoenix-tail shrimp, and duck tongue and feet. Meiren gan was a little more expensive, but you didn't have to eat it. Food was never as unreasonably expensive in Nanjing as it is today. Eating in Nanjing is more expensive than in Guangzhou or Shanghai, and Nanjingers' incomes are nowhere near that of the residents of either of those two cities. In those days, braised abalone at Dasanyuan was 2.5 yuan; duck feet with tangerine peel was cheaper, at only 0.8 yuan. At Shouxihu Dining Hall near Xinjiekou on the eve of the war against

Japan, one could have a feast of four cold plates, four hot plates, and five main courses for just 5 yuan. People would go to Qifangge to drink tea and chat, and when they were hungry, they would spend 5 fen [cent] on a plate of shredded tofu; for 7 fen, they could have a bowl of noodles. Braised beef with soy sauce would be carved into thin slices on a chopping block and served upon freshly picked lotus leaves at an extremely reasonable price. In the late 70s and early 80s, in Sichuan restaurants, one could eat one's fill for 10 yuan. Save for when it came to eating, people at the time spent money and consumed goods far less than they do today. They did not have much money, but they could eat heartily and have enough to spare. Eating thus became earnest and sincere, both simple and delicious. People ate for the sake of eating, and they ate well.

People today will not expend much effort in eating. Compared to the past, people's lives are richer, and it seems like food will not become a problem again. If food itself is not a problem, then that means that new problems have arisen. Today, people eat for convenience, for appearances, for quality, for friendship, for money, and for all sorts of strange reasons; my one regret is that no one eats for the sake of taste. But people's ultimate goal in eating at a restaurant should still be for flavor. Otherwise, Nanjing's food will never attain glory. In truth, cuisine in Nanjing nowadays has been severely punished. I live near the busy Hunan Road. When I am walking in the evening, I see rows of glimmering lights outside restaurants, with awkward-faced girls standing outside to greet customers who pay them no attention. If someone opens a restaurant simply to make money, then people may refuse without the slightest hesitation. Presuming that Nanjingers know nothing of food is really quite silly.

I will never forget when I was young, over 20 years ago, and I lived in an alleyway where a man would sell wontons. In his tiny shop front, he had a big wok where he boiled bones for soup year-in and year-out. The wontons tasted heavenly. In those days, there were countless places in Nanjing where one could eat small plates that were ordinary and yet delicious. Nowadays, as I speak of it, I cannot help but salivate.

Drinking in Nanjing (Part 1)

One

Many years ago, on a warm day, an American friend of mine came to visit Nanjing on vacation. I went to the train station to meet him. He was a tall, strapping fellow, and it was not particularly difficult for us to recognize each other in the crowd. He was an expert on China, and he had flown up from Hong Kong. He was staying in Nanjing for a day or two, and he knew the black market for currency like the back of his hand. When I asked him for his impression of Nanjing, he thought for a moment, then gestured to the can of Sprite he was drinking and laughed. "This stuff isn't very popular in America."

I was somewhat surprised. "But it's an American soft drink, isn't it?" I asked him. He didn't deny that, but he insisted that he had never drunk it before, and that it was a new product in America, too. That year, Sprite had only just entered the Chinese market. "Crystal clear, ice cold"—many children knew the advertising slogan. The American food and drink industry is truly formidable. I have met many people like me—who do not care for KFC or McDonald's but have had no choice but to sheepishly accompany their daughters there to spend frivolous sums of money. Similarly, I do not like Sprite. I did not like it at the time, and I still don't. Many of my friends don't, either. But there is nothing we can do to obstruct the unbridled American moneymaking machine. Perhaps the reason for this is joint venture companies in Nanjing. In any case, guileless Nanjingers are easily swindled, swallowing up advertising and moving crates upon crates of beverages back to their houses because work units seem to have gone mad in their pursuit of wholesale trade.

The term yinliao, meaning "beverage", has in fact only become widely used in the past few years. It seems that almost anything can be termed yinliao. As long as it has some sort of a pull-top can, or some sort of nutritional value, or it can nourish yin and boost *yang* energy. Traditionally, Chinese people would only consider drinking tea or liquor. Nanjing is a city of consumers; not only does it pay attention to eating, but it also pays attention to drinking. Historically, Nanjingers drank tea and grain liquor. They were connoisseurs, with palates just as sophisticated as those in any other place. The Nanjing area does not produce tea, and nor does it brew wine. But Nanjingers still drank high-quality beverages.

As they say, tall mountains produce the best tea. There are a few mountains surrounding Nanjing, but they are all small hills, lacking the conditions to produce top-quality tea leaves (one thing that Nanjing produces a lot of is experts in tea). Tall mountains produce the best tea because they are sparsely populated and unpolluted. It is impossible for there not to be pollution in the area surrounding Nanjing, but Nanjing does in fact produce one famous variety of tea: the high-priced Yuhua tea. Twenty years ago, I was a factory worker, and a young colleague quietly informed me that Yuhua tea had been developed by his father. Once, I visited his house and sampled some genuine Yuhua tea. It was heavenly. Afterward, whenever I sampled tea that called itself Yuhua tea, I found that it was completely incomparable.

I am not sure whether what the young man said was true about Yuhua tea having been developed by his father. I have never seen any records that suggest so, and I have heard many different explanations. One book says that Yuhua tea was developed collectively, to commemorate revolutionary martyrs of the Yuhuatai district of Nanjing. It resembles pine needles in form, signifying the eternal steadfastness of the revolutionaries. This cannot help but arouse some suspicions. I do not believe that it was developed collectively. As a form of commemoration, it is rather insufficient, and feels something like sloganeering. Good tea is good tea. After my father was branded a rightist, many of the scripts he wrote were dubbed "collective works". As his son, I knew that these collective works were written entirely by my father. From these two matters, I am justifiably convinced that that young worker's father was just like mine; someone who could not sign his work with his own name. I remember that, at the time when I was sampling my colleague's Yuhua tea, his father had been locked up for many years, and had just been released from prison.

Yuhua tea was just a little too good, finer than the average person could bear. The price of Yuhua tea has remained high from the start, rather lacking in the spirit of "Serving the People". The common people rarely have the chance to sample true Yuhua tea. Yuhua tea has become a precious gift that people begrudgingly drink; it is sent back and forth before finally landing in the cup of someone who does not know how to appreciate tea. Someone once earnestly invited me to his house to drink Yuhua tea from the last year's harvest. Good green tea must be fresh; how could he offer me last year's crop? It was truly a waste of resources to make one sigh.

Two

Much like its food, tea in Nanjing has gone downhill, with each generation being worse than the last. Nanjing's old teahouses are a thing of the past. According to historical records, one could once find a teahouse on almost every street in Nanjing. In 1935, there were nearly 300 teahouses in the city. At the time, there was no television, and fewer newspapers than there are today. News and information of all kinds was concentrated and circulated most quickly in the teahouses. When disputes arose between people, they would often go to teahouses to reconcile their differences with the aid of family and friends or intermediaries. Thus, teahouses became places to keep the peace. Zhang Henshui's *Great Changes in the Bottom of a Cup* records the splendor of Nanjing's mid-century teahouses:

No matter how early you go, the teahouse will be full of the chatter and laughter of people in good company. When I arrived, it was between seven and eight o'clock. A few groups of tea drinkers had already satisfied their craving and departed. Here there were public servants and merchants. They were not neglecting their jobs by being here; this was an accepted part of tea-drinking in Nanjing.

A tea server came by, clearing everything away like a strong breeze. He pulled a cleaning rag from over his shoulder and immediately wiped the table clean. In his left hand, he clutched lidded teacups with saucers. In his right, a large tin pot. Setting out the crockery in front of each person, he poured out the hot water with a rush of heated air, and added the tealeaves, immediately closing the lids on top of the cups; this was where the fun began. A number of wooden stools surrounded the square table and were sat upon casually; there were very few high-backed chairs and no couches at all. This was the proprietor's way of making sure you could not get too comfortable and forget yourself. If you were a regular customer, the tea server would bring you your own personal teapot and teacup which were yours and yours alone. Whether it was a plain teapot, decorated with flowers, in the "gourd" or "horseshoe" style, or even copper, it would not be sold to another customer.

Nanjingers would drink any kind of tea, but that did not mean that they were not picky. Nanjingers want their choice of tea to embody their own individual mastery of the subject. Since their own region does not produce tea, they have no choice but to accept what they are given. A tea connoisseur can never fixate solely on one type of tea. Different seasons and different surroundings call for different teas. This is a fundamental principle of tea-drinking. When a new tea appears on the market, attention is paid to its freshness, and to which season it was harvested in. On a warm day, one might as well drink a smokier tea, such as Lu'an Melon Seed tea, to help beat the heat. In midwinter, Keemun black tea will warm the cockles. Some love Pi Lo Chun, grown in the Dongting Mountain region of Jiangsu, some love Longjing tea from Shifeng in Zhejiang, some love Huangshan Maofeng tea from Anhui, and some love Lushan Cloud tea from Jiangxi. There are also teas from Fujian, Yunnan, and Sichuan. Different teas have different tastes. When Nanjingers drink tea, they pay close attention to the taste. The wealthy drink high-quality teas. When they have drunk one or two famous teas, they will look down on any other kind. They are by no means aficionados of tea.

Modern manufacturing techniques have caused great steps to be taken in the production of tea. For example, tea no longer needs to be baked. During the manufacturing process, the liquor is kneaded from every leaf and it is dried. One merely needs to soak it in water, and it will overflow with fragrance. This revolution in production has made tea-drinking much more convenient but means that we have shed the elegance of the old process. Sometimes, the pleasure of tea-drinking is in sitting around a stove. Drinking tea should be a process, and there is no harm in having a sequence of steps for it—such inconvenience is a prelude to pleasure. A similar argument can be made regarding the invention of the thermos flask. In the past, one reason why people went to teahouses to drink tea was due to the unending supply of hot water. Nowadays, the thermos flask has taken the place of the tea-server. Tea-drinking is becoming more and more convenient, but the kind of joy that comes as a result of overcoming inconvenience will never return.

Three

Convenience is not necessarily a good thing. Nanjing's tea shops are fewer and fewer, the prices higher and higher. True, genuine famous teas are becoming rarely-seen things. Nowadays, the kind of people with a sense of refinement—those who will go to a tea shop, buy one or two fine teas, and invite other tea connoisseur friends to drink tea for the sake of tea, sampling it for the sake of its flavor—are increasingly rare. No one treats tea-drinking as an end in itself. It is only a custom, an almost mechanical action. Over the past few years, when teas have entered the market, they are purchased wholesale, and this has been a disaster for tea-drinking. Many teas are produced by work units, then distributed, and thus this creates passive tea drinkers. Since they are not spending money on it, people have no choice but to drink what they have at hand. Merchants will pay bribes to those with the authority to use public money to buy tea, and poor-quality leaves stealthily make their way into countless houses. There are some high-quality leaves, but because people have forgotten how to carefully appreciate tea, they are overshadowed.

There are also some problems with the water used to boil tea. Nanjing's water quality is better than that of many other big cities, but it is still incomparable to the past. Water pollution has ultimately become a common problem. As far back as 1937, the city government installed free drinking water taps in the Confucius Temple and Daxinggong areas, allowing the common people to quench their thirst. When I was in middle school in the early 70s, when summer came, at the very moment we finished class, boys and girls would rush to the water taps, clasping the copper faucets and taking big slurps. The water was cool and refreshing, and no one ever heard of experiencing an upset stomach as a result of it. At the time, the Qinhuai and Jinchuan rivers that flowed through Nanjing were crystal clear right down to the bottom, and when the Yangtze swelled its banks in spring, the waters were a wonderful blue. With such fine water as that, making good tea was not a problem. If Nanjing's water had not been good, then the historical saying, "I would rather drink the water of Jianye than eat the fish of Wuchang," would not exist.

When drinking tea, one absolutely cannot neglect the water, or the leaves, either. Historically, due to the favors bestowed upon them by nature, Nanjingers have rarely had to consider such issues. Over the past years, however, water quality has fallen, and people have begun to become aware of it, but they have no choice but to adopt a laissez-faire attitude. One cannot open one's own water processing plant. I once heard people discussing this issue and saying that Nanjing's water was better than Shanghai's. It is said that Nanjing's water quality is still higher than that of other major cities. An attitude of unconscientious tea drinking is spreading throughout Nanjing's tea-drinkers.

To ensure they had good water, old Nanjingers would collect snow from the branches of plum blossom trees and store it in a jar, boiling it in summertime to make tea. Tea connoisseurs will not re-boil water. In those years, tea-drinkers would take their "purple sand" pots and wait patiently in front of an old-style kitchen stove, making tea with the water at the moment that it boiled. Because boiling water took a long time, the dissolution of oxygen and CO_2 was greatly reduced. Using this sort of water to brew tea gave it a fresh taste. If the water had not been brought to a rolling boil when the tea was brewed, the tea's effective components would not be released, and its flavor would suffer greatly. Nowadays, all this ceremony seems to have fallen by the wayside. Nanjingers are called "radishes" for so many reasons, and you might as well add tea to that list. The traditional stoves are rarely seen these days, but there are all kinds of water-heating implements and vacuum flasks of varying quality, all of them springing up suddenly in homes and offices. People reheat water over and over again like they do soup, and they use this water to brew tea. Good tea leaves are wasted.

Now, the current fad is to use expensive, stainless-steel, heat-preserving flasks. In meetings, everyone who is anyone has one. I have asked questions to many people in meetings who own these flasks, and many of them were given the flasks by their work units or sent them by other people. Some own multiple flasks. Unfortunately, using these to brew tea is also a great offense. Putting soft young tea leaves inside such a flask quickly makes for overly stewed teas. Drinking tea such as this is even worse than drinking the Americans' beverages.

Drinking in Nanjing (Part II)

One

Good wine and good poetry are seemingly inseparable.

At Qingming Festival, the rains fall, and people wander the streets like lost souls.
"May I ask, where are the taverns?" The shepherd-boy points at distant Apricot Blossom Village.

Many scholars have argued over the exact location of Apricot Blossom Village (Xinghuacun) in this poem by late Tang poet Du Mu. Guichi in Anhui Province, Macheng in Hubei, and Fenyang in Shanxi all lay claim to Apricot Blossom Village as their own, and each has their own logic. The people of Shanxi brazenly advertise it on television, claiming Du Mu's Apricot Blossom Village to be theirs.

There is plenty of evidence to suggest that Du Mu's Apricot Blossom Village is in fact in Nanjing. So far, the earliest records of Du Mu buying wine in Apricot Blossom Village are from the Song dynasty's Taiping Huanyu Ji, in a passage regarding the Jiangning area of Nanjing: "Apricot Blossom Village is in the west of the county, and it is said that Du Mu bought wine there." The Sunchu Restaurant in Fenghuangtai, where Li Bai drank wine and composed poetry, is adjacent to Apricot Blossom Village. Records of the Historical Sites of

Jinling, compiled during the reign of the Jiaqing Emperor in the Qing dynasty, also confirms without doubt that the Apricot Blossom Village where Du Mu purchased wine is in Nanjing, and includes verse on the subject: "South of the Yangtze, spring rains fall and one's dreams are vast, and wine is bought in the bannered pavilions by the gate of Baixia [Nanjing]/when mention is made of Fan Chuan [a sobriquet of Du Mu], people speak to this day of the Apricot Blossom Village."

The poem suggests that when Du Mu was mentioned, people in Nanjing fell over each other in their eagerness to remind the speaker of the location of the village. In fact, the exact location of Apricot Blossom Village is not particularly important. It is only a celebrity making mischief. Du Mu was a celebrity, and he wrote famous poetry, which serves as the best advertisement. I am citing resources on the original location of Apricot Blossom Village in Nanjing simply because I wish to explain the long history of wine-drinking in Nanjing.

Nanjingers enjoy wine; there is nothing unusual about it. During the golden age of the Six Dynasties, wine was abundant. The area around the Qinhuai River was nicknamed the "Lake of Wine and Forest of Meat" (Jiuchi Roulin). "In Apricot Blossom Village, the tavern banners stand at an angle, and spring trees bloom within its walls." A Taiwanese friend of mine came to Nanjing and was surprised to see so many restaurants calling themselves "wine houses" (jiujia). In Taiwan, he said, the term "wine-house" had erotic connotations. I found this quite amusing. Wine is a great sexual matchmaker; it is no surprise that such a connection is made. But there are many reasons behind the names of Nanjing's taverns. The tavern in "'May I ask, where are the taverns?'" and the tavern in "Mooring at evening in Qinhuai and entering the tavern" were perhaps not also houses of ill repute. Although drink was also served in brothels, there was a clear division of labor between brothels and taverns.

Much like when they are drinking tea, Nanjingers are connoisseurs when it comes to drinking wine. Nanjingers may love to drink wine, but they are not expert winemakers. The Nanjing area has not produced any famous wines. The city consumes a lot of wine, however, and there are plenty of famous wines on offer from other areas for those who wish to drink. The area produces more drinkers than it does drink. Many people came to settle in Nanjing, so it is only natural that they brought the drinking habits of their various regions with them. Wine produced in Nanjing cannot compete. The Apricot Blossom Village truly produced fine wine, and no other place can compete with such a branding. Back then, a spring flowed down from the Purple Mountains; it was named Thunderbolt Spring (Pili Quan). It is said that the water of this spring was particularly well-suited to making wine, creating a particularly well-received type of wine named weijiu. Unfortunately, the Nanjing area is too large, and the small spring could not produce much wine, and so it was soon overshadowed by other types of wine and died out.

Two

The wine that the great poet Li Bai drank at the Sunchu Restaurant was named "Jinling Spring" (Jinling Chun). When he had finished, he wrote poetry, and that poetry has lasted through the ages. "In Baimen [Nanjing] the willow trees are plenty and the tavern fragrance fills the air/a beautiful local woman calls to customers, asking them to try the wine." What I find odd is that Nanjingers are not natural businessmen. Seeing as we now have "Confucius Family Baijiu", "Mencius Family Baijiu", and even "Cao Xueqin Family Baijiu", why have Nanjing's wine factories not created the "Jinling Spring" brand to try to make money from their compatriots? When it came to drinking, Li Bai was more of an expert than Confucius or Mencius, and even more of one than Cao Xueqin. Li Bai's wine-sodden poetry serves as a ready-made advertisement. If Nanjingers wanted to perform such a deliberate excavation, there would be countless essays on drinking culture to be written.

During the Song dynasty, Nanjing had four great winehouses:

the Eastern Winehouse, the Southern Winehouse, the Northern Winehouse, and the Ministerial Winehouse. By the time of the Ming and Qing dynasties, Nanjing's drinking culture had blossomed, and taverns and winehouses could be found everywhere. Zhu Yuanzhang once "ordered the Ministry of Works to build ten buildings outside the gates south of the Yangtze, so that the people may set up wine houses and receive travelers from all places." Drinking was once an activity extremely close to the hearts of Nanjingers. It became a part of everyday life for the common people. It is worth mentioning that, historically, the alcohol that commoners drank was not particularly expensive. The lower classes could get drunk for a few copper coins.

Nanjing's wine houses were particularly skilled in procuring good-quality wine from outside the region. During the Republican era, the Laowanquan Winehouse would stick their own logos onto wine bottles and sell them on to the restaurants. They mainly dealt in Shaoxing wine, as well as the sorghum wine of the same type that is distilled today by the Yanghe Company. The Shaoxing wine that Laowanquan stocked had been aged for 30 or 40 years. This type of vintage wine was difficult to find even in Shaoxing itself.

Writers like Chen Jimin—in Tales of Jinling, in this case—have recorded how there was a fashion among the common people of Nanjing for drinking seasonal wines. The Nankinese have always had a romantic spirit, loving to drink wine and loving to drink different wines in different seasons. Romanticists are often unconcerned by the inconvenience. For example, at Duanwu Festival, they will drink "Calamus wine"; on Double Ninth, they will drink "chrysanthemum wine"; and at New Year, they will drink "Tusu wine". The manufacture of these wines is not difficult, but it is also uneconomical; they are all, to an extent, medicinal wines. "Calamus wine" is made from extracts of the calamus plant and yeast rice, and "chrysanthemum" and "Tusu" wine are both brewed with additives. Many people who like to drink wine are opposed to medicinal wines. They feel that such additives alter the original flavor of the wine. But the Nankinese are unconcerned; because they are attracted to novelty, they do not wish to stick to one type of wine. Nanjingers also enjoy drinking a type of wine brewed from the scorched rice found at the bottom of the pan, creating a wine with a burnt aroma.

The Record of the Seasons of Jinling notes that the herbalist Sun Simiao developed Tusu wine, and that this wine was clearly very popular in Nanjing. The recipe was as follows: seven mace and five candareen of cinnamon; one tael of siler; five mace of China root; five mace and seven candareen of Sichuan pepper, Chinese bellflower, and rhubarb; two mace and five candareen of wolf's bane; and 14 azuki beans. Grind them all together into a powder, wrap this powder into a triangular purple-red bag, and suspend it over a well on the eve of the lunar New Year. Early in the morning of New Year's Day, take it out, put it in wine, boil, and serve.

Tusu wine was drunk at breakfast on New Year's Day. Hence why Wang Anshi wrote "The firecrackers on New Year's Eve and the spring breeze brings the warmth of Tusu." Kong Shangren, the writer of Peach Blossom Fan and a descendent of Confucius, drank Nankinese Tusu wine, and wrote: "Drinking many cups of Tusu, huddled around the stove in accordance with custom." It is said that there is a tradition that one must face east while drinking Tusu wine, "drinking in the order of youngest to eldest" as the sun rises in the east, signifying upward mobility and prosperity. Kong Shangren's poetry points out this custom.

Three

When it comes to drinking, times have changed. In times past, low-strength rice wine was drunk. Drinking 60% baijiu is a modern phenomenon. For example, my father loved to drink Yanghe and Shuanggou from northern Jiangsu. For a long period of time, these two brands were on sale in stores all across Nanjing at a retail price of 1.37 yuan for a catty. This price remained constant for a long while.

When I was young, I often bought alcohol for my father. After the Cultural Revolution, these two brands were in very short supply. At New Year and other festivities, one had to rely on a ticket system to buy them. My father would often ask for such tickets from his friends. At the time, there was no problem with fake alcohol, and like many other drinkers, my father was happy to slowly sip his liquor with a few handfuls of shelled peanuts, either by himself or with friends. I never saw him 'binge-drinking' with anyone. In the past few years, I have had the opportunity to enjoy myself in all sorts of places, and I have come across a number of people who find courage in their drunkenness. Wine makes them blunt, and they do not care about its taste, being able to drink it only due to their cast-iron stomachs. I see this as completely different from the traditional drinking culture of Nanjing. What makes drinking in Nanjing special is not the volume consumed. Nanjingers are not particularly capable drinkers; it is not the custom to drink heartily and then eat a big meal to sop it up. True Nanjingers' drinking is like that depicted in *The Scholars*. Drink must be accompanied with some light snacks—half a duck or a bit of tofu (either the fresh or stinky kind)—and that will do just fine. Drinking is drinking, and not that much effort needs to be put into it.

There is a strong sense of individualism in drinking for Nanjingers. Excitedly carrying home a bottle of wine, pouring it into cups, drinking one at a time, as one wishes, to one's heart's content—keeping in mind one's ability to pay and one's health, not drinking to show off, and not forcing those who do not drink to drink. Nowadays, only those who are seasoned drinkers will frequent small stores set up in doorways, coming home with bottles of Jinfenting baijiu. The tangible benefit of this liquor industry is that it prevents poor people and those without plenty of cash at hand from drinking often.

Although I am not a seasoned drinker, I am very happy to see others do so in happy moderation. For example, my father drank leisurely, and when he drank with his friends, it was on a foundation of gentle enjoyment. Drinking is a personal matter and drinking by oneself is fine; there is no need to force others to drink. There are many different schools of thought when it comes to drinking, and the Nanjing style is not to make a raucous scene when doing so.

In fact, Nanjingers like to drink the cheaper alcohols because, as a whole, they are not particularly well-to-do. The most important factor for Nanjingers is low price and decent quality. Nowadays, there are many different kinds of liquor, all to be served at dinner parties and banquets. Often, serving top-brand liquor at a banquet is merely a matter of gaining face. Drinking cup after cup of baijiu at a party with no regard for taste is a waste of good liquor as well as good food. At too many feasts, there are too many who will not foot the bill for their own drinking, and this is a major factor in the decline of liquor standards.

A seasoned drinker cannot be satisfied by freeloading at a restaurant. Often, those with a real taste for liquor are those who do not have the opportunity to go to banquets. I remember that, when I was young, someone in our courtyard made props for a theatrical show. He was a married man, and he was cooling off in the evening shade. He would often bring a small wooden stool with him, sit by the doorway, and drink grain liquor called liangshi. This liquor was somewhat heady, and it was cheaper than both Yanghe and Shuanggou. During the Cultural Revolution, when my father's wages were docked so much that we could only just about survive, he drank this type of liquor. I remember the propmaker would drink nothing but this kind. Every day, when the time came, he would sit there drinking alone with a blank look on his face. His wife and children were in the countryside, and it seemed he had not thought to bring them to the city. Other than his propmaking, the only thing about him that left an impression on me was his drinking. For this propmaker, without liquor, life would have had no meaning. He kept up this single-minded devotion to alcohol until the day he died. One day, he could finally drink no more, and his life had come to a head.

I had a friend who was a drinker, and after a while, the porch of his house was filled with bottles. Drinking is a very individual thing. He would rarely brag to others about his ability to drink or what famous liquors he had drunk. For drinkers like him, high-grade liquors are out of the question. I have always thought that there were two kinds of people in the world: those who like to drink and those who do not. There are not many Nanjingers who truly love to drink, and nor are there many for whom alcohol is a significant part of their lives. Those who like to drink but are capable of not becoming roaring drunk are often the most likeable people.

Nanjing's drinking has not changed the disposition of its people. For Nanjingers, drinking also embodies a kind of Nankinese spirit. Unfortunately, nowadays there are few in Nanjing who will drink Tusu wine.

Leisure in Nanjing

One

I live near Xuanwu Lake Park in Nanjing. As a result, I have a pass to the park and I go for a walk there every afternoon. One day, I bumped into an old university classmate by the gate. He was accompanying the mayor, inspecting Xuanwu Lake Park with plans to turn it into a World Park theme park. He had already linked up with investors, and that day was merely meant for a quick look into the feasibility.

I did not attempt to hide my ardent opposition. I told them that a space as fine as Xuanwu Lake Park was a rare find in Nanjing and asked them to stay their hands. A city, perhaps, cannot avoid the possibility of being defiled, but a place like Xuanwu Lake Park would be best left as is. In terms of personal interest, I am far from enamored of places such as World Park and European City even though they may appear to be places for entertainment, bringing economic benefits. During the Republican era, Xuanwu Lake was renamed Five Continents Park (Wuzhou Gongyuan). This change in name was merely a curiosity, symbolizing the islands in Xuanwu Lake. They were dubbed Asia, Africa, Europe, and America. Thankfully, they were an original feature of the lake, and were not a result of destruction.

Xuanwu Lake has always been the pride of Nanjing. Friends who come to visit Nanjing are awed by the sight of the lake. There is a long wall in Xuanwu Lake which separates it from the clamor of the noisy city center outside. It is rare that one can find such a large, quiet park in a busy urban center. In terms of visual effects, this dark-colored city wall also blocks out the sight of many of the modern buildings that one may not want to see.

Strolling around Xuanwu Lake, you may entertain yourself as you please. You can row across the lake, which due to its size takes quite substantial effort; those less inclined to exertion may take an electric boat. You may walk along the dike, and whether the weather is fair or foul, whichever direction you walk in, as long as you have the stamina, you can walk all day without taking the same path twice. You can find a scenic spot to sit, alone or with friends, and enjoy a flask of tea, waiting for sunrise or sunset. You can sit on the old wall with its twisting vines; sit beneath the pines that have seen thousands of years of the vicissitudes of life since the Six Dynasties; sit by the lakeside, watching the ripples of boats in the blue-green water; or sit by the clear waters of the Wumiao Lock. Before your eyes stands a wonderful scene, and you yourself become a minor detail in this painting.

It is hard to find a place that is suitable for such entertainment all year round. At heart, Nanjingers love to enjoy themselves. Since antiquity, there has been a saying: "In spring, Niushou; in autumn, Xixia." In spring, one should go to Niushou Mountain to wander through its greenery; in autumn, one should go to Xixia Mountain to watch the leaves turn red. And no matter what time of year one visits Xuanwu Lake, there is always something to do to amuse oneself.

In spring, the flowers are in bloom at Xuanwu Lake, with pink peach blossoms and green willows, winter jasmine, flowering crabapple, apricot blossoms, plum blossoms, both Japanese and Chinese cherry blossoms, Dutch tulips, and all other kinds of flowers. I particularly love the fire-red poppies that grow along the dike in Xuanwu Lake.

Nanjing is known as one of the country's "great furnaces". As the summer heat draws near, a cooling breeze blows gently along Xuanwu Lake and the lotus flowers open, making it a natural scenic spot in which to while away the warm summer days. In my novel, *Nanjing*

1937: A Love Story, I wrote this of the warmest days: "The best place in the north of the city to enjoy the summer heat is Xuanwu Lake. So that everyone could have a place to cool off in the summer, the authorities opened the gates to Xuanwu Lake, and so the whole park was filled with the sound of laughter and chatter all day long." Xuanwu Lake was a place to spend the summer in the old days, too. When night fell, people would come to admire the lotus flowers, chatting all through the night. In the past few years, air conditioning has begun to become widespread, taking the place of such cooling-off spots. People hide away in their air-conditioned apartments watching TV, and Xuanwu Lake has become a place for lovers to meet while the people of Nanjing feel disinclined to join in the fun.

In autumn, as well as enjoying the fragrance of osmanthus flowers, you can gather the ginkgo and the walnuts from the trees (the walnut trees having been introduced by the Americans). As winter approaches, the walnuts fall from their tall branches onto the cement pathways with loud thuds. Years ago, when the walnuts fell from countless walnut trees in Xuanwu Lake Park, there seemed to always be a few people who would come to collect them on certain days. I never saw the authorities interfere with their collecting. Perhaps some of those collecting the walnuts were the authorities themselves.

As snow falls on Xuanwu Lake, people will also rush in to observe the scene. In Nanjing, snow melts quickly, and anyone who wishes to take a decent photo must act with speed.

Two

There is another place in Nanjing that fills people with pride: the scenic area in the eastern suburbs. Historically, Nanjingers' sites for leisure were located on the southern outskirts of Nanjing rather than the east. The reason may have something to do with Zhu Yuanzhang's burial on the eastern outskirts. During the Ming and Qing dynasties, this area was forbidden ground, with large numbers of troops garrisoned there and thousands of sika deer. The common people did not think it worth the trouble to travel there. And the southern outskirts were not far from the Qinhuai River, nor far from where the common people resided.

Nanjingers have only cast their attention eastward in the past few decades. While the waters of Xuanwu Lake are enchanting, the Purple Mountain is the heart of the eastern scenic area. There are still plenty of historical sites and scenic spots here. Fifteen-hundred years ago, Purple Mountain was the home of 70 different temples, and when Buddhism became prevalent during the Liang dynasty, there were too many temples there to count. A number of rulers, generals, and ministers came here for leisure, including the Kangxi and Qianlong emperors of the Qing dynasty. Countless literati also left their mark on the area. One could write an endless list: Wang Yizhi of the Eastern Jin; Li Bai, Gao Shi, and Yuan Zhen of the Tang; Su Shi, Wang Anshi, Lu You, and Li Gang of the Song; Zhao Meng of the Yuan; Liu Ji and Fang Xiaoru of the Ming; Kong Shangren, Gu Yanwu, and Huang Zongxi of the Qing, and so on and so on.

The eastern scenic area is well known for its mausolea. Going back in time, there was the tomb of Sun Quan. Later came the tomb of Zhu Yuanzhang, founder of the Ming dynasty, and, in modern times, this was the burial site of Sun Yat-sen. Nanjing's natural scenery has always been connected to its history. If leisure in Nanjing does feel like one is investigating the past, then it loses much of its pleasure. For young people with no interest in history, visiting the tombs of long-dead figures can at times be nothing more than a formality, simply done to show that one has visited such places. Often, all such visitors remember of them are the exhausting flights of steps and the stifling atmosphere of solemnity.

But for one who is familiar with the history of the Republican era, the feeling one gets from such a place is completely different. In the eastern scenic area, one can easily come into contact with the history of the Republic and the buildings left over from the era. It is a museum of the Republic. One can find the writings of many figures from the Republican era, as well as their tombs. Tales of the Republic abound.

For someone who has an interest in excavating the past, spending a day in the scenic eastern suburbs can result in quite the historical haul. Deep within its forests, a depository holds 138 stone tablets nearly two meters tall. Upon them is written the entire text of The *Three Principles of the People*, which is 155,000 characters long, inscribed by the most famous calligraphers of the time. The stone for the tablets is said to have been chosen personally by General Feng Yuxiang from Mount Song in Henan Province. There is also the nine-story-tall Linggu Pagoda. Nowadays, many people do not know how it came about, and young people merely gambol up it thanks to their youthful vigor. In fact, Linggu Pagoda is a memorial, built to commemorate the fallen soldiers of the National Revolutionary Army, much like the contemporary monuments we have today for the martyrs of the revolution. Above the door are four characters reading "Absolute Dedication to the Service of the Nation" (Jingzhong Baoguo), inscribed by Chiang Kai-shek. Inlaid between the second and fourth floors of Linggu Pagoda are 12 stone tablets upon which is engraved Words of Parting upon Heading North by Sun Yat-sen, inscribed in cursive script by senior Republican figure and noted writer Yu Youren. From the fifth to the eighth floor are 16 tablets, on which another Republican figure, Wu Zhihui, inscribed Sun Yat-sen's Verse on the Foundation of the Whampoa Military Academy.

These hills have the good fortune to have heroes buried within them, and much like West Lake where Yue Fei is buried, they are greatly enriched by the presence of the remains of Sun Yat-sen. After the Xinhai Revolution, the Guomindang's first leader, Sun Yat-sen, went hunting and expressed his wish to his subordinates that Purple Mountain was where he wanted his remains to be interred. Without the mausoleum of Sun Yat-sen, the eastern scenic area would be markedly worse off. After the Sun Yat-sen mausoleum was completed, it was the greatest honor that the area could receive to have Sun's remains buried there. For example, in the cemetery for fallen officers and soldiers of the National Revolutionary Army at Linggu Pagoda, 1,029 officers and men are buried there. These are only representatives. Many of them gave their lives during the Northern Expedition and the January 28th Incident. Their names are all carved upon countless memorial tablets.

During the Cultural Revolution, many of those who took part wanted to destroy such places, their desire borne out of a righteous indignation directed against the reactionary Guomindang. The emblem of the Guomindang was erased from the roof of the Sun Yat-sen funeral hall, and Sun's bronze statue was also almost destroyed. Severe damage was done to the graves of the NRA soldiers. History is easily forgotten. The young and impetuous revolutionaries knew nothing of the Northern Expedition. Those who gave their lives as part of the NRA included both Nationalists and Communists because they were in a phase of cooperation at that time. And the soldiers of the January 28th Incident deserve to be immortalized as heroes of the people for their role in resisting Japan. During the January 28th Incident, there were many brave patriots who sacrificed themselves, and they could not all be buried in the martyrs' cemetery at the Sun Yat-sen Mausoleum. They were chosen, then, so that one member of each unit would represent those who had sacrificed themselves. Of those, General Cai Tingkai's 19th Route Army had the most, with 70. Fifty-eight were chosen from Zhang Zhizhong's 5th Army and the Military Police, for a total of 128—a subtle reminder of the incident that had started on the 28th day of the first month.

At the foot of the north side of Purple Mountain, behind the Sun Yat-sen mausoleum, there is a cemetery of Air Force martyrs. Here are buried the heroic pilots from China, America, and the Soviet Union who gave their lives fighting the Japanese. When the Japanese occupied Nanjing, it suffered damage, and was repaired after the end of the war. It suffered more damage during the Cultural Revolution. What we can see today is the result of joint repair efforts carried out by the Sun Yat-sen Memorial Park authorities and the Nanjing Air

Force in 1985.

It is worth noting the music stage in the eastern scenic area. In my novel, *Nanjing 1937: A Love Story*, I wrote:

For Nanjingers, the twelve small circular lawns that make up the 3,000-capacity music stage are the most interesting thing about the Sun Yat-sen Mausoleum. It was planned jointly by the noted architects Guan Songsheng and Yang Tingbao, and it cleverly makes use of the original low-lying terrain. The entire place seems to open out like a great green half-unfolded fan, with excellent acoustics. The music stage's significance does not lie solely in its existence as a performance venue, but importantly in its location as a place for assembly. In the beautiful spring weather or the cloudy fall, huge groups of security guards line the streets, and Party luminaries and diplomats accompany their wives around the ambulatories surrounding the stage. The reinforced concrete path is 150 meters long and six meters wide, and the lofty wisteria twist freely around it, forming a beautiful green passage. When the wisteria bloom, swarms of bees fly between the beautiful, fragrant blossoms.

This sort of assembly is usually seen after a public memorial service and was a common sight in Nanjing during the Republican era.

Three

In Nanjing, leisure is perhaps inextricable from the past. When outsiders come to Nanjing for leisure, it is best that they read a few books on the history of the city. Nanjing is not a shopper's paradise, and its natural atmosphere is not completely in line with people's expectations. If you have no interest in exploring the past, it is best not to come to Nanjing.

When I was at university, a friend and I visited the Two Mausolea of the Southern Tang on the city's southern outskirts. At the time, they were yet to be opened to the public. We cycled a long way to get there, purely because we were partial toward the poetry of Li Houzhu, the final ruler of the Southern Tang. Telling the tale these days feels like a fantasy. I remember that, at the time, the Two Mausolea of the Southern Tang had been damaged so badly that they were practically unbearable to look at. One of them was locked with a big old-fashioned iron padlock. We found a group of officials and borrowed the key from them, and then carefully opened the door to make our way in. Inside, it was pitch black, and barely a few steps in, I took quite a substantial tumble.

At the time, there was no difference between the mausolea and an abandoned air-raid shelter. The Southern Tang royal court of the day was, likewise, just as decaying and unstable. Many years later, I went once more to the mausolea, which had become a tourist destination. With the passage of time, everything had changed. But it was rather a failure of a visit. It felt as if they had repaired it as good as new, and there was an unspeakable awkwardness about it. The mausolea, having become a tourist trap, felt as if they had suddenly lost all sense of history. The heaving, chattering crowds of people and vehicles, alongside peddlers of all sorts, all reminded one of the reality one inhabited. You became aware that you were located in this reality, and that history was nowhere to be found.

Coming to Nanjing for leisure, it is best to have nothing to do with these time-pressed "one-day tours". The result of the one-day tour is that you make a cursory visit to each location, simply seeing the exterior of Nanjing's landscape and never its soul. You can only take photographs to prove to others that you have visited Nanjing, and, in truth, you feel nothing of what sets Nanjing apart from other cities. Rather than wasting your money on these one-day tours, you are better off seeing a movie in a theater, or hiding yourself away in your home to watch television.

Fragments of historical civilization are scattered all throughout

Nanjing. In Nanjing, leisure cannot be separated from roaming the spiritual world. On the city's outskirts, you may find bixie—mythical, lion-like statues left behind from the Six Dynasties that were built to ward off evils. Each unique bixie statue weighs around 15 tons, and it is difficult to imagine how people from over 1,000 years ago managed to transport such things. You can visit the Yangshan Quarry, which holds semi-finished stelae constructed by the Yongle Emperor to commemorate his father. If they were ever erected outright, they would be 73 meters tall, the height of a 24-storey building. This would mean a monument the size of the Xuanwu Hotel or the Nanjing Grand Hotel. You can climb atop Purple Mountain and look out upon the landscape. You can reach the top of Yuhuatai and watch the sun set, with the air of the Six Dynasties around you, like the waiters and barmen of The Scholars. You can stroll through great streets and small alleyways, following the Qinhuai or the Jinchuan river, and with the guidance of an expert, you can imagine how those derelict historical remains might once have looked. You can even wander along the desolate riverbank, looking on the reeds by the shore and feeling a sense of uniqueness, which is perhaps even better than strolling by the bustling Confucius Temple.

Nanjingers don't really care how much of their city could be entered into the Guinness World Records. Nanjing's history is passive; it requires you to discover it and experience it with your heart. In Nanjing, leisure brings with it an intense flavor of human affairs.

The Seasons of Nanjing

One

Nanjing's climate arouses much complaining from outsiders. Summer in Nanjing is truly summer. Only people who have stayed here can understand its ferocity. I remember when I was at university. In the days before the beginning of summer vacation, a heatwave hit the city. Some of my classmates who had come from the north had never seen such vicious heat in their lives. In the evening, it was so hot that sleeping was impossible. Carrying sleeping mats over their shoulders, people scattered all over the place, lying down in any place where there was a slight breeze. Clad in only their underwear, they were absolutely indifferent to matters of public decency. When the Nanjing summer truly heats up, the breeze in the evening disappears completely, and the air seems to congeal.

Electric fans have only come about in the past few decades; air conditioning has an even shorter history. Six years ago, I sneakily installed a small window-mounted air conditioning unit. It was completely illegal to do so, and there was a notice in the newspapers saying that private residences were not authorized to do so without permission from the board of electricity. At the time, regulations stated that only provincial-level cadres and above could enjoy air conditioning. Nowadays, air conditioning has brought about a fundamental change in significance for Nanjing's summers. And in the past few years, one question has become rather unpopular in Nanjing—that is, asking people where they intend to spend their summer.

Surviving a summer in Nanjing is a Herculean feat. For the elderly, surviving a summer means they have survived another year. In those days without electric fans and air conditioning, people wore very scant clothing, and the sweat would drip down them in an endless cascade as they fanned themselves as best they could. When it came time to sleep, because of the heat, they would all soak themselves in baths of cold water. Cooling off in summer was once a significant part of living in Nanjing. When their houses got so warm as to be uninhabitable, people would gather in the spaces outside their front doors. Many of the children of Nanjing grew up lounging around on couches in the cool evening air, listening to the grown-ups and their grown-up talk. In the deep, still night, the adults let down their guard toward children, chatting amongst themselves and telling racy tales that children were perhaps not meant to hear.

When the Republican government designated Nanjing as the capital, Nanjing was filled with bureaucrats. When the summer heat approached, their heads swam, and they found themselves unable to complete their countless official tasks. Thus, the Nanjing government had no choice but to make a getaway, spending their summers in the renowned scenic spot of Mount Lu. Mount Lu, 500 kilometers away from the city, became the summer retreat of the Nanjing government. Once the time came to escape the heat, the bigwigs from each and every government department, led by Chiang Kai-shek, would make their way there like migratory birds, travelling by all different means of transportation—by land, by river, and by air.

Summer in Nanjing can reach highs of 36°C to 37°C, even reaching 40°C. According to records, in August of 1959, the temperature reached 40.7°C. Regular human body temperature is 37°C. Temperatures above this are difficult to bear. If the temperature reaches or even surpasses 40°C, this essentially means that the entire city is running a fever. In the warm season, anything you touch will feel hot.

Nanjing is famously known as one of the "great furnaces" of China. Thankfully, there are still trees in the city center, allowing for cool shade in any case.

Two

Nanjing's rainy season, which arrives during spring and summer, can also make people feel uncomfortable. Its endless drizzle can last for two to four weeks. In 1996, the rainy season was particularly long, lasting for 40 days. Northerners cannot imagine such a monsoon season. One can almost wring the water from the air with one's hands. Those who live on the ground floor of a building are those who suffer most. All of their possessions are left dripping wet, beads of condensation condense upon the outsides of their refrigerators, and their beds and mattresses are damp to the touch. Mold grows everywhere, the scent of it hovering in the air, and rust abounds; in times like these, it feels as if one's bones are rusting.

The long monsoon season is a time for flood control precautions. As the rain falls daily, the Yangtze's waters rise, and the accumulated water in the city drains into the river. The river water upstream makes its way downward. Thus, on television, there are daily scenes of mayors and provincial governors making public appearances, giving urgent instructions on how to defeat the rising waters.

The monsoon season is an ideal time for tree growth, however. The trees of the south are fond of water and moisture. As the hot summer arrives, the plain trees are inundated with water and they become huge umbrellas, completely shading the streets with their leaves. Unfortunately, in order to widen the roads, many trees have been felled in the past few years. If this were not the case, then Nanjingers would not have to fear the heat nor the rain when they ventured outdoors. The majesty of Nanjing's trees would not be possible without the annual rainy season. When the monsoon is over, people who live in single-story houses or on the first or second floors begin to take their belongings outside to dry off. In Nanjing, this is commonly referred to as shai mei, "drying mold". While shai mei is happening, people will also surreptitiously compare their households to others. Expensive clothes hidden in the backs of closets, unused fresh bedsheets, silk quilts, leather jackets, fleeces, down coats: they all come out into the sunshine. Many housewives have no choice but to specifically ask for time off work in order to complete the difficult task of shai mei.

In the past, rich people would damp-proof their homes by placing empty wine jars in the floors of the foundations of their homes, then laying floor tiles on top of those jars. When building a house in Nanjing, one does not only have to consider ventilation in order to handle the summer heat, but one must also consider moisture-proofing against the mold and dampness of the monsoon season.

Three

I cannot think of anything particularly special about autumn in Nanjing. Nanjing is a city with four clearly delineated seasons, all types of weather being represented. Summers are hot, winters are cold, the rainy season is wet, and the autumn is dry, cool, and refreshing. This is unlike the year-round summers of the island of Hainan, or Kunming's four seasons of endless spring, or the far north where snow falls for most of the year. Autumn in Nanjing seems quite pedestrian. When the days come, they come quickly, and, just as quickly, they take their leave. Autumn is a season of ripening, but Nanjing does not produce its own fruit. Neither the apples and pears of the north nor the tangerines of the south have any relevance to the city. Nanjingers are used to self-assuredly eating the fruit of other regions.

Nanjing is an awkward place. In autumn, one goes to Qixia to see the leaves turn red, but these red leaves are not in fact native to Nanjing at all. Firstly, they are not red; secondly, they do not grow into forests. In Nanjing, perhaps only the ginkgo trees are worth paying any attention to. The autumn winds rustle past their golden leaves as they fall to the ground like snow. Swathes of ginkgo trees stand on the campus of Nanjing University and on Liang Island in the north part of Xuanwu Lake. But one must act quickly to appreciate their golden leaves, as they are shed completely within a matter of days. They say that Nanjing has a regal air. It is quite mysterious; heaven knows what this actually means. Autumn enters Nanjing in a hurry and leaves likewise. The rulers who designated Nanjing as their capital did much the same. Historically, Nanjing has produced the last emperors of many dynasties. The last emperors of the Chen and the Southern Tang dynasties were more enamored by beautiful women than beautiful scenery and were destined to become the emperors of vanquished nations. The fashionable women of Nanjing all complain that autumn is too short, and that the cold arrives too quickly. They buy beautiful clothes, and as soon as they bring them home, they find it is not possible to wear them anymore. Autumn in Nanjing is dynamic. It does not stop to rest, and it changes in a myriad of ways. Women who wish to appear beautiful must be prepared to feel cold. Beauty comes at a price, and women who want to look pretty may find themselves catching cold.

Autumn in Nanjing prevails precisely due to its brevity. Beauty is always fleeting, and it is transience that defines beauty. Only those Nanjingers who have lived through the city's intense summer heat can feel the significance of the first autumn winds. It is a gladness which comes with surviving by the skin of one's teeth. In those scorching days, the phrase re si le ("so hot I could die") became something of a mantra for many people. The autumn winds cool the ferocious flames of Nanjing's furnace. Just as autumn makes its way through, day by day, then when winter stealthily approaches, Nanjingers appreciate autumn more than people from other regions. Winter in Nanjing is often more difficult to live through than winters in the north. When northern students come to Nanjing University, the cold moist air often leaves them constantly complaining. The orderly procession of seasons is one of Nanjing's merits, though. Only in a city like this can people truly experience the changing of the climate and of the season. Spring, summer, autumn, and winter are precious gifts from nature given in vain to humanity, and to miss out on any one season is a great loss. Autumn in Nanjing is not as beautiful as one might imagine, but beauty has always existed only in one's imagination.

Four

Winter in Nanjing is not that great, either, with annual lows of -8°C. In 1977, the temperature reached -13.3°C. Low temperatures in Nanjing are not the same as they are in the north. In the north, it is a dry cold, unlike Nanjing's damp frigidity. When Nanjingers go to the north for the first time and experience a northern winter, they are both enamored by the warm atmosphere of northern homes and incredulous that temperatures outside could reach as low as -10°C.

To say that northerners are constantly complaining about the damp chill in Nanjing is no exaggeration. When describing the cold in Nanjing, northerners all say the same thing: that it's as cold inside as it is outside. There is no place to hide from the cold in Nanjing. For northerners, this is unbelievable. Many Nanjingers choose to settle in the north, all the while thinking of everything that the Yangtze River region has to offer and feeling great homesickness. But when they think of winters in Nanjing, they are completely disheartened. This was the case for my grandfather. He was from Suzhou, and he lived in the north for decades. He was accustomed to his central heating, and when he returned south of the Yangtze, he dreaded the hard winters.

Winter in Nanjing is truly winter. When it gets cold, it is unambiguously cold. When I was working in a factory, Xuanwu Lake froze one winter. I even dared to venture across it. It is no easy feat for a lake so vast as Xuanwu to freeze completely. And if the ice had not been thick, it would not have been able to withstand people walking across it. Winter in the south can see significant fluctuations in temperature. As a result, days on which the ice is genuinely sturdy are rare. In fact, there were a few people who fell into holes in the ice and drowned that year. It was 1977.

One can sense a spirit of adaptability in Nanjingers when winter approaches. Examining the old houses of Nanjing, one can understand that, historically, Nanjingers have had their own ways of coping with winter. Chimneys still remain in many old houses, and when winter came, Nanjingers would once light fires just like northerners did. The common people would have braziers in their homes, filled with cheap charcoal. These charcoal braziers are rarely seen nowadays—outside of folk museums, that is. We once had one in our house with handles on both sides. It was quite pretty, looking something like a vase in which one would grow lotus flowers. It might have been produced in Jingdezhen, a city famous for its porcelain. Because we never burnt charcoal, it was used to store rice. I once saw a copper charcoal brazier, which looked a lot like the military helmets worn during the Republican era.

Nanjingers gave up on such methods of heating in the 1950s. At the time, a regulation was put in place to subsidize heating. North of the Huai River, there were heating subsidies; south of the Huai, there were no such subsidies. Although it was only a very small sum of money, the common people south of the Huai all happened to agree to give up on heating their homes. Nanjingers' ability to resist the cold has greatly improved. Although the north is colder than the south, northerners have no choice but to concede that, out of all the southerners, Nanjingers are the ones truly capable of withstanding the cold.

Nanjingers

One

The term "Nanjingers" is a rough approximation meaning those who live within this city.

True Nanjingers can only be examined theoretically. When it comes to living in this city, the real Nanjingers are you and the people around you. Nanjingers are the streams of people who you see going about their lives every day right in front of your eyes. It doesn't matter whether this is your ancestral hometown or whether you were born and bred here. People are a reflection of their environment. However, many years after you have lived in this city, you have breathed its air, drunk of its waters, and eaten rice bought within the city. Thus, you are a Nanjinger. Nanjingers are those men and women who hurry around the streets at rush hour, the young fellows making collect calls in the telephone booths, and the young women eating lamb skewers by the roadside. They are the people who you see and hear every day.

The concept of the Nanjinger is a wide-ranging one, but a wide-ranging concept will inevitably mention some things but omit others. Lenience is a particular characteristic of the Nanjinger. Nanjing has always been a tolerant city. In fact, people living in this city will rarely probe into whether or not you are a true Nanjinger. Surveys show that many people whose Nankinese credentials have been called into question will, after a moment of surprise, think first of their ancestral hometown. People are used to answering such questions with the location of their ancestral hometown, and thus many people may tell you that they are not Nanjingers.

An agency surveyed 171 Nanjing residents and found that only 10% said that Nanjing was their ancestral hometown. Nearly 50% did not consider themselves to be Nanjingers even though they had been born in the city.

Nanjingers are not particularly fond of this topic, unlike the Shanghainese and others who will frequently use the dialect expression aklak zaanhe nin, "we Shanghainese". Nanjingers lack the cohesiveness of the Shanghainese. The composition of the Shanghainese population is even more complex than that of the Nankinese, but the Shanghainese have an innate gestalt, a natural recognition of themselves as Shanghainese. Nanjingers have never been xenophobic. Shanghainese will often use words like waidiren ("outsider") or xiangxiaren ("country folk") with a tone of disdain. These words, which exclude others and center oneself, reflect a sense of superiority.

This is a sense that Nanjingers do not have. History and reality have rarely given Nanjingers much to feel superior about. Nanjingers have at times naively tried to assert their own might—for example, setting up the ningpai school of literature to compete with Beijing's jingpai and Shanghai's haipai literary movements. But such assertions fell on deaf ears, and not only did other regions not acknowledge the ningpai school, but even Nanjingers themselves did not recognize it. Nanjingers are used to disorganization, to disunity among groups and an inability to form factions. Their ideology has never been unified. Nanjingers are hard to summarize specifically because their innate character has always been difficult to grasp.

Two

When Xiao Fuxing discussed how Beijingers saw the TV drama Sinful Debt, he said that it showed the small-mindedness of the Shanghainese because its story was so full of suffering. The protagonists are abandoned by their own flesh and blood, handed over to others to be raised with no trouble at all. They are essentially adopted for no good reason, too late for them to find their own happiness, and they must risk life and limb to meet their own needs. Beijingers would not allow five children to make such an arduous journey, resulting in three children returning to Yunnan, one being left with a permanently crippled leg, and another one ending up in a police station cell. This conclusion, for Beijingers, shows that the Shanghainese have no compassion. And when Shanghainese watch the works of Wang Shuo, they also feel an inexplicable irritation. On multiple occasions, I have heard their criticisms of glib, superficial, frivolous Beijingers, even indignantly calling "No Way to Love you", "No Way to Watch You".

Nanjingers are entirely different. Nanjingers do not have a single view on anything. Some will praise something, others criticize it. Today, they may say something is good, and tomorrow they may change their minds. Nanjingers like to blab and have a natural fondness for soliloquy. Once, in a market, I heard two women sales assistants joyously discussing Wang Shuo, their excitement making them look all the prettier. "I'm a huge fan of Wang Shuo. Anything he's in, I'll love watching it." They were speaking entirely in the Nanjing dialect, but to express their feelings toward Wang Shuo, they stiffly rolled their tongues in a strange approximation of the Beijing accent— Nanjingers have a rather difficult time speaking Mandarin. While Sinful Debt was being broadcast, it was discussed everywhere. The author of the book it was based on, Ye Xin, came to Nanjing for a book signing, and many passionate readers clamored to catch a glimpse of him. Nanjingers have the stomach for pretty much anything. They are quite happy to go mad and join in the fun over almost everything.

Nanjingers are not obstinate in their beliefs. They will weep at the works of the haipai school just as they do over the works from the jingpai school. They are easily deceived.

Others can easily sense the notions of haipai and jingpai, even if they are not spoken of much by Shanghainese or Beijingers. Neither side can rid themselves of their feelings of superiority on the national stage. The Shanghainese arose as a result of commerce, so they will frequently talk of money. Beijingers lived under the foot of the emperor, and so they will often speak about unconfirmed internal rumors. The Shanghainese are money-makers; Beijingers are bureaucrats. The Shanghainese ideal is a pocket stuffed with money. For Beijingers, the higher up the bureaucratic ladder they can climb, the better. This separation of money and officialdom is the way that both Shanghainese and Beijingers can keep up an air of haughtiness. If you have money or an official position, you can dare to feel superior, to have self-respect, to do anything you like. Shanghainese with no money or Beijingers with no official positions are still products of their environment, and because they have been influenced by this atmosphere, they have the same shortcomings.

Nanjingers are at best apathetic. Unlike Shanghainese and Beijingers, Nanjingers do not think much of themselves for being Nanjingers. This feeling of superiority coming from others has nothing to do with them, and really, they have nothing to feel that superior about. Nanjingers do not have great self-confidence. They have little in the way of ego, but they also do not feel in any way inferior. The typical Nanjinger is carefree and lazy, apathetic about many things. He does not admire bureaucrats and nor does he envy the rich—because the majority of Nanjingers are neither. The bureaucrats of Nanjing are all outsiders, as are the city's wealthy. When a Nanjinger sees outsiders come to take up official positions or make money, he is not jealous, but rather indifferent.

Three

On the national stage, the Nankinese are neither northerners nor southerners. Within the boundaries of Jiangsu Province, Nanjing, its provincial capital, one is still neither in the north nor the south. The people of south Jiangsu are accustomed to seeing Nanjingers as being jiangbeiren ("people from north of the river") even if they are clearly located south of the Yangtze on a map. Jiangbeiren is much like the Shanghainese epithets of waidiren and xiangxiaren; it carries a sense of disdain.

The common people of south Jiangsu have, historically, paid little attention to the citizens of their provincial capital city. Once, on a train from Chongqing to Shanghai, the Shanghainese author Chen Cun joked to me that Nanjing was a suburb of Shanghai. I took up the argument with him. To put his theory to the test, we found another passenger nearby. When I asked him where he was from, he boastfully stated that he was Shanghainese. Chen Cun and I were rather surprised, because this supposed Shanghainese man was clearly not speaking Shanghainese. After careful questioning, it turned out that he was from Liyang in Jiangsu Province. I was suddenly rather furious. No matter what distance they were at, or whose jurisdiction they were under, there is no way that someone from Liyang could call themselves Shanghainese. Liyang is now under the jurisdiction of the city of Changzhou. It is much closer to Nanjing than it is to Shanghai. This response left Chen Cun feeling rather pleased with himself.

It seems as if all of southern Jiangsu has forgotten where its provincial capital is actually located, and that their superiors once lived in the ancient city. When the city of Wuxi advertised itself as a superior tourist destination, it publicly labelled itself "Shanghai's back garden"—and when it said so, the leaders of the Jiangsu Tourist Board sat upright on their rostrum. This attitude of publicly fawning over the Shanghainese, even if it is for the purposes of parting them from their cash, also shows Nanjing's awkward position as the provincial capital. It indicates that Nanjingers clearly lack money, not having enough to catch the discerning eyes of the shrewd people of Wuxi. Economically, Nanjing stands somewhere the middle of the province. As the provincial capital, Nanjing does not seem to have enjoyed the same blessings that Beijing has had as a capital city. Nanjing has long been this way, its fortunes never stable for long. The economy in south Jiangsu is somewhat stronger than the economy in the north; Nanjing finds itself in neither prosperity nor poverty. When Nanjingers have money, they will think of the rich south and feel listless. When they are poor, they will think of the impoverished north and count their blessings. Nanjingers seem to have a natural willingness to live in the middle, neither envying the haves nor mocking the have-nots. Nanjingers do not think that they should be first in all of Jiangsu, and they never worry that they will fall behind. Nanjingers have never had much awareness of suffering. They did not have it in the past, they do not have it now, and it is quite possible that they will not have it in the future.

Four

Nanjing is not much of a high-pressure city. This lack of pressure is what has created the specific characteristics of the Nanjinger. Nanjingers are not particularly competitive. Some are, but they are often still less so than others. Not only are Nanjingers tolerant, but they are also simple people, naturally unruffled. The "Nanjing radish" is innately calm, knowing nothing of worry or urgency. Even if the sky were to fall tomorrow, Nanjingers still would not change their pace; they would chatter in the street, sleep in their beds, watch TV, and play majiang.

It would be a mistake to think highly of Nanjingers for this, but it would not be right to look down on them for it, either. Nanjingers epitomize the middle way. Early in the morning of November 2, 1995, over 20,000 vases of flowers arranged outside the Gate of China were looted by a large number of people. This incident aroused substantial public ire, with a feeling that Nanjingers had lost face. At the same time, something else also caused indignation on the part of the intelligentsia: a number of the city's ten newly-installed, card-operated payphones had already been vandalized. One could draw a simple conclusion from this: Nanjingers were bad people.

In fact, to be fair, these two incidents cannot speak of the innate qualities of Nanjingers because these kinds of disgraceful incidents could happen in many of China's cities. Stories of looting flowers clearly did not begin with Nanjingers, and nor can one come to a conclusion about Nanjingers on the basis of such a scandal; I do not believe that we can simply continue paying close attention to the newspapers. As for the telephones, Nanjing is far from the only city to undergo such an infuriating incident. Perhaps only Shenzhen is better. Thus, we can only use undamaged payphones to evaluate how a city is good, and we cannot conversely demonstrate how a city is bad.

A year ago, Nanjing's Mochou Lake Park held an event for the outdoor goods brand, Dadi Zouhong. The whole time, not a single one of the thousands of umbrellas was stolen. This was a credit to Nanjingers. However, this is no cause for excitement. Looting flowerpots and surreptitiously stealing umbrellas both clearly show one aspect of the Nankinese character: that they have no fixed rules. Nanjingers are inherently moderates. They have always been easy-going types. Before doing anything, they do not spend too much time worrying over whether or not they should. Nanjingers are Nanjingers, and they don't care all that much one way or another, for better or for worse. Nanjingers have also almost never cared how others see them.

The Outsiders of Nanjing

One

Nanjing is heaven for outsiders. They are a fascinating point of cultural interest. Like all of China's major cities, Nanjing is at its heart a city of migrants. Outsiders in Nanjing do not feel excluded and discriminated against just because they have lived in other places. Nanjingers themselves do not feel any particular sense of belonging in Nanjing. For real Nanjingers, it isn't important whether or not one is a Nanjinger oneself, let alone whether others are Nanjingers. Outsiders in Nanjing do not feel as if they are inferior because they are not the masters, playing host to others. Nanjing has no masters, and thus there are no guests. In Nanjing's land of plenty, the idea of "doing as the Romans do when in Rome" is not particularly popular.

The majority of outsiders in Nanjing are from Jiangsu Province. In terms of character, because they are the cream of the province's crop, they are significant figures in their careers. Anyone can mingle in Nanjing, and it is easy to do so. Likewise, outsiders find it difficult to develop a sense of belonging in Nanjing. The memories of children and adolescents have always been most important. No matter how long they have stayed in Nanjing, they do not consider themselves to be Nanjingers. Those of the second generation, born of outsiders who have settled in Nanjing, can be considered to be real Nanjingers. Thus, Nanjing's outsiders are the ancestors of future Nanjingers.

Outsiders from south and north Jiangsu have two different views of Nanjing. South Jiangsu is well-off. People from south Jiangsu who come to Nanjing often feel they have no alternative but to do so. They settle in Nanjing, raise their children here, and enjoy its atmosphere, yet deep down they absolutely look down upon Nanjingers. People from south Jiangsu who have moved to Nanjing often feel that the Nanjingers are a vulgar people—that they eat poorly and dress badly. They enjoy a sense of complete superiority because they implicitly feel that others have little positive going for them, while also feeling that they themselves are extraordinary. People from south Jiangsu are much like the Shanghainese in terms of character; they are both smarter than true Nanjingers and more competent. If they were to go to Shanghai, they would be thoroughly discriminated against as outsiders. But in the tolerant city of Nanjing, no one looks down on them. Instead, they go from being the city's guests to being its lords, looking down upon Nanjingers.

People from north Jiangsu are different from those who've come from the south. North Jiangsu is poor, and many people from north Jiangsu rely on strenuous academic efforts in order to be able to come to Nanjing. It is not easy for them to get here, and because of this, unlike the people of south Jiangsu, they are not arrogant, and they do not feel disdain for the indigenous Nanjingers. Their approach is subtler and much warmer. They are marked by a commitment to mutual aid and assistance. Although Nanjingers do not cheat strangers, they are careful in their intentions in this respect. Nanjingers are not cliquish, but people from north Jiangsu tend to be more community-focused and committed to their common strengths. People from north Jiangsu in Nanjing have a deep understanding of the old adage that unity is strength. They undergo hardships in the city together and weave a wonderful network of connections, intentionally or otherwise. As to those from north Jiangsu in Nanjing, when compared to those from south Jiangsu, their priorities lie elsewhere. The northerners do not feel as if they have no alternative but to come to Nanjing. They do not live their lives in the city with fussy attitudes. They did not come to this city to enjoy a feeling of superiority. Speaking generally, northerners in Nanjing are more mature than southerners. They do not feel wronged, as if they are beleaguered aristocrats; they come quietly to the city, and not only do they plan to put down roots here, but they are filled with the ambition to subdue this ancient city. They build their world around them with honest work, and their contributions toward the city are greater than the contributions made by the southerners.

Two

Historically, many people who settled in Nanjing from south Jiangsu came solely for business. They devised countless ways to make a profit and, having done so, they wanted to leave. In comparison, the impoverished people of north Jiangsu do not disparage the city. When they settle in Nanjing, it is often in pursuit of one of two paths: the first is as coolies who earned money serving business and decided not to move on; the other is as wildly ambitious people who worked solidly in all kinds of businesses so that they might one day find themselves a part-time government position. The magistrates of Nanjing are very rarely true Nanjingers. The same can be said of top-ranking provincial leaders, as well as the top-ranking municipal leaders. It was thus in the Republican era, and it has not changed to this day. When one hears leaders talk on the television, one rarely hears a genuine Nanjing accent. It is not because the Nanjing accent is unpleasant to the ear, but because the leaders who speak on television are very rarely Nanjingers. Nanjing does not produce bureaucratic talents, and the larger government organs have no Nanjingers in them at all. There are hardly any Nanjing bureaucrats who go on to hold positions in central government. Nanjing is a city that owes its development to the leadership of outsiders. If, one day, Nanjing was left completely to be managed by Nanjingers as a result of an outbreak of regionalism, it would find itself a complete laughing stock. History proves that Nanjing cannot be without outsiders. It would not be what it is today without such people. Nanjing has provided endless opportunities for outsiders and has always been a friend to them.

Real Nanjingers are happy to admit that they are not bureaucratic material, and also happy to admit that there are a number of areas in which they do not measure up to outsiders. Nanjingers are used to disorganization, they are not stubborn in their opinions, and they will follow the latest trends. Nothing is set in stone. Nanjingers are not xenophobic and are always happy to accept things from other places. During the Northern Expedition, because the soldiers governing Nanjing came from the north, it became the fashion to eat scallions and garlic and to speak with a rolled tongue. When the Nationalist government established Nanjing as its capital, because Sun Yat-sen was from Guangdong and the Nationalist revolution had originated in the province, Cantonese restaurants became all the rage. And after the victory against Japan, when the Nationalist government returned from Chongqing, Sichuan restaurants became popular. It was as if eating a dish at a Cantonese or a Sichuanese restaurant meant reliving the history of the revolution. Nanjingers have always found it hard to avoid engaging in rather immature behavior. At that time, many Nanjingers followed the Nationalist government into the interior; these were good men. After the war against Japan finished, they returned to Nanjing, and after such a long period of time, their speech was peppered with Sichuanese mannerisms.

Outsiders in Nanjing took full advantage of the Nanjingers' natural naivety. This is also why, for a long time, there has been no fixed character to cuisine in Nanjing. Not only is Nanjing not xenophobic, but on the contrary, it has always taken a thorough interest in outsiders and their customs. Outsiders may move through Nanjing like fish through water. Whether we speak of western tastes for foods such as KFC, beef noodle soup from California, or the products of other places, it doesn't matter whether they are authentic or a facsimile just as long as the companies and foods are new and have the audacity to position themselves as a brand, in which case they will part Nanjingers from their cash. Outsiders in Nanjing can fully enjoy the easily-swindled nature of Nanjingers. Nanjingers like clothing from Shanghai, electronics from Japan, and all manner of products that advertisements tell them to buy. Nanjingers do not worry about being fooled at all, or even worry about being fooled time and time again.

No matter whether outsiders are settled in Nanjing or just passing through, they will never feel at a loss for what to do. Nanjingers may not have much money, but they are always gracious with it. Singers and movie stars from outside always like coming to Nanjing for their first performances. Whether from the north or south, and whether talented or otherwise, they can always count on a good reception in Nanjing. The TV series Ke Wang ("Yearning") was very popular in Nanjing. The singer Mao Amin became popular in Nanjing. The already-popular singers Na Ying and Li Lingyu also both like to kick off the publicity for their new records in the city. Nanjing is not the best cultural city, but it is certainly one of the best cultural cities in China. Achieving success in Nanjing brings unimaginable prospects for marketing potential. In fact, those in the culture industry look favorably upon Nanjing as a land of plenty. Southern businessmen see Nanjing as a frontline in their own northern expeditions, and when northerners want to expand their power southward, they also see Nanjing as a site for struggle.

Three

Many people feel that Nanjing is a conservative city. Outsiders often hold this incorrect view. In fact, this is a false impression of the city because Nanjing has always had liberation in its blood. Its gates have always been open to outsiders. Nanjing welcomes northerners and southerners alike. It accepts all travelers on the hunt for opportunity.

Outsiders in Nanjing can therefore live in harmony with Nanjingers, and this is inextricably linked to Nanjingers' own tolerance.

For those from distant lands, cities like Nanjing are hard to come by. It has its traditions but does not cling to bad habits. It has culture but is not elitist. It welcomes the new but does not tire of the old. Nanjing gives outsiders a place to fully display their capabilities—a stage on which they may manifest their talents to the utmost. Outsiders in Nanjing may find themselves to be desperate or find themselves the beneficiaries of great and immediate success. They may find themselves the protagonists in brave tragedies or gentle comedies.

Regardless, they have become an important part of the people of Nanjing. Unknowingly, they have been integrated by Nanjingers. From a certain angle, one could even say that the history of Nanjing is the history of its outsiders. Real Nanjingers may look three generations back and soon find that they are not real "Nanjingers" after all. Nanjing opens its arms to outsiders and ushers in talents from north and south Jiangsu using differing methods. Nanjing's tolerance has meant that many outsiders have stayed. As it accepts outsiders, it changes them, just as those outsiders have changed the city itself. Nanjing and its outsiders accommodate each other, and they slowly but surely become true Nanjingers. Because of the constant influx of outsiders filled with vitality, in fact, pure, authentic Nanjingers no longer exist.

Nanjing's Authors

One

Nanjing's authors are all but countless. People often ask me: how does Jiangsu have so many writers, the majority of whom are from Nanjing? At first, I didn't care about this question at all. It was a case of my not seeing the forest for the trees. Sometimes, counting on one's fingers, Nanjing seems to have plenty of authors. There are writers of every age group, gender, and writing style: poets, novelists, essayists, journalists, and writers who will tackle just about anything. It is no surprise that commissioning editors from outside of the city will frequently turn up in Nanjing on the hunt for writers. The forests are rich with game and firing off a few indiscriminate shots will bag plenty of prey.

A journalist once asked me why I never considered pursuing another career outside of writing, such as bureaucracy or commerce. "I wouldn't mind being an official, or making money, either," I said with a laugh. "But in a place like Nanjing, the streets are filled with people who think the same as I do. If I were an official, I'd worry that I couldn't serve the people wholeheartedly. If I took the plunge into the world of business, I'd feel ashamed of defrauding people, as well as being defrauded by others. The streets are full of petty schemers like me. If I didn't write, what else could I do?"

People who write in Nanjing rarely have any other aspirations. It is not that they do not want to do more; it is that they know that there is no use in wanting such a thing. There is no sense in letting one's brain cells go to waste. Whether you are unoccupied or focused on a task, it is reasonable to realize that there is no use in trying not to think about it. Fantasy is not a strong suit of Nanjingers. True Nanjingers feel that they lack the aptitude and are reticent to think about such things. Nanjing's writers embody the first-rate qualities of Nanjingers. They are suitable as neither bureaucrats nor businessmen. Their merit is their cynical approach to materialism and their indifference to glory. Their flaw is that they are lacking in ability and in luck. Writers often have little in the way of future prospects.

Nanjing is a thoroughly appropriate place for writing. There is not too much competition, and when you've done well for yourself, not that many people will admire you, so your pride will be all for naught. If you don't make it, no one will want to mock you. They couldn't care less about your suffering. That's your own business. Nanjing produces true literati. It invites you to choose between right and wrong, and you may do as you please, good or bad. If you write a fine essay, people will not necessarily say so; if you write badly, people will not necessarily scold you. Sometimes, an essay full of both praise and censure will arise; no one will truly take it seriously. Writers seek only a moment of happiness. For them, to not speak is like having a fish bone stuck in one's throat, and thus they write. People chance upon it, are unconcerned by it, and soon forget it. This is essentially how the literary world works. Nanjing's authors have written a number of essays which have indeed been read by many, but that does not necessarily mean that those readers have read them in earnest. Nanjing's authors understand this and know how they should rely on their consciences to write. If you do not write well, the person you cannot face most is yourself. One can never satisfy one's readers, and thus there is no need to pander to them.

The aspect in which Nankinese writers are most blessed is that they are interfered with relatively less than writers in other places. In a city where competition is not fierce, the pressure is lowered somewhat. Nanjing is neither too modernized nor too backward. A city that has been overly commercialized or closed off is not a suitable cradle for a literary scene. Creation is a thoroughly individual act. External factors have never been of much help, but they can cause some minor chaos from time to time. Those who understand and support literature most know that writers' work should not be interfered with. Writers are often weak. They are not arrogant, but they can be rather delicate; they are very able people who, all the same, cannot eliminate such interference. For better or worse, this has had a wide-ranging effect on writers. Deliberating on awards and titles should be kept separate from a writer's work. If not done well, it can interfere with the mood of writers. Writers are still, at heart, ordinary people who want to be of use. Sometimes, leaders are careful and kind to them, and yet writers do not know how to accept such honors. When writers are too self-involved, they end up unsure of how to handle themselves.

Two

Nanjing is fertile ground for writers. Going back, we find that Cao Xueqin, author of *Dream of the Red Chamber*, was born here. Going further back, we have Last Lord Li (c. 937-978)—"How many sorrows do you have? / They flow eastward like the river in spring."—as well as Crown Prince Zhaoming, who compiled *Selections of Refined Literature*. There are a number of writers who were born in Nanjing yet made their living elsewhere. Closer to the modern day, there are Lu Ling, Wu Mingshi, Zhou Erfu, and Zhang Xianliang. More recently still, there are popular young authors such as Wang Anyi, Wang Shuo, and Fang Fang. Nanjing's status as the birthplace of authors is an interesting phenomenon. In an essay, Wang Anyi said that she left Nanjing perched upon a spittoon. At the time, she was a child, and was probably relieving herself on it. This was her particular way of waving goodbye to Nanjing. It is a shame that Nanjing could not retain such literary talents; otherwise, Nanjing's literary scene would be much livelier today.

If memory serves me correctly, Zhang Tianyi, who is Hunanese, was also born in Nanjing. At the very least, he spent the formative years of his childhood in the city. His family's house was on Ba Fu Tang. His ancestors were definitely members of the Hunan army who fought and destroyed the Taiping Heavenly Kingdom before coming to Nanjing to take up posts as officials. The family of the late Eileen Chang had even greater influence, with a bigger house which later became the site of the Legislative Yuan of the Nationalist government. They were practically neighbors of Zhang Tianyi. Eileen Chang was born in Shanghai, but Nanjing was her hometown. This is something understood by anyone who has read her novels. The people in her novels who come from her hometown all have traces of the Nanjing dialect in their speech.

A particular topic of discussion regarding Nanjing is its open-armed embrace of authors from other places. There are writers who were born in Nanjing but did not stay; there are even more writers from elsewhere who eventually made Nanjing their homes. In *Records of the Capital*, published during the Republican era, the great poet Li Bai is but one impressive entry in a list of authors who settled in Nanjing. Others include: Liu Xie (The Literary Mind and the Carving of Dragons); Wang Anshi, one of the Eight Giants of Classical Literature; Yuan Mei (Poems from the Sui Garden); Kong Shangren (Peach Blossom Fan); and the poet Chen Sanli, who was a leading light of the poetry world during the reign of the Qing emperors Tongzhi and Guangxu. Historically, Nanjing has always been a suitable place for the literati to make their homes. All it takes is a cursory reading of Wu Jingzi's The Scholars to be convinced of this. A work like *The Scholars* could be written in every era of Nanjing's history.

In Nanjing's contemporary literary scene, those writers who have settled in the city have far more grandeur than the city's indigenous writers. Of course, I myself am one of those native sons of the city.

Other authors born and raised in Nanjing include Han Dong and a number of authors who write in their spare time. Most of those writers who are active within the Nanjing literary scene are outsiders. Su Tong is from Suzhou; Zhao Benfu and Zhou Meisen are from Xuzhou. Chu Fujin says he is from either Jintan or Shangha. Huang Beijia, similarly, is from either Taizhou or Rugao. In any case, neither is from Nanjing. Soldier-turned-writer Zhu Sujin is from Fujian. Wang Binbin, the writer from Anhui who rose to fame for his prolific essays on literary criticism, is also a military man (though I have never once seen him in uniform). Likewise, the literary critics Wang Gan and Fei Zhenzhong are also not from Nanjing.

Many of the new generation of Nanjing writers are also outsiders. Apart from Han Dong, other writers such as Lu Yang, Bi Feiyu, and Zhu Wen are also not from Nanjing. These writers, who are not true Nanjingers, are now receiving high praise in the city's literary circuit. They have settled down in the city to raise families, and they should be thankful to Nanjing. People are a product of their environment. Nanjing's air has purified them; its waters have brought them good fortune. On the other hand, Nanjing should also be grateful to them. Without them, Nanjing's so-called literary boom would not exist, and commissioning editors would not come from far and wide to prowl the city for new talent.

Three

Though it is said that writers do not like each other's company, Nanjing's authors will often meet up. It is said that writers will disparage and envy each other, always ready to quarrel at the moment they bump into each other. In fact, Nanjing's authors will very rarely get into such red-faced shouting matches. Perhaps it is a result of the city's tolerant atmosphere. Nanjingers do not like to fight. Even the bullish young lads of the city are reluctant to throw punches in the street; why should the city's meek, docile writers be any different?

Nankinese authors will rarely sing the praises of their own work in public, and nor will they disparage the works of others. This is not necessarily a case of world-wise writers who know that one cannot easily judge the quality of a work. Coming together to admire remarkable work, and debating and analyzing points of doubt, is certainly the best approach. If this cannot be done, and everyone simply remains cordial to each other, then this is acceptable, as well. Quarreling is of absolutely no help to writing. A lack of argument over a work does not mean that a literary work will turn out badly. The Nanjing literary scene is united in its admiration of authors from other places. People will often call me long-distance to argue about writers from elsewhere, phoning me so that they may enumerate their shortcomings to me. I have no choice but to half-heartedly chuckle and try to smooth things over, speaking well of these writers, and thus the caller will tell me: "You Nanjing writers really are great; you never argue."

Authors from other places who live in the same city will often go years without seeing each other. Sometimes, I will go to a literary conference in one place or another and bump into two authors who live in the same city, only to discover after everyone has departed that this is the first time that they have met each other. Nanjing's authors will often meet each other—on a weekly basis, even. There are many different ways they will meet up. Sometimes it is for playing chess or just in collecting mail from the post office, or at a dinner party or for one of countless other reasons. There are no hermits in Nanjing, and nor are there any clearly defined factions. Everyone knows everyone, and everyone helps where they can. Everyone is polite when they meet, and when they depart, they will quickly forget each other. Nanjing's authors are not excessively intimate with each other. There is gentlemanly friendship between writers, but they need not see each other as brothers. Those authors who like to call others their brothers are often those who like to quarrel most. Those who will praise others are often those who will scold them, too.

Nankinese writers' greatest strength is their diligence. Although they may not produce iconic works, they write honestly and earnestly. To them, nothing is more important than writing.

The Salaried Classes of Nanjing

One

The salaried classes of Nanjing constitute a large group, and compared to the salaried classes in other places, they are not necessarily all that different. It is difficult to describe them without leaving out much more than one includes. The salaried classes make up an overwhelming majority of the city's working population. When day breaks, public officials of all ranks hurry to their workplaces on their bicycles. Bureaucrats, security guards, university lecturers, kindergarten teachers, bank tellers, doctors, nurses, factory workers, foremen, sales assistants... all of them are part of the salaried classes.

The Chinese character xin, meaning "salary", had the original meaning of "firewood". The salaried classes are those who could never be thought of as rich. To have a salary means having enough to eat and having the necessary means to keep oneself warm and to support one's family. A salary is a livelihood. In the years since China's reform and opening up, the "iron rice bowl" (a term meaning "secure employment") has become of less value, and at times, it has taken on a negative connotation. The thoroughly coveted status of the salaried classes is not only less stable but is up against a severe challenge. Now, those who are doing well for themselves are those who dared to break out of the iron rice bowl. I have known a number of people who are temporary workers. From an old-fashioned perspective, there is always a sense of precarity to such labor. If these people have daughters, they cannot afford to marry them off. But society does not transform itself based on the wills of the old-fashioned. With careful investigation, we discover that the temporary workers are those who spend the most money. Those without a fixed professional income are the most extravagant. Nowadays, there are many young people without stable jobs who work according to their own interests. Whatever they do, they are not at it for long. They will work for a while, lose interest, and then change jobs. These young people live free and easy lives. Old-fashioned types always worry that these people will go hungry later on in life, but they are often shown to be living better than ever. If a tree is moved from its roots, it will die, but people must keep moving to live. The most wretched among the salaried classes are those who jealously guard their paltry salaries, not daring to imagine any sort of change.

Although stable employment has been challenged, Nanjingers still fix their sights upon it more than those in most other economically developed cities. Everybody talks about the drawbacks of the iron rice bowl, but in fact, a great majority of people still believe in it. The temporary workers I spoke of before should really be classified among the salaried classes, but simply because their employment is not secure, they are, intentionally or otherwise, counted as being outside such a class. A salary is a reward for labor, but it has become a byword for a fixed income. It is not only the conventional types who hope that their children will find proper, stable employment. Those young people who are enjoying the sweet taste of their freedom will also one day find themselves searching for iron rice bowls like the others. People look down on stable jobs, but deep down, they can't be without them. This is the typical mentality of Nanjing's salaried classes.

Two

The Nankinese mentality is most suitable for becoming a member of the salaried classes. Salaries can weaken intense competition between people. Although they both may draw a salary, there are countless differences between one career and the next. But surrounding one person who draws a salary is a group of others making roughly the same amount of money. Nanjingers are not given to competition. They are kind and honest to others, and sluggish in their responses. They may compare wealth, but only with those directly around them. The greatest advantage of the salaried classes is that, from the perspective of a payslip, you are mostly the same as others. You are no better than others, and others are not worse than you. In Nanjing, there is a saying: dage kan erge, dajia chabuduo—"big brother, look at your little brother; everyone is more or less the same." The word chabuduo—"more or less"—is the best way to bring comfort and balance to one's state of mind. The old attitude of neither envying the rich nor mocking the poor is perhaps not something one can keep up at all times. Nanjingers will compare themselves to those around them, and to those roughly on the same level as them. Compared to those above them, they are lacking, and to those below them, they have plenty. They are perfectly contented and worry-free.

 Those in different trades are worlds apart. Wages in different industries are an entirely different matter. The street where I live is near the busy Hunan Road, filled with all kinds of offices offering benefits for employees. At lunchtime, they will all go out to buy boxed lunches. Five yuan for a boxed lunch is by no means expensive, but if one's company is in dire straits, then boxed lunches do not appear particularly cost-effective. People can only save themselves the trouble if they have money and saving oneself the trouble requires one to spend money. In the average office, the majority of those who buy boxed lunches are young people who are inevitably more carefree sorts. In such offices, employee benefits have changed with the overall trends. At lunchtime, they will dispatch people to buy a few dozen boxed lunches. Nowadays, the smaller offices tend to offer better benefits, and the less formal enterprises are the ones that thrive. Being lighthearted is considered rather important, so people avoid dwelling on such unimportant things. Those who have money will spend it, and those who don't have money will also spend it. Of course, some workplaces have better benefits than others, such as businesses or banks, who are naturally wealthy and might as well spend the money they have. Every day, someone will come obediently to their offices with boxes full of food, and the salaried classes will eat lunch without employees having to spend any money at all. This is the best way of doing things.

Nanjingers tend not to engage in this kind of comparison between workplaces, however. If your workplace grants you benefits, then that's just your luck. Nanjingers are not the kind of people who bite off more than they can chew. Besides, there's no particular reason why one person might work in one office and not another. Sometimes, it's just coincidence. If one has a good workplace, that's simply good fortune. If one doesn't, there's nothing to be done. Income for the salaried classes can differ between workplaces and industries, but it pales in comparison to those wealthy people who have managed to get rich quick. The factor that truly defines one's living standards is still how much money one has in one's pocket.

Three

I know a Beijinger who somehow managed to make a quick fortune. I once ran into him at the Jingu Hotel. He complained to me about Nanjingers' lack of purchasing power. He had been commissioned by a foreign company to look into Nanjingers' purchases in the busy streets of Xinjiekou. The conclusion he came to was that, although there were many people in the streets, few of them actually had the money to buy anything. And the more luxurious the products were, the less interest they held for people. The foreign company wanted to buy a plot of land behind the Dongfeng Theater and erect what would be Nanjing's largest office building. After some investigation, they felt that this investment was potentially risky. They launched survey projects in Shanghai, Beijing, and Guangzhou, and finally decided to abandon their plans. "You Nanjingers aren't willing to part with your cash," the man said to me. He was somewhat lacking in understanding.

    To say that Nanjingers are miserly is truly an unjust accusation. Nanjingers don't have nearly as much money in their pockets as people from other provinces think they do. Although the economy in Jiangsu is developed and GNP is high, Nanjingers are by no means the rich masters of a big city. That is the case when compared to other provinces, and even when compared to the small- and medium-sized cities of south Jiangsu. The economic base forms the superstructure, and it also determines the common people's purchasing power. Having money but not being willing to spend it is not a typical part of the Nankinese mentality. Nanjing's salaried classes are fundamentally rational consumers. If you spend too freely, then having food and warm clothes can become an issue. Nanjing's salaried classes don't like to treat others to meals, and neither do they like being treated by others, because that means they will have to return the favor. Nanjingers are not shrewd people. I can give an example of this. When a new KFC or McDonald's opens, business will be booming. People will line up outside in crowds. Investors see such scenes and are unimaginably happy. In fact, this kind of investment just about manages to fit in with the salaried classes' levels of consumption in Nanjing.

    Abroad, people eat fast food to save time, but in Nanjing, going to KFC or McDonald's is an absolute waste of time. Fortunately, outside of the office, Nanjing's salaried classes are time-rich. Nanjingers have always retained a level of childish innocence. If you look at the people who are going to KFC and McDonald's, alongside children, you will see young people flirting with each other. Nanjingers don't particularly like eating KFC chicken or McDonald's hamburgers. The people who eat there are those who just childishly like that sort of taste. In this society, elementary school students are all only children with no siblings, much beloved and catered to. There is no way they will not be spoiled with a trip to KFC or McDonald's. My daughter has never said that she particularly likes eating KFC. She doesn't look all that happy when she eats it. But if we haven't been to KFC in two months, she treats it as a sign of parental neglect. We even feel ashamed of our own parenting as a result.

Nanjing's salaried classes cannot go gorging themselves at restaurants whenever they please. Those who spend all of their time in restaurants are those who live off the public purse. The majority of Nanjing's salaried classes usually stay at the level of being able to afford to take their children to western-style fast food restaurants. This kind of consumption is a good reminder for investors. If you bite off more than you can chew, then you will find yourself utterly defeated. Luxury goods' purveyors often find themselves at an impasse in Nanjing. The moral is that rich investors do not take the salaried classes seriously. The oft-vaunted Nanjing Hong Kong City shopping center is a dead duck. All people do is talk endlessly about how expensive everything is there. If things are expensive, people won't buy them. If your cash stays in your pockets, people can't steal it. Over the past few years, brand-name outlets have opened up across Nanjing, and they see little traffic. It might be that they have a prime location for a shopfront, but if people only come to window-shop without buying anything, or if they don't even come to look at all, then one is left in a rather awkward position.

One year, in Guangzhou, a Giordano outlet had a huge sale. The people of Guangzhou went mad over such cheap accessories. The people of Guangzhou care a lot about brands. Even if they are the salaried classes, they are naturally unwilling to let such an opportunity go to waste. It is not quite the same in Nanjing. The general appetite among Nanjing's salaried classes is for middle-of-the-road consumer goods. They have no desire for things that are either too expensive or too cheap. The rich like to parade their wealth around; the shrewd will try to save money wherever they can. Neither of these approaches is the strong suit of the Nankinese. Nanjing's salaried classes tend to have a more serene outlook. They feel that they are getting along just fine at the moment, but there is always room for improvement.

The Men of Nanjing

One

The men of Nanjing are neither macho nor effeminate. There are inevitably a few sloppy types among them who don't care about their appearances at all. For southerners, and particularly the women of south Jiangsu, the image of Nankinese men is not only uncouth, but somewhat barbarous. I think that this image comes about as a result of their familiarity with the gentleness of the men in south Jiangsu. In fact, the manly men of the north think that Nankinese men are lacking in vigor. Talking of the men of Harbin, Ah Cheng, a writer from that same city, said that northeastern men are quick to come to blows. He spoke of his own experience on a business trip to the south, where he saw two men arguing for quite a long time without getting into fisticuffs, and who eventually concluded their business and parted ways. Ah Cheng was quite puzzled and wondered how southerners could keep such moral integrity.

I shall not say which southerners Ah Cheng was talking about for the time being, but in any case, they were from one of the cities south of the Yangtze. There are plenty of southerners who are not lacking in vigor, such as the Hunanese. If you don't believe me, pick a fight with a Hunanese man; you will learn quickly. The Hunanese are fighting types, and they make good soldiers—thus the saying, "If you aren't Hunanese, you won't make a good soldier." Likewise, the people of Guangxi, who are also southerners, once made up the Guangxi Clique, one of the most powerful armies of modern Chinese history. Armies made up of troops from south Jiangsu, meanwhile, have never been particularly outstanding. When one thinks of south Jiangsu, one thinks of useless scholars. There are also obviously very few generals from south Jiangsu.

In geographical terms, Nanjing should be considered as being in the area south of the Yangtze. But when people speak of the southern Yangtze region, they often leave Nanjing out. The expression *jiangnan* ("south of the river") refers to the area east of Zhenjiang. In Jiangsu, it refers to the cities of Suzhou, Wuxi, and Changzhou, where they speak dialects of the Wu language family. People from Suzhou, Wuxi, and Changzhou will never admit that Nanjingers are also from *jiangnan* (South of the Yangtze River). The men of Nanjing are not as gentle as those of the Suzhou-Wuxi-Changzhou area, but neither are they military material. They are somewhat awkward, being neither as macho and imposing as the men of the north who excel in flaunting their bravery and fighting skills, nor as tender and graceful as the men of south Jiangsu, who excel at making careful plans and dealing in economic matters. Nanjingers are not fighters. Nankinese men are never willing to argue that much about anything and are indifferent to profits and losses alike. One increasingly popular phrase sums up the mentality of Nankinese men: duo da de shi—"Is it a big deal?" This saying can only take on true life in the mouth of a Nanjinger; if the Beijingers say it with their rolled tongues, then the sound becomes higher and it takes on an entirely different meaning. There is a particular low sound to the Nanjing accent, and as such, these four words not only take on a tone akin to a rhetorical question, but also an element of soliloquy.

Two

Every afternoon, I go for a walk in Xuanwu Lake Park. Sometimes, I catch sight of park workers catching fish in their seine nets. The water of Xuanwu Lake is not particularly clean. There are many fish, and quite large ones at that. Catching fish is a rather long process, and the workers must divide their tasks appropriately between them. What caught my eye was two young men who sat on a stone bench by the side of the water. While the others worked the net, these two men had bought some salted duck and were drinking in a leisurely fashion. The booze was more or less finished, and the net more or less reeled in, so those two men could have jumped into the water and caught fish. It is worth pointing out that those two young men appeared even more vigorous than all of the other men who were employed to be there.

The crux of the matter was that, in their leisurely, somewhat childish approach, these two young men were typical Nanjingers. Whether it was in their laid-back drinking or their leap into the cold lake waters to catch fish, they acted on a whim in a somewhat immature manner.

Really, Nankinese men should make for natural scholars. In Chapter 29 of *The Scholars*, Du Shenqing and other scholars reflect on the past and present. It is worth reproducing one particularly wonderful passage:

They had sat there for most of the day, and the sun was already setting in the west. There were two manure-carriers, each carrying two empty buckets on shoulder poles, who had stopped on the hill for a rest. "Brother," said one of them, clapping the other on the shoulder, "we've sold our goods for the day. Let's go to Yongning Temple and drink tea there, then we can come back to Yuhuatai and watch the sunset!" Du Shenqing laughed. "The waiters and bartenders truly do have the vapor of the Six Dynasties."

History changes, and Nanjingers change with it, and Nankinese men naturally have done so. "The vapor of the Six Dynasties" changed early in the Ming and Qing dynasties. By the time the Republic was established, there was very little of it left. Though the people did not cling to the old, there were still some remnants left behind, and, for Nanjingers, that was a source of pride. It is worth noting that the famous scholarly air of the Nankinese did not show itself in the literati. Their scholarly airs were put on, learned from books. The scholarly airs of the Nankinese were passed down from their ancestors, innate and by no means unpresentable. There is a certain leisurely attitude among all true Nankinese men, and if they have it, they don't care who calls them a "radish".

Three

The healthy attitude of Nanjingers governs a great many things. Innately indifferent, they do not care to flaunt their manliness, and nor do they fear that others will mock them for being weak. Machismo and effeminacy are entirely trivial matters to them, if they even matter at all. Nankinese men are simple sorts, and this came about as a result of the conditions of the city. People are a product of their environment. If we were to compare people to the stages of human life, we would conclude that Nanjingers are more like children, and Nankinese men are like adolescent boys. When they insult others, they like to call them dai (dumb), erbaiwu (literally "two hundred and fifty", meaning an idiot), or say naozi li you shi ("shit-for-brains"). All of these insults have a rather childish ring to them.

Without leaving Nanjing, you can't realize just how laid-back Nankinese men are. Arriving in an economically developed city, you get the feeling that all of the men who line the streets are hustling for money any way they can. On the streets of Nanjing, you see men leisurely riding their bikes, absolutely unconcerned about arriving late to work. Nankinese men are not the sort to leave their house early, following schedules down to the minute. They don't spend all day glancing constantly at their wristwatches. They are not particularly conscientious people, and naturally, they don't take time all that seriously, either. If you come across such a petty, small-minded man in Nanjing, it is quite likely that he is not a born-and-bred Nanjinger. Nanjingers are not the type to split hairs; Nankinese men, especially so. Nankinese men are moderate in temperament. They frequently end up losing out, but that doesn't really matter to them. The ones who win aren't going to live forever.

Nankinese men can be almost excessively laid-back at times. I once came across a man who had been hit by a bicycle. He'd stopped the cyclist and was not permitting him to leave.

> The cyclist was a man in a well-ironed suit, and he offered an apology.
> The other man did not bat an eyelid, saying, "I don't care if you're sorry—I'm not letting you go."
> The cyclist said he had urgent business to attend to, and he was clearly telling the truth, showing the other man an official document as proof.
> "I don't care if you've got business," said the other man, "I'm not letting you go."
> "Are you looking for a fight?" asked the cyclist.
> "Let's not be uncivilized," said the other man calmly, "we're not going to fight."

This went on for some time, with one man desperate to leave and the other unwilling to let him. Eventually, the cyclist lost his temper. "What the hell are you doing? If you want a fight, we'll fight. If you say I've injured you, then I'll send you to the hospital. Why the heck are you wasting my time?"

The whole time, the injured party was calm, unmoved by force or persuasion. He told the man that he was unemployed and lacked unemployment insurance. He didn't dare get into a fight. If the cyclist didn't care about paying for his medical bills, then he could freely take a swing at him; he promised he wouldn't hit back, or even answer back. A number of people gathered around to watch the scene. The injured man had been waiting for just such a hubbub. This was the result he wanted. There was a big green bruise on his leg, and blood was trickling from his knee, but these were trivial injuries, and he didn't want to use this as a pretext to extort anyone. His aim was to make sport of the man who had hit him, and once he had had his fun, he would let him go.

Such excessive insouciance can sometimes be close to knavery. If anyone else were in the same situation, they wouldn't waste anyone's time in such a way. Nanjingers can overdo it, making mischief in their nonchalance. Nankinese men can be rascals at times, yet still retain a certain childishness.

Nankinese men are children at heart—more so than men from other places. It seems that they are unwilling to truly grow up. Some years ago, I had a reunion with my elementary school classmates. At the time, there weren't as many taxis on the roads as there are today. When the party had finished, a number of people ran out to telephone for a cab. As a result, when the cabs all came at once, it wasn't clear which taxi had come for whom. In fact, those male classmates of mine who'd called for them didn't necessarily need to get a taxi; there was nothing urgent they had to do that day. Their motives were simple: they only wanted to show off in front of the female classmates. Grown men would usually look down on such behavior, but Nankinese men are children at heart.

Four

When Nankinese men look to get married, very few of them look for women who aren't Nankinese. Non-Nankinese women who settle in Nanjing very rarely seek Nankinese men. Nankinese men are not shameless experts at chasing women. As a result, your average Nanjing radish does not tend to be valued highly on the marriage market.

Women from south Jiangsu who work in Nanjing will always prioritize a husband who is also from south Jiangsu and works in Nanjing. If they cannot find him, then they will reluctantly settle for the next best thing: a Nankinese man. When women from outside Nanjing look for Nankinese husbands, it seems that they feel a sense of resentment from the very beginning.

If an outsider woman is unwilling to lower herself to the level of a Nankinese man, or a simple-hearted Nankinese man is angered and unwilling to accept her haughtiness, then she will have no alternative but to end up a spinster. There are a number of spinsters in Nanjing who became so because their standards were so high and they wasted their youths looking down on Nankinese men. Nankinese men should also keep in mind an old saying: "In marrying off a daughter, one should marry her into a family better than one's own; in finding a wife, one should marry into a family worse than one's own." Biting off more than they can chew is not one of the Nankinese men's more majestic characteristics. If a woman does not love me, why should I love her? Besides, if a woman's standards are too high, she is unloveable.

Conversely, non-Nankinese men who settle in Nanjing have a great opportunity when it comes to marriage. Outsiders who settle in Nanjing are sophisticated types. This is enough to arouse the ire of born-and-bred Nankinese men. They can't easily marry non-Nankinese women. If they do manage it, then those women also feel somewhat humiliated. They are looked down upon by such women, and non-Nankinese men often capture the hearts and minds of their women. Outsider men can easily take what Nankinese men feel is theirs and thus sow their own wild oats.

Women in Nanjing are not that bothered about whether or not they are married to a born-and-bred Nanjinger. For them, it's fine either way. It doesn't matter whether they're from north or south Jiangsu, or if they come to Nanjing for work; those merry bachelors will brazenly and unrelentingly woo Nankinese women without the slightest hesitation. Since it's easy for them to mingle in Nanjing, they're quite capable of chasing after women. The grass is always greener on the other side, and Nankinese women will sometimes find it hard to resist their curiosity. It's not snobbishness; if there are other men with better prospects available, then it's only natural that they renounce the Nanjing radishes.

Nankinese men aren't really angry about it, either. There aren't that many Nankinese men who remain single.

The Women of Nanjing (Part 1)

One

In the previous essay, I spoke of how the men of Nanjing tend not to marry outsiders. As if deliberately singling out my shortcomings, the moment I had finished the essay, a local evening newspaper published the following, under the headline "10,000 Non-Nankinese Women Marry Nankinese Men":

In a survey of armed forces members who had come from outside Nanjing, this paper has discovered that the number of non-Nankinese women marrying and settling down to start a family in Nanjing is increasing. According to statistics, between 1993-1995, 10,000 non-Nankinese women married Nankinese men, a 1.4x increase on the previous 3-year period, and the number continues to rise.

This seemed a powerful riposte to one of my points, because it proved that Nankinese men, undervalued on the marriage market, are seemingly and increasingly becoming objects of interest—perhaps offering cause for optimism. In fact, it's not that Nankinese men are unexpectedly choosing non-Nankinese spouses. The issue is that many non-Nankinese women come to Nanjing and inevitably become Nanjingers, but still hesitate when it comes to choosing a Nankinese husband. Women who come to Nanjing from the *jiangnan* area south of the Yangtze and women who come from elsewhere have two different ways of thinking. Outsider women are willing to marry

Nankinese men; some *jiangnan* women, even after they have settled down in Nanjing, still would prefer that their daughters did not marry Nankinese men. These two differing views show the awkward position of Nankinese men.

But, for Nankinese men, there is no use in worrying. There are plenty of Nankinese women to pair up with. And Nankinese men are still better off marrying Nankinese women. Nankinese women have never been the slightest bit inferior to women from other places. Compared to Nankinese men, Nankinese women are even more worthy of discussion.

The young men of Nanjing never talk of the women who surround them as being particularly pretty. This, of course, is a case of not seeing the forest for the trees, or actually ignoring them altogether. Nanjingers do not feel that their region produces great beauties. On the street, the feeling is that Nankinese women are eye-catching; it is not right to say that Nankinese women are ugly, but one can not realistically say that they are particularly beautiful. In fact, no matter what city one may be in, one will catch sight of beautiful and not-so-beautiful women. However, in the speech and writing of non-Nankinese writers, one can sense a heartfelt admiration for the beauty of Nankinese women.

I think that this is for historical reasons. The fact is that words and phrases with historical connotations—such as the qinhuai ba yan ("Eight Beauties of the Qinhuai") or the Jinling shi er chai ("Twelve Maidens of Jinling")—can make strong impressions on the way that people think and confuse their senses. There are plenty of beautiful women from other places, like Xi Shi, Wang Zhaojun, or Yang Guifei. But these historical beauties lived more than a millennium ago, and they seem to stand alone, unmatched. Meanwhile, Nanjing's beauties were not only produced relatively recently in the Ming and Qing dynasties, but they were also seemingly produced wholesale, in groups of eight or twelve. Of course, there could be a few placed in there just to make up the desired numbers, but the same is true for other places. It's not easy to gather together as many beauties as Nanjing has.

Two

What exactly makes a woman beautiful is an eternal topic of debate. Beauty is not in the face alone. It is in a pair of alluring eyes, a smooth nose, and a delicate mouth. It is in the measurements of the bust, waist, and hip. It is height and weight. Beauty has demanding standards; without them, it would not exist. Beauty has never been about ranking in any contest. Incidentally, however, Nankinese women would certainly score well in a beauty contest. The third-place contestant in a Nanjing beauty contest went on to compete nationally in Shenzhen, and effortlessly brought home the trophy. It is hard to say exactly what the problem is with defining beauty because beauty is more of a spiritual thing.

To call someone beautiful is different from calling someone a hero. It is easy to say who is a hero. Heroes perform painstaking deeds that shake heaven and earth. There have always been approximate standards for heroism. Heroes are visible and tangible. Either you are a hero, or you are not. It is hard to say for sure who is beautiful. With one smile, frown, or sideways glance, beauty can bring a state to its knees. It is a mysterious thing. No one says exactly how beautiful the Eight Beauties of Qinhuai were, or what made the Twelve Maidens of Jinling so stunning. When describing a woman's beauty in Chinese, there are customary and set phrases—guose tianxiang ("grace of a nation, fragrance of the divine") and chenyu luoyan ("fish sink, geese alight", suggesting beauty that captivates even the birds and beasts). Were the so-called Eight Beauties of Qinhuai not simply courtesans who plied their trade along the banks of the Qinhuai during the Ming and Qing dynasties? Many years ago, in the midst of its Six Dynasties golden age, Nanjing had countless famous courtesans, but people only remember a handful.

The historical distinction of the Eight Beauties is perhaps due to the fact that they were unlike other beauties, who themselves were specially presented to the emperor. They did not assume responsibility for the fall of nations. In terms of love, they enjoyed much more freedom than other beauties. They had the right to choose. In other words, normal men could fall in love with them, and they could love common men. Compared to Xi Shi, Zhao Feiyan, and Wu Zetian, the Eight Beauties were commoners. Of course, the crux of the Eight Beauties' true significance lies in the fact that they were not slaves from a defeated nation, and they were outstanding when it came to their cultural accomplishments and their political knowledge. Outer beauty is easy to find, but inner beauty is much harder to come by, appearing only in times of great calamity. Only at the final juncture, when one's country is on the brink of ruin, can one see a person's moral integrity.

The Eight Beauties were a mirror. The Peach Blossom Fan uses these oustanding courtesans to look back on the previous dynasty. We see the decline of Chinese culture and the hypocrisy and pretension of China's male intellectual class. Qian Muzhai and Hou Fangyu were both talented scholars of their age. Both started off speaking fine but empty words, and ultimately ended up risking it all in their disloyalty. They discovered the downsides of the ideals they agitated for; they climbed high and fell hard. Meanwhile, the Eight Beauties were righteous, and put men to shame.

Three

I don't know why Lin Liguo wanted to come to Nanjing to choose a consort. There is a historical tradition of the emperor coming to Nanjing to choose from its women, however. When the Jiajing Emperor of the Ming dynasty chose his concubines, he chose six women from Nanjing alone, among whom were those from the renowned clans of Fang and Wang. Lin Liguo's modern-day choice of a concubine caused a stir in Nanjing that was known all over. Perhaps, initially, it was not Lin Liguo's intention, but rather the blind enthusiasm of his subordinates. Yet, ultimately, he still came to Nanjing to make his choice. And, like many beautiful women in history, the women of Nanjing are often unintentionally caught up in the maelstrom of politics, becoming political sacrificial lambs. When Lin Liguo died alongside his father Lin Biao in Mongolia, Nanjingers ferociously discussed the time he had come to "choose a consort". I once personally heard a description of the scene from a woman who was part of this selection. There is one small detail I have never forgotten: the demand that the candidate be thin but without any bones showing—suggesting that this was the mark of true beauty. At the time, I had just begun middle school and was a young, undeveloped boy. I had no idea why you would want to be thin but without bones showing. I remember the woman who was part of the selection extending her own snow-white arm, talking about this and that. To this day, I still don't quite understand it.

Lin Liguo did not take up the position of "crown prince", and although the "concubine" was chosen, it is said that there was no time for the marriage ceremony to take place.

Nanjing eventually loses its finest beauties. It lost Zhang Lihua, the imperial consort who sang "Flowers of the Jade Tree Hall" for the last emperor of the Chen dynasty. It lost Queen Zhou the Younger, consort of Li Houzhu, who wrote *The Spring River Flows East*. The beauties of Nanjing are destined to be unsuitable for the power wielded by women such as Wu Zetian (Empress Wu: 624-705) and Cixi (Empress Dowager: 1835-1908). For them to become the Eight Beauties of Qinhuai is nearly impossible.

Beautiful women are much like generals. They cannot be seen to age. A beauty past her prime is much like an old general; to speak of them invokes a feeling of melancholy. If beautiful women live to old age, people rarely remember them for their beauty.

Four

To speak of the famous beauties of Nanjing evokes a sense of melancholy. The Eight Beauties of Qinhuai and the Twelve Maidens of Jinling have this in common: they all met unhappy ends.

Take, for example, Zhang Lihua and Queen Zhou the Younger. These unlucky belles have historically taken responsibility for disaster. It is as if the blame for the sub-par reigns of Chen Houzhu and Li Houzhu, and their respective national downfalls in Nanjing, has been wrongly shouldered entirely by these two consorts. Zhang Lihua was torn from the well in which she hid and beheaded on the orders of Emperor Yang of Sui. The spot where this happened stands today on the Sixiang Bridge. For a beauty to lose her head is already tragic enough, but Queen Zhou the Younger's misfortune was even more so. After the nation fell, she and Li Houzhu were taken north by the Song army and kept under guard by the Emperor of Song. Spending those difficult days where they "could not bear to think back on the country's past in the bright moonlight," she was summoned to meet the victorious emperor. A Yuan dynasty poem has this to say of it:

> *Left behind in Jiangnan, Li Huakai*
> *Was also beheaded by the emperor.*
> *It is no surprise that the autumn winds rushed forth*
> *And the imperial gardens were covered in purple-red sand.*

This poem was written upon a well-known erotic painting which circulated in private. The Compilation of Anecdotes of the Song records with shock: "The painting *The Emperor visits Queen Zhou the Younger* was painted in the Song dynasty. The emperor wears a turban, his face is dark, and he is stout. Queen Zhou is delicate of limb, and a number of palace attendants hold her down. Queen Zhou furrows her brow, distressed."

The emperor raped her, in a scene that was made into a painting to be gawked at by many. It is truly pitiful that the innocent Queen Zhou should have to suffer such humiliation.

According to popular belief, revenge for the shame of his deeds was borne by his descendants in the Humiliation of Jingkang. Women bear things on the part of men, sacrificing themselves for the nation; for a long time, it seems that this has been a matter of course. In a city like Nanjing, which has seen the chaos of war countless times, women have borne more humiliation than in any other city. Women have not only been blamed for the downfall of nations but must also suffer the consequences of such downfalls. In Chinese history, each time Nanjing has suffered in war, it has been a disaster for women. It goes without saying that the Japanese invasion of the city in 1937 is the clearest example of this.

Historical records show that, in December of 1937, when the Japanese invaded Nanjing, during the nightmarish incident in which 350,000 people died, there were around 20,000 cases of rape.

The Women of Nanjing (Part II)

One

Nanjing's Mochou lake is named after a beautiful woman called Mochou (whose name means "no worry"). There are three different ways of thinking as to the origin of Mochou. The first comes from the people of Henan, who take their proof from a poem about Emperor Wu of Liang: "The river's waters flow eastward, and in Luoyang there is a fair maiden named Mochou." The second comes from the indigenous population of Nanjing. The chapter "Records of Music" in *The Book of Tang* records: "In the city of Shicheng (Stone City) lived the maiden Mochou, who sang fine ballads of the city." The third comes from *Rongzhai suibi* (Notes taken in Rong Study) by the writer Hong Mai. It repudiates the second, saying that "Shicheng" in *The Book of Tang* does not refer to Nanjing, but rather Shicheng in Jingling (now Tianmen), Hubei—referring to Jingling rather than Jinling.

Where exactly Mochou came from is not particularly important, but some people take it very seriously, writing deadly earnest books like *In Search of Mochou of Jinling* and *Was Mochou a Prostitute?* Not only do they strive to prove that Mochou was from Nanjing, but they also emphasize the fact that she was absolutely not a prostitute of lowly birth. It is as if only Jinling can produce good women, and good women are surely chaste. There is really no need to be quite so serious about this matter. Since there are so many different tales about

Mochou, it is clear that she is an amalgamation of many different women rather than being one woman in particular. Even if she was a prostitute, it would be nothing to make a fuss about.

For many years, though, there have been countless boring essays penned on just such a topic. Wang Xiangqi, a Hunanese, came to Nanjing to visit Mochou Lake and wrote a couplet on the Mochou of legend:

> There are none as beautiful as the rouge-cheeked woman of the north; watching the painted boat come forth, the women south of the river are without color.
>
> The gold and splendor of the Six Dynasties has been enjoyed and exhausted; only the green hills remain, and when spring comes, the peach and plum are rich once more with fragrance.

Wang Xiangqi was a famous scholar from Hunan. He wrote this couplet in Nanjing, in a discourteous attempt to flatter Mochou, and it unexpectedly touched a nerve among Nanjingers. This was because the Hunan army was, at the time, most pleased with itself. Zeng Guofan had defeated the Taiping Rebellion and his brother Zeng Guoquan led troops into Nanjing, freely slaughtering all and sundry, taking advantage of the situation to defile the women of Nanjing. Nanjingers look on the Hunanese as their enemy, feeling an unspoken anger toward them, and thus they made a great fuss about this couplet, nitpicking and discussing neither Mochou's place of ancestry nor how one could exhaust the splendor of the Six Dynasties, but wanting to clarify the line regarding how the women south of the river are without color.

This anger put Wang Xiangqi on the spot, and he had no choice but to change the poem, changing "without color" (*wu yanse*) to "freshly colored" (*sheng yanse*). As for what "freshly colored" actually meant, it didn't matter. The second line "only the green hills remain" was also changed to "only the green hills are in good health" (*wu yang*). *Wu yang* seems to admit the plundering undertaken by the Hunan army—

while the green hills remained untouched, everywhere else fell afoul of their ravaging. It is no wonder that Huang Chang jokingly said that this was yue gai yue fandong, "more reactionary with each alteration."

Two

Where Mochou actually came from, or which dynasty she lived in, is ultimately irrelevant. In any case, she can be considered a Nankinese woman like the historical Eight Beauties of Qinhuai or the Twelve Maidens of Jinling.

I don't like turning such a beautiful woman as Mochou into a tragic figure. The Mochou of The Maiden Mochou, as staged by the Nanjing Shaoxing Opera Group, is a figure so pitiful as to make one feel uncomfortable, and her influence has been great, making many people wrongly presume that such a historical figure truly existed. The historical Mochou was probably not accurately reflected in this portrayal. I have always felt that Mochou could serve as a representative of Nankinese femininity, but entirely due to the meaning of her name. Mochou knows no worry. A woman in ancient times being called Mochou, by interpretation, suggests that she was an innocent, vivacious young woman. Historically, the women of Nanjing have undergone countless hardships, but these difficulties have not changed their innocent, vivacious natures.

Let us return to the modern day and talk of the women of Nanjing as they are now. It is not enough simply to be beautiful. As Confucius said, "If three walk together, then one can be my teacher," and if three women walk ahead of me, then one of them must be good-looking. Because external beauty is often compared, as long as there are women in a place, then there will be beauty. Speaking of the beauty of Nankinese women, there are a few particular details that differ from other cities.

For example, they indeed do not know worry, just as Mochou did not. There have been no great historical changes within the hearts of Nankinese women as time has passed. This sort of melancholy seems to be the destiny of men. Nankinese women are often carefree. There is a descriptive word in Nanjing, mugu—it is unclear which characters are actually used to write it, but it means someone who does not care, who has no perception of things, and who is easy-going.

Nankinese women are, at heart, free spirits, more so than Nankinese men.

Three

The allure of Nanjing's most beautiful women is often expressed in this word, mugu.

In the past, the saying "Clear water produces lotus flowers" was used to describe the nature of young women. Beauty, it seems, does not require one to meticulously adorn oneself, but rather quite the opposite. One cannot say that Nankinese woman do not like to adorn themselves. On the contrary, if a Nankinese woman likes to get dressed up, she is often bold in her attempt to prevail over her opponents. I have on more than one occasion heard people say that Nankinese women "dare" to make themselves up. This word "dare" is remarkably similar to the way that Nankinese women would express it. Nankinese women are like Shi Xiangyun, one of the Twelve Maidens of Jinling.

To dare is to be bold, that is, is foolhardy. There is no place where women are quite as daring in their clothing choices as Nanjing. The secret of the most stunning of Nankinese women is their bold and chaotic clothing choices. Such brazenness dazzles others and leaves them dumbstruck. For many Nankinese women, the fashion rulebook is thrown out the window. They are eye-catching not because they wear expensive designer brands, nor because they wear bizarre clothes. Sometimes, it is simply because they dare to dress and accessorize themselves in such a random manner. One should not underestimate the effect of randomness. In martial arts, an indiscriminate blow may strike down a master. To dress in such a way is to win without having made a single move.

There is no clothing that a Nankinese woman dare not wear. For them, "dare" is the watchword. It seems as if there have never been any such taboos, and the more unsuitable something seems for their dress, the more likely it is that they will wear it. For a pretty, shapely woman with the right assets, anything can look good. Of course, there are those who do not look so great, whose assets are not quite so strong. Petite women will wear dark colors, and fat women will wear light colors, and in these days where leggings are now in style, one can often catch sight of short, chubby legs stuffed into pants like glutinous rice in a dumpling. What brings one success can also bring one defeat, and, for Nankinese women, their brazenness can make them look either beautiful or unsightly.

The carefree way that Nankinese women dress is truly unique. Many non-Nankinese women who come to settle in Nanjing say that they have little good to say about the way that Nankinese women dress. Nankinese women seem to be innately ready to shock the world, naturally beautiful dressers whose skirts may be long enough to drag along the floor or short enough that they might catch cold. In hot weather, they might still wear leather jackets; in the cold, they might expose their necks to the elements. They will go out on the streets in multi-colored, plastic flip-flops. They will go out garishly dressed according to whatever whim pleases them—faces plastered in makeup, lips red, fingernails and even toenails bright crimson, without a care in the world for how others on the street will see them. They will sit on the streets next to the wonton stalls, sitting with one leg crossed over the other, slowly eating with a spoon. When wang jidan (partly fertilized eggs) come on sale, they will squat next to the piping hot pots, their slender fingers picking through them, eating a dozen in a sitting.

Thus, are the women of Nanjing. What makes them loveable is their carefree spirit. Whatever others think is completely unimportant to them. There is a Chinese saying: "A true gentleman will sacrifice his life for a friend who understands him, as a woman makes herself beautiful for her sweetheart." Sometimes, Nankinese women only care about what interests them, but still their mothers come first. To be honest, doing as one pleases can sometimes bring about victory completely by accident. Following one's desires can bring about a particular state of affairs. This is unlike women from other places, who live under far too many regulations and restrictions only so that they can show their own white-collar status or how they are unwilling to fall behind. They are clothed from head to foot in the same outfits as everyone else, and they speak the same way everyone else does. Nankinese women would not do such a grievance to themselves.

Four

In the bathroom of a bar in Taiwan, I once saw some writing that served as a word of advice to men. It was targeted toward those men who were about to get intimate with women, reminding them that a woman's psychological age can never exceed forty.

For Nankinese women, this reminder is rather conservative. Because, in truth, a Nankinese woman's mental age often never exceeds the age of eighteen. On the plus side, this means that Nankinese women always have a lively, youthful attitude. On the downside, it means that Nankinese women will never grow up.

Often, you will see Nankinese men and women arguing on the street. This is unique to the streets of Nanjing. Nankinese women do not bother to avoid trouble, unlike Nankinese men. If they feel they have lost out, then they will say so. Nankinese women do not like to repress their feelings. Any man who argues in the street with a Nankinese woman is particularly stupid, however, because in the eyes of Nanjingers, to quarrel on the street is already outrageous, let alone with a woman. Nankinese women particularly like to argue with those men who choose to split hairs with women.

When Nankinese women express their feelings, they are used to being direct. When they are happy, they will show it; when they are unhappy, they will not hide it. Their work environment usually determines their attitude toward work as well as their emotions. For example, women working in hotels will be affable, and it is said that airlines, who recruit staff from across the country, are most satisfied with Nankinese women as employees due to their diligence and tenderness. In Nanjing, the women you see will often leave you with many different impressions. The women who work in banks will just as often have a face full of smiles. In universities, the female students are full of vitality—probably because they're yet to meet with the pressures of life. And anyone who gets on the bad side of the women selling meat and vegetables at the market will soon hear them turn the air blue. Shop assistants at the state-run stores of Nanjing, ticket sellers on buses, and on-call nurses in the emergency rooms are all not to be crossed. They are rarely in a positive mood, and always ready to argue with others.

These differing environments have accordingly produced differing dispositions in Nankinese women. Many outsiders wrongly presume that either one of these temperaments is representative of all of the women of Nanjing. As a result, some outsiders feel that Nankinese women are particularly gentle while others think them rather fierce.

The carefree women of Nanjing can not only make good wives and good mothers, but also good friends. Nankinese women don't have any shrewdness to them, and don't tend to pursue vendettas against others. They do as they please, and, as they get older, they become less self-restrained, less concerned... more mugu. As the years pass, both their merits and shortcomings are magnified and developed. From a general standpoint, Nankinese women are lacking in restraint, and perhaps also in humor. Nankinese women will not look down on their husbands for not bringing home much money, and nor will they pressure their husbands to become government employees. And if they do become the wives of wealthy businessmen or important politicians, their personalities will not change all that much.

Nanjing, 100 Years Ago

One

Lu Xun and and his brother Zhou Zuoren's descriptions of Nanjing a century ago are perhaps the most apt descriptions of the city written. Both of them spent a large part of their youth in the city. Lu Xun attended two different schools in Nanjing—the Jiangnan Naval Academy and the School of Mines and Railways. He was not particularly enamored of his schooling, but this did not prevent him from achieving high marks, and he was eventually sent abroad to Japan to study there. After the Xinhai Revolution, the Jiangnan Naval Academy changed its name to the "Thunder and Lightning Academy". Lu Xun felt that this name was reminiscent of the Ming dynasty novel, *Investiture of the Gods*, and he later wrote an essay on this very topic. Zhou Zuoren spent even more time in Nanjing—five years in total—so his descriptions are more plentiful and more detailed.

One hundred years ago, Nanjing was utterly dilapidated. There was absolutely no comparison that could be made between the cities of China a century ago and the cities of the west. Such ruin does not come about in one day. Many of the sumptuous buildings of St. Petersburg were built over a hundred years ago, and yet, after a century of wind and rain, they still stand just as elegantly as before. In Nanjing, one simply cannot find a hundred-year-old building, and we can attribute this to war—either civil war or foreign aggression. St.

Petersburg once suffered heavy shelling by the German army. From a chemical and physical perspective, the city suffered far worse than Nanjing did, but the Russians stubbornly stood their ground and many of their sturdy buildings thus remain intact. Stone structures show their superiority with the passing of time. The majority of our buildings are made of wood. Although gaudy-looking firewalls may abound, one large enough blaze can raze a vast section of the city.

One hundred years ago, Nanjing was much calmer than the north. The Hundred Days Reform had failed, the Boxers were rising up, and the Eight Nation Alliance was about to invade. The Qing Empire was being buffeted from all directions. At that moment, Nanjing did not find itself in a vortex of contradictions. It had found peace and stability by staying out of things. The pendulum had swung back. At that moment, northern society seemed that it was about to fall into chaos just as the south had. For Nanjing, the Taiping Rebellion's Kingdom of Heavenly Peace had been anything but. Nanjingers had endured horrifying turmoil. The Taiping armies had come, invaded the city, and established their capital. Then, the Qing armies came, encircling the city. Salvo followed salvo, attack after counterattack.

There is something I have never quite understood. After the Taiping rebels designated Nanjing as their capital, the Qing armies were stationed on the outskirts of Nanjing for a long period of time. The camps north and south of the river were like hands around the throat of the Taiping Kingdom. This was a rather absurd situation of confrontation, and it was the common people who suffered. In the time of the Kingdom of Heavenly Peace, the people of Nanjing saw no peace at all. There were small battles every day, with larger confrontations also happening frequently. Eventually, Zeng Guofan's Hunan Army entered Nanjing and scores of people were killed. In the decades that followed, the people spoke bitterly of the chaos caused by the "Long Hairs"—a name for the Taiping troops.

One hundred years ago, the Taiping Kingdom had perished nearly 30 years prior, and the Nankinese had shaken off their state of terror. As the new century dawned, the wounds of war faded into the past and Nanjing slowly began to change. Everything was in a state of recovery, and the Viceroy of Liangjiang (modern-day Jiangsu, Jiangxi, and Anhui) was the prominent statesman Zhang Zhidong. Zhang was a member of the modernizing faction of the Qing government, and he played a major role in the "New Policies" of the late Qing era. Under the heavy pressures of imperialism, Shanghai developed quickly, but it was still yet to become the most prominent city of the southeast. Nanjing still held that position, and the Viceroy of Liangjiang who oversaw it all was a celebrated figure. In comparison to the governors of other regions, the Viceroy of Liangjiang was not only a commander of the armed forces, but also the equivalent of a logistics chief in the Qing Empire, who had to constantly ensure a steady supply of financial assistance to the Qing government. The prosperous southeast was an economic pillar of the Chinese government. There was a popular saying: "With the prosperity of Suzhou and Changzhou, All-Under-Heaven may have plenty." The Viceroy of Liangjiang's major responsibility was to ensure the stability of the region's booming economy. Stability is the foundation of prosperity, and if the beaten-down Chinese economy wanted to recover, then stability was paramount.

One hundred years ago, Zhang Zhidong was already showing his age, though he was by no means a doddering old man. As Viceroy of Liangjiang, Zhang Zhidong did many things for Nanjing. Its earliest railways, its greatest public works, and its first university all came about under his leadership.

Two

It is somewhat awkward to talk about the life force of Nanjing: the once-flourishing Qinhuai River. Regional officials, all men of reason, knew that if they wanted Nanjing to come to life, there were two major actions that needed to be taken. The first was to quickly reinstate the imperial examinations, raising up talented scholars and giving them the chance to stand out. Presented with an opportunity like this, the intellectuals would surely be unable to cause trouble. Scholarship produces hormones that must be given a release. A revolt of scholars would come about not ten years later as a result of such belittling as they had seen and experienced in the past. In truth, the climate of revolution would not have been possible without the work of the intelligentsia. So, in the second year of Taiping rule over Nanjing, examinations began. Hong Xiuquan was obstinate on this point, and not confused in the slightest. It is a historical experience worth noting that, when the Manchu Qing took control of the country, there was an important factor in their victory that went beyond military strength alone. They lost no time in reinstating the imperial examinations, using high posts and generous salaries to bribe the Han intellectuals. Scholarship is the most noble of pursuits. Those with integrity are few, and scholars are the most noble. In the face of the imperial examination system, all of their anger dissolved.

Another action necessary for Nanjing's rebirth was to "build brothels as Guan Zhong did." The shuttered brothels were opened once more, a red-light district was established, and commerce—as well as all other professions that accompany the sex work trade—immediately developed. Hong Xiuquan had made a significant mistake. He was a clear prohibitionist. Not only were men and women separated and not permitted to have sexual freedom, but prostitution along the banks of the Qinhuai was completely cracked down upon and eliminated. A direct result of this action was that prostitutes and their patrons were all expelled to the Shanghai International Settlement, and thus the settlement instantly flourished just as the Qinhuai immediately hit a slump. We cannot say that Hong Xiuquan's defeat was directly related to the prohibition of prostitution, of course. But, after the chaos and destruction of the Taiping Rebellion, the renowed Zeng Guofan and all of the successive viceroys of Liangjiang, without exception, adopted a liberal attitude toward prostitution on the Qinhuai.

The liberalization along the river had an instant effect. Many of the prostitutes returned from the Shanghai International Settlement, and the wealthy also returned. The red-light district thrived more and more each day, and merchants congregated alongside scholars and courtesans. According to historical evidence, the lifting of the ban had a direct impact on the economy of Shanghai. The population of the settlement suddenly lowered, and business subsequently slumped. But the sex trade alone could not bring true prosperity. The golden age of the Six Dynasties and the splendor of the Qinhuai had long since passed, never to return. Feudal society cannot rise once more from the dead. The glories of the past cannot be recaptured.

One hundred years ago, Nanjing was utterly ragged and in turmoil. This ancient city, and likewise, ancient China itself, was beyond cure. There was no panacea that could treat it.

Neither the imperial examinations nor the beautiful women who lined the Qinhuai could save old Nanjing. The river aided and abetted the wicked, intoxicating them with the sound of paddles on water and the shadows of lamplight. In his autobiography, Chen Duxiu wrote of his experience taking the imperial exams at the turn of the century. In August of 1897, Chen Duxiu came from Anhui to Nanjing to sit the exams. In the exam hall, he could not focus; this was because, two hours prior, he had been staring blankly at something. The strange sight of another student, plump and wearing a long braid, had set Chen Duxiu's mind wandering. Perhaps it was Nanjing's unbearable August heat. The student had left his cell and wandered naked through the exam hall, muttering: "Very well, very well, I shall pass these exams now!" This had made Chen Duxiu consider the strange situation of all of the students. If that band of "animals" accomplished their ambitions, the nation and the people would suffer.

Chen Duxiu compared the exam candidates to "an exhibition of animals"—within a few years, the exam system had become a show of performing monkeys. The superiority of the exam system was no more. "Selecting Ministers from the Intellegentsia"... "Seeking the Worthy for the Nation"... these slogans had become empty. Feudal society had finally come to its end, and an end-of-days atmosphere had enveloped Nanjing. One hundred years ago, Nanjing was lifeless, a dirge for the olden days. Old Nanjing was on its deathbed. A few years later, the exam system would be abolished, the Tongmenghui established, and the Qing monarchy overthrown. This was an era of the new replacing the old. With the coming of the new century, Nanjing had no alternative but to change with the times. It had to be born anew.

Three

Zhou Zuoren once made a joke about the scholarly scene of Nanjing. In one of the so-called "new schools", an old man who taught Chinese literature spoke of geography. He said there were two worlds: one acted while the other was acted upon. One was the Western Hemisphere, and the other was the Eastern Hemisphere. There were many jokes like this one hundred years ago, and from this point we can see the atmosphere of society at the time. Lu Xun and Zhou Zuoren both studied at new schools in Nanjing. When they began, they were looked down upon somewhat. For example, Lu Xun was born as Zhou Zhangshou. His great uncle felt that it was indecent for members of their family to study and join the armed forces, and that taking such a name from one of his ancestors was inappropriate, so he encouraged him to change his name to Shuren, meaning "learned person". Many works treat Zhou Shuren as Lu Xun's original name, but this is not correct. By the same reasoning, Zhou Zuoren's original name could be expressed as Zhou Xiazhou. One hundred years ago, modernizers and conservatives stood in intense opposition, with each side despising the other. Conservatives look down upon modernizers only for a short time, but modernizers forever disdain conservatives, and have the complacency of those who have seized total victory. Reading the Zhou brothers on Nanjing a century ago leaves a particularly deep impression.

After Zeng Guofan, the position of Viceroy of Liangjiang was taken up mostly by Han people. On the face of it, the ethnic conflicts of the time were not particularly fierce. The Han people had been subalternized and the Manchus had been Sinicized. Men wore the queue, the long pigtail that was a Manchu custom, and enough time had passed for it to become customary. Women had their feet bound, a tradition which had then been passed down for centuries; Manchu women did no such thing. Men wore pigtails and women bound their feet: this was the result of compromise. One hundred years ago, no one dared to challenge the queue because it was a choice between wearing the queue or losing one's head. If you wanted to cut off your queue, you had to exile yourself from your country. Domestically, the modernizers wanted to make a difference, so they had no choice but to campaign loudly against foot-binding. Thus, the Foot Emancipation Society was born.

Ethnic conflict had not completely disappeared, however. An anti-Manchu mood was slowly being fermented among the people. At the time, there was a Manchu barracks on the eastern outskirts of Nanjing. The children of Manchu bannermen made up most of the army and they rode roughshod over the people, frequently bullying Nanjingers. If anyone approached the camp, they would shout loudly and aggressively throw stones. This practice was somewhat absurd, and as a result, Nanjingers became rather angry. They boldly rode in on horseback to protest, and Lu Xun and his classmates were involved on more than one occasion. The reason for doing this was simple: to show that the Han were not afraid of the Manchus. One hundred years ago, no one would have thought that the Green Standard Army, made up of the sons of Manchu bannermen, had no strength save for their proficiency in feasting, drinking, whoring, and gambling. When the Xinhai Revolution broke out, the allied armies of Jiangsu and Zhejiang—made up of militia and revolutionary armies—quickly captured Nanjing.

When western missionaries and gunboats came to China, they

became a target that the modernizers could utilize, and sometimes they became their most powerful supporters. The power of the Christian church could not be ignored. The Boxer Rebellion very quickly failed, with the missionaries and converts of Nanjing spending some time in a state of panic. Their arrogance had not diminished, and instead, thanks to the military interference of the Eight Nation Alliance, they had become even more arrogant in the knowledge that they had secure backing. The special rights of foreigners in China were clear. Officials and commoners alike were all subservient to some extent. On the streets of Nanjing, there was nothing particularly new about catching sight of blonde-haired, blue-eyed foreigners. Various Christian denominations practiced throughout the city. Nowadays, if we want to get a feel for the situation at that time, the photographs and writing left behind by missionaries offer our best chance and evidence.

The number of converts was clearly exaggerated. In order to win over the Chinese traditionalists, western missionaries ran all kinds of emergency relief organizations, refugee camps, medical clinics, schools, and universities. Western-style constructions became the most important buildings in Nanjing, and some of them have been preserved to this day. When people were hungry or sick or wanted to be educated, they had no qualms about exploiting the missionaries' kindness. Among them were a few who would perhaps pray afterwards, or even join the religion, but truly believing Christians were still few in number. The majority of converts were pragmatists. The missionaries offered a sugar pill which would gladly be sucked on; once the layer of sugar had dissolved, converts would spit it out.

Modernization had already begun to take shape in Nanjing. The first effects of the Self-Strengthening Movement could be seen, and the Nanking Arsenal had become the largest factory in Nanjing. The firearms produced there "could be used to destroy domestic foes, but none dared believe they would resist foreign aggression." Domestically produced goods gave no one any cause for relief. Somewhat more effective were the building and restoration of public roads and railways, which was pioneering work that created something from nothing. Many years ago, waterway travel had always held top priority. When Lu Xun and Zhou Zuoren had come to study in Nanjing, they'd had no other choice but to come by boat, coming ashore at Xiaguan Wharf. Now, the first signs of good-quality, land-based infrastructure had begun to surface. The Shanghai-Nanjing Railway had become a gold mine, and the British, under extremely harsh terms, had signed the "Shanghai-Nanjing Railway Lending Contract" with the Qing government. It was a prime thoroughfare, and the year that it was properly repaired, passenger volume reached over 3,000,000. Nowadays, such a volume is nothing impressive, but one hundred years ago, it was exceptional.

Four

One hundred years ago, Nanjing was like an expectant mother past her due date, reclining with her protruding belly and awaiting the onset of labor pains. It was also like an abandoned child lingering at a crossroads, looking helplessly in all directions in the boundless night, unsure of which path to take through the vast and open wilds. In the century that followed, Nanjing would be turned on its head, and it was destined to face a great many things. It was here that Sun Yat-sen was proclaimed the first interim president of the Republic of China, opening the first page of the history of modern China. This was considered a significant break with the Nanjing of old. This new chapter did not come about with the turn of the century, and as with many other aspects of China's development, there will always be regret about the tardy progress of the Chinese revolution. This turned out not to be so important: in the end, history cannot be impeded. Time flies like an arrow, and a century passed in an instant. But if we suddenly look back, we find ourselves shocked by the massive changes this city has undergone.

Nanjing, History, and Culture

One

 Nanjing is a city which one must mull over carefully in order to appreciate it. Unable to see the forest for the trees, its inhabitants do not know their own luck and often complain that there are no places where one may enjoy oneself. I have a friend who is, to put it simply, not short on money, and who is always happy to brag about the places he has visited. Yet, walking along Wanli Road is one of life's great pleasures, but pleasure can at times simply become conventional, like clocking in at work by swiping one's punchcard—a kind of transaction between oneself and others.

 The world is large... so large that it is impossible to visit every single place. The cash in one's pocket is limited, and as travel becomes more popular, costs also rise. In 1986, the writer Wang Zengqi came to Nanjing. I accompanied him and my father to the castle at the Gate of China, which was still yet to be renovated. Standing at the highest point, Wang said nothing for a long time, and then finally sighed and spoke. "This truly is a wonderful place. To come to Nanjing and just visit this place alone would be enough." We thought he was simply being polite. We certainly didn't expect him to go on to speak so loftily about it, saying that it was as great as Shanhai Pass, the eastern pass of the Great Wall, if not even greater. The tourists surrounding him heard what he said and turned around to re-appreciate the scene.

People can end up paying no attention at all to the familiar sights around them, and sometimes they continue to do so unless someone with something of a celebrity status points things out to them. I don't want to say that the castle at the Gate of China is superior to Shanhai Pass. A comparison like this will usually set off debate. But, for those of us familiar with history, climbing to a high point and looking outward inevitably leaves us feeling deeply moved. "Looking worriedly upon Jingkou, I see the armies defeated. I speak with pain of Yangzhou, besieged for 10 days." Shanhai Pass is the gateway to the nation, the Gate of China a barrier to the city. If either fell, then it would be nearly impossible to escape destruction. When the Qing armies entered the pass, their movement sounded the death knell for the Ming regime. When the Japanese tanks entered the Gate of China, their movement made for the prologue to the Nanjing Massacre.

I know an old soldier who served at the time. During the fight to protect Nanjing, his artillery unit was stationed nearby, and he travelled several times to the headquarters stationed at the Gate of China, reporting to Sun Yuanliang. On the eve of battle, everything looked solemn. The autumn wind was cold, the setting sun red as blood. The Gate of China towered majestically. At the time, Sun Yuanliang was spirited, a red-blooded youth in command of an army division; he was an elite commander tasked with defending Nanjing. Nowadays, the younger generation has barely heard of Sun Yuanliang. The best way to bring him up is to tell them that he is the father of Taiwanese movie star Chin Han, the one who always stars in romances with Brigitte Lin. Popularity is the best way to fight historical amnesia. Or perhaps time will pass, and people will forget Chin Han, too. It is said that, when Sun Yuanliang's troops were defeated, he hid in a brothel on the Qinhuai River, sheltered from danger by patriotic prostitutes. I'm not in the mood to verify this story. It's hard to get it out of one's head, however—part of the scenery before the outbreak of war. Sometimes, disregarding the outcome and picking out only a part of the beginning of a story can better evoke one's imagination. For me, the brief moment of peace before the outbreak of war is perhaps more thrilling than the spectacle of a bloody battle.

Where the Gate of China Castle ranks on the global stage, one cannot say. In China, it could place highly without much argument. It occupies an area of over 15,000 square meters. There are 27 holes along the barbican in which soldiers may hide; the largest of these can hold 1,000 troops. During the Battle of Nanjing, the Gate of China Castle was the site of the fiercest fighting, with both sides firing and bombing indiscriminately. Corpses piled into mountains; blood ran in rivers. The viciousness of the Japanese army after their entrance into Nanjing cannot be separated from the fierce resistance they encountered during their assault. They could not have dreamed that the besieged city, completely defeated, would struggle so fiercely even upon its deathbed.

Two

If the Great Wall was tasked with protecting the nation, the old wall of Nanjing, considered to be the greatest city wall in the nation, was intended to protect the city. In one sense, a city can be considered a microcosm of the nation. Zhu Yuanzhang, the first Ming emperor, proudly built one of the largest cities in the world, directly along mountains and rivers and wide expanses of arable land. "To the far east is the foot of Mount Zhong; the way west is blocked by solid stone. To the south is Changgan, through which the Qinhuai flows. To the north, Mount Fuzhou and Lion Mountain are how the lake beyond them is controlled." Thus, the territory was defended through the ages by rivers and mountains. As a result, the easiest way to take the city was from within. Zhu Yuanzhang died not long after construction was finished. His fourth son Zhu Di rushed to Beijing to seize the throne, claiming the Ming empire as his own.

Nanjing as a city is almost always destined to lose the fight. Its forbidding terrain is of no aid, just as the Great Wall did not stop the armored horsemen from the ethnic groups of the north. The poet Lu You once strongly advocated for the Southern Song dynasty capital to be moved to Nanjing. As a result, on the pretext of "cultivating moral integrity and not choosing a strategic location," Emperor Gaozong of Song refused to move from the city of Hangzhou, intoxicated by its warm breezes as if he were a tourist. Since time immemorial, monarchs have never been content to simply hold the territory they own. Gaozong's approach has always been criticized as one of surrender, but the period during which Hangzhou was the Southern Song capital was much longer than any period in which Nanjing was the capital of any of its ten dynasties. Those familiar with history may have their own doubts. "Three hundred years have passed, disappearing like a dream at daybreak." "On the ramparts, the banners are lowered." With its advantageous territory, and the regal air of Jinling, how could Nanjing fall again and again, becoming the graveyard of one empire after another?

Nanjing has produced too many so-called last emperors. Sun Hao, the last emperor of the Eastern Wu, carried his coffin with him to report to the Western Jin army. The Final Lord of Chen jumped into a well alongside his beloved concubine. Li Houzhu, the last emperor of the Southern Tang, "shed tears gazing at the palace maidens." It is hard for people to avoid superstition at times. After their victory in World War II, a few Guomindang elders advocated moving the capital to Beijing. Their reasoning was that Nanjing was located in the southeast, and the people were too listless — throwing their weight around there would not be enough to inspire awe throughout the nation. The shadow of defeated empires lies too heavy upon Nanjing. In *Records of The Viewing-River Tower*, the Ming dynasty historian sang the praises of Zhu Yuanzhang, the first Ming Emperor Taizu, starting his work in this way:

Jinling has served as the seat of royalty. From the Six Dynasties to the Southern Tang, each one has been forced to relinquish its territory, unable to live up to the regal air of its mountains and rivers. That is, until His Majesty founded His capital here, worthy of such a place.

Song Lian's suggestion was that, with the coming of Zhu Yuanzhang, Nanjing would no longer be the site of defeated empires. But Emperor Taizu, full of wisdom, was not willing to listen to such flattery. In *On Sacrifices to the Kitchen God*, written in his later years, he lamented his unfulfilled wish to move the capital, bemoaning that his old age and lack of strength meant he had no choice but to drop the matter. He realized the many different ways in which Nanjing was unsuitable as a national capital. Although he had made a big fuss over building the city, Zhu Yuanzhang had known that its distance from the constantly shifting Central Plain concealed great danger. It was Zhu Di, the Yongle Emperor, who fulfilled his father's wish. It is often said that Zhu Di was the Prince of Yan, bestowed the city of Beijing, and came from Beijing and brought the power of the Ming state back with him. The truth is that Zhu Di spent 18 years as emperor in Nanjing. During that time, 22,000 scrolls of the first great encyclopedia, *The Yongle Great Encyclopedia*, were composed, and Zheng He sailed westward on his great expeditions. Thus, Zhu Di's position was already thoroughly secure. Moving the capital was clearly not a result of his own selfish calculations. Zhu Di's reign was arguably more remarkable than that of his father, and for this he is praised as Yongle ("perpetual happiness"). Another equally famous ruler is the Kangxi Emperor of the Qing dynasty.

The Yongle Emperor's decision to move the capital was an important move in the 300-year chess game played in an effort to preserve the power of the state. In terms of ruling over and uniting the country, Nanjing was inferior to Beijing. It is much like how the American capital is best suited to Washington, rather than the financial center of New York or Hollywood in Los Angeles. In the past, the establishment of Beijing as a capital has been emphasized as being good for preventing invasion by the ethnic groups of the north. In fact, being far away from the listless people of the southeast is also an effective way to ensure political stability. During Kang Youwei's

Hundred Days Reforms, he strongly advocated moving the capital to Shanghai. His reasoning was that Beijing was too conservative and decayed, "surrounded by Manchu bannermen, full to bursting with conservative factions, with opportunists among the lowest ranks of officials of which there is plentiful evidence, and all kinds of relics of a defeated nation." "Without moving the capital, it will be difficult to build a new city, and reform will be impossible," he claimed. As a result, the Guangxu Emperor wanted to take a few people with him and flee to Shanghai in the hopes of easily solving many of his problems. This was a thoroughly naive way of thinking, but in a sense, it showed "cultivating moral integrity and not choosing a strategic location." Nothing about Beijing makes it a natural stronghold, and like Nanjing, it is an old city that, once surrounded, can only succumb to its tragic fate. A sturdy wall cannot protect a national capital from danger; the fort is usually breached from within.

"Geographical superiority does not come from moats; the victory of the republic depends on the will of the people." One dynasty must give way to another: this is a historical necessity. There may be external factors to the downfall of an empire, but the most important factors are internal.

Three

It is impossible to avoid nostalgia when discussing Nanjing. In the poems and songs of the Tang and Song dynasties, one can find much lamentation regarding the city. The history of Nanjing cannot be separated from the defeat of the nation. When the nation is defeated, one's thoughts turn to prosperity; in times of prosperity, the nation's downfall is forgotten. "The singing women do not know the regret of the vanquished nation, and across the river they still sing Flowers of the Jade Tree Hall." This is a vivid portrayal. On the eve of the Xinhai Revolution, a young southern poet, Zhou Shi, wrote of his passionate feelings after reading Peach Blossom Fan:

In the thousand-year brothel only can she be seen; on the rooftop, a steadfast refusal of trousseau,

The Central Plain is far away and lifeless, and the strong-willed heroes have left daughters behind.

Not long after writing this poem, Zhou Shi was martyred in the revolution. He was barely 27 years old. Nanjing's prosperity always seems to be tied up with the intoxicating splendor of the Qinhuai River. "The strong-willed heroes have left daughters behind" can be seen as conceding a point; had they left no progeny behind at all, the nation would truly fall to its wretched fate, and its downfall could only be accepted. In fact, historically, Nanjing has produced not only the rulers of fallen empires and the Eight Beauties of the Qinhuai, but also heroes who were willing to risk life and limb for their ideals. "If they die, they shall be heroes, and worthy of such praise." The existence of men with lofty ideals has made the weak city stronger and more beautiful.

Not far away from the Gate of China is the famous Yuhuatai. It is said that, over 1,400 years ago, the Master Yunguang recited the sutras there, and the Buddha, moved by his recitation, immediately caused petals to fall like rain—thus the name Yuhuatai, "terrace of raining flowers." Discussing Yuhuatai brings to mind Fang Xiaoru. As Zhu Di was amassing his troops, the royal court sent soldiers out to fight them. They were under the command of Fang Xiaoru, a highly cultured man. After Zhu Di entered Nanjing, he forgot his former enemies and ordered that Fang draft an imperial edict, saying: "You must write an address, that I may subjugate All-Under-Heaven."

Fang, in mourning for his former liege, threw his pen to the ground, weeping and scolding Zhu Di. "If I am to die, let me die; I shall not write your address."

Humiliated, Zhu Di flew into a rage. "This is a matter for the royal family; what business is it of yours?" He threatened Fang, saying that if he did not comply, then his entire family would be exterminated—a practice known as "extermination of the nine degrees of kinship". Fang was loyal to the end, saying that even ten degrees of kinship would make no difference. Thus, Zhu Di had the entire Fang clan arrested, and, one by one, in front of Fang Xiaoru, they were executed. After the ninth degree was executed, in order to fulfil the "tenth" degree, all of his students and peers were also shockingly murdered. In total, over 870 people were executed.

Although Fang Xiaoru's death came about as a result of his steadfast loyalty to his former ruler, and although it involved so many innocent lives, we must affirm this spirit of laying down one's life for one's beliefs. What should be criticized is Zhu Di's brutality: right and wrong cannot be obscured; we cannot claim that black is white. When the Japanese army entered Nanjing, the Chinese army was massacred, even after having already given up their arms. This is much like not criticizing the atrocities committed by the Japanese army, but rather blaming the Chinese army for not fighting with all their might. Presuming a course of events based on the outcome can often make one fall victim to bias. Fang Xiaoru struck a blow for men of culture. His remains were buried in Yuhuatai, where a shrine was built to commemorate him. The hills are fortunate to have his loyal bones interred within them. In fact, before Fang Xiaoru, Yuhuatai also held the remains of Yang Bangyi, a magistrate of Liyang County during the Northern Song period. When the Jin armies entered Nanjing, Du Chong was left behind to surrender. Yang chose to die rather than submit. He cursed Wanyan Zongbi, the leader of the Jin, and died on Yuhuatai, his heart cut out from his chest.

The romantic air of Nanjing is only one aspect of the city. The lamplight and sound of oars on the river merely make for an idea. People should not forget such bloody events. The listlessness of the people of the southeast was a result of the brutality of victors. The intoxicating atmosphere of the city is both a cause and a result of the downfall of nations. "One kingdom flourishes, and another dies.

The Six Dynasties flourished and died far too hastily." In this way, Zheng Banqiao wrote emotionally of Nanjing. The fall of a city means disaster every time it happens. When the Sui army entered Nanjing, Emperor Wendi of Sui employed the most extreme methods to fight, razing the entirety of this beautiful city to the ground. The common folk of Nanjing are no strangers to mass murder. It remains fresh in their minds. Within the space of a century, the Taiping Kingdom rose and fell; the Second Revolution ended when Zhang Xun recaptured the city; and the Japanese army invaded Nanjing and massacred its inhabitants. Whether through the changing of dynasties or the invasion of foreigners, Nanjing has been plagued by terrible nightmares.

The more a history is written in blood, the deeper it is etched into the memory of man. The luminaries buried in tombs on the outskirts of Moscow and St. Petersburg are the pride of Russia. The graves of famous figures are best visited with a written guide. Tour guides can prattle on and on at you—Pushkin is there, Dostoyevsky is over there, and Tchaikovsky is that way. Leisure in Nanjing, in a sense, cannot be separated from tombs. On the eastern outskirts are the Ming tombs, the Sun Yat-sen Mausoleum, and the graves of Deng Yinda, Liao Zhongkai, and Tan Yankai; in the south, alongside the aforementioned Fang Xiaoru and Yang Bangyi, there are the graves of Zheng He, Liu Zhi, and the King of Boni.

Nanjing's famous figures are all closely connected to the city's rise and fall. They are not a source of pride, but of melancholy and deep consideration.

Four

The city of Nanjing is a fine history textbook. If one pores over this city, one will evoke the history of China itself. Every historic site in Nanjing is saturated with the character of human affairs. Whichever ruins one might visit, they are all part of a deep historical dialogue. In terms of scenery, Nanjing has mountains and rivers enough to match any city. But the city's strength is in its history, and in its unique culture.

No city can provide a clear outline and framework for contemporary history quite like Nanjing can. The cemetery for the fallen soldiers of the National Revolutionary Army on the eastern outskirts of the city and the Revolutionary Martyrs Cemetery in Yuhuatai to the south represent China's opposing sides: the Nationalists and the Communists. The sizes of these cemeteries and the magnificence of their buildings are unmatched in the country. In desperate times are brothers found; on meeting, one smile erases all enmity. In any case, Nanjing is a tolerant place. It cherishes the details of history that are left behind and protects the historical heritage that remains. On the streets of Nanjing, it is as if one walks in history's murky shade. Every place has a story, every inch a remnant of history. History has bequeathed upon Nanjing a most abundant inheritance. One must recall the past in order to understand the future. Nostalgia is an innate part of mankind, regardless of whether one is satisfied with one's life and environment. People cannot avoid bringing up the past, turning their heads to peer back into the mists of time. I may as well end with a quote of my own:

Nanjing is not the only ancient capital city of China. But few cities have undergone such great, intense changes as Nanjing; few are as worthy of the nostalgia of later generations. It is of no matter whether you seek to understand it or not. The people of Nanjing cannot escape the nostalgia complex. For those of us au fait with culture, the city of Nanjing is a window through which we may look back on history.

Hexi, 5 September 2001

On the Qinhuai River

During the Republican era, a work called *Treatise on the Qinhuai* was written on the subject of the Qinhuai River. Many things have been written in books, and if one wishes to truly understand the Qinhuai River, it doesn't hurt to find something on the subject. Most people are happy with only having a vague understanding of the river. Sometimes, knowing too much can only leave one confused.

The Qinhuai is long, with inner and outer reaches. In a vague sense, Qinhuai is a mother river. Nanjing could not live without it. Its development is representative of the city's own development. "Mist shrouds the cold water and moonlight covers the sands, [and] in the evening boats moor by the taverns of the Qinhuai." Whether the "Qinhuai" that Du Mu wrote of was the inner or outer Qinhuai has long been a subject of debate. For most, the Qinhuai is simply seen as the bustling stretch of water by the Confucius Temple. Its splendor and its dishonor are summed up as "flowers in every doorway, jade in every home." An outsider comes to Nanjing, finds somewhere to rest, and strolls around. Even if the river is but a tiny stinking ditch, such visitors will be unable to restrain their emotions, and they will wonder if this is where Li Xiangjun walked the streets. If a pretty girl approaches them, they will wonder if she is a descendent of the Twelve Maidens of Jinling.

Historically, Nanjing has been filled with wharves crisscrossing the river, and with boats paddling along from all across China. All of the cities along the lower reaches of the Yangtze, whether north or south of the river, tend to make an issue of the course of the river. But only Nanjing could become a strategic town in the southeast. If you think of how important Shanghai is nowadays on the national stage, then it is not difficult to understand how Nanjing could once hold such authority in Chinese territory. Back then, before the opening of the Treaty Ports, Shanghai was little more than a fishing village. Some people joke that, with the rise of American imperialism and the fall of the British Empire, poor Nanjing has declined like the British, and now one can only look on helplessly as Shanghai rises meteorically, becoming an international metropolis—the so-called pearl of the east.

Few people think about any historical connection that Shanghai's modern-day prosperity might have with the Qinhuai River. They say that old Shanghai is the Shanghai of foreign settlements, and that its prosperity is inextricably tied up with the International Settlement. It is possible that many are unaware that the initial profits made by the International Settlement trickled out of the Qinhuai River in Nanjing. As the Taiping army was murdering its way through Guangxi, wealthy people south of the river fled to the Shanghai International Settlement. Before this, the place which the wealthy most liked to loiter around had been the Qinhuai. The Taiping armies came, and clients fled. Hong Xiuquan sat on his throne as Heavenly King, and forbade all prostitution. With this ban, the prostitutes had no choice but to flee, as well—all the way to Shanghai. The truth is, clients and prostitutes went hand in hand when it came to invigorating the Shanghai economy.

Zeng Guofan led the Hunan army into victory against the Taiping Kingdom. In order to revitalize the war-wracked city of Nanjing, he made the simple choice to reliberalize prostitution along the Qinhuai, reopening the "Six Houses". He would be praised as a paragon of virtue, and historians are unclear as to why he only chose to reopen the Six Houses. These so-called Six Houses were those that the government had granted a license for prostitution. After they had opened for business, there were no hard and fast rules on exactly how many women could operate within. Historical records only show that this move worked very well. With this shot in the arm, the economy recovered almost instantly. Nanjing quickly returned to prosperity. The population of the Shanghai International Settlement fell, and business subsequently declined. "The markets quickly faded; their brocade cast aside, the generosity of the past did not return."

Historically, Nanjing has always been the center of the *jiangnan* region. *Jiangnan* was once quite a broad concept. Its scope has decreased more and more, and now it is often understood in a much narrower sense. "Above there is Heaven, below there is Suzhou and Hangzhou." *Jiangnan* had come to represent the affluent Jiangsu-Zhejiang-Shanghai region, with its only limit being the southern bank of the lower reaches of the Yangtze. In fact, *jiangnan* can be split into east and west. Chinese territory during the Northern Song dynasty resembled a city map; at a provincial level, the regions were called "roads". For example, the lower reaches of the Yangtze were divided into Jiangnan West Road and Jiangnan East Road. The historical Greater Jiangxi and today's Jiangxi Province are not completely the same, but there are some important areas of overlap which have been inherited. As a counterpart to Jiangxi ("west of the river") stood Jiangdong ("east of the river"). Jiangdong was the area which is now referred to as *jiangnan*.

Nanjing was also known as a meeting of the two. Perhaps due to the natural moat formed by the Yangtze, the first thing that *jiangnan* collides with would be the meeting of east and west, and Nanjing's Qinhuai River was just such a meeting point. If we go all the way back to King Fuchai of Wu and King Goujian of Yue, we see that Yue eventually emerged as the victor, taking over Wu territory. In order to resist the stronger state of Chu, walls were built along the Qinhuai, running from the city of Yecheng to the city of Yuecheng. The area reaching from Yecheng to Yuecheng was the embryonic form of the city of Nanjing. Not long afterward, the powerful state of Chu vanquished the state of Yue, and Yuecheng was renamed Jinling. There have been countless discussions regarding the name Jinling ("golden hill"). The most popular explanation for it was that the King of Chu felt that this place had a "regal" air which he felt needed to change. Thus, gold was buried in places surrounding the city—in order to assert domination over its royal aura. When Qin Shi Huang launched his southern expedition, feng shui masters felt that Jinling's royal aura was still abundant. In order to protect his successors, Qin Shi Huang ordered that dragon-shaped channels be dug into the land, and he changed its name from Jinling to Moling ("horse-feed hill"). This change embodies the interesting nature of Chinese characters. Of the five classical elements—metal, wood, water, fire, and earth—metal is considered paramount, the most expensive. Meanwhile, horsefeed was clearly the lowliest.

In victory or defeat, its regal aura remained. Jinling was the seat of kings, and the Qinhuai is beautiful territory. Nanjing's prosperity was not brought about by victory; instead, its luxuriant growth was a result of defeat. The defeated *jiangnan* holds too many unbearable memories. Northward assaults and southward attacks still linger in the hearts of northerners and southerners alike. When the south wishes to strike back against the north, they encounter desolate winds and rain, requiring endless effort, diligence, and a long-suffering desire for revenge. When the north attacks the south, though the winds are bitterly cold, should they wish to slaughter their way across the land, they become an irrefutible force, with millions of troops crossing the river.

Xiang Yu the Conqueror led 8,000 troops across the river, destroying everything in their path, until finally, surrounded on all sides by enemies, he was forced to say a panicked farewell to his concubine. History shows that whoever controls the Central Plain can control China. The subtext of the Chinese saying "hunting deer in the Central Plain" is that one is contesting the right to ultimately unify China. Ultimately, a country can only have one center. If we are to say that "Yellow River culture" or "Yangtze River culture" is actually an existent thing, then the center has always been the Yellow River region. Whoever controls the Central Plain may rule All-Under-Heaven and control *jiangnan*. The Yellow River is both our mother and our father. Defeat is a common part of war, yet one cannot anticipate it; one who may bare such humiliation is a true man. The men of Jiangdong were many and talented, but none could know for sure if they could ever fight back. In fact, in conflicts between the north and the south, the south has been no match. It has always found itself in a state of defeat, attempting to make a comeback. This is the view of many scholars, but they are armchair strategists engaging in idle talk.

Jiangnan seems naturally destined to concede the middle ground, a child deficient since birth and completely unlike strapping heroes of indomitable spirit. For a long time, the Qinhuai River—as the cultural center of *Jiangnan*—has seemed to only spend its days in a drunken stupor. As a survival strategy, ceding ground is the safest option. Only when you are stable can you stand a chance of overpowering others. "The singing women do not know the regret of the vanquished nation, and across the river they still sing Flowers of the Jade Tree Hall." The women of *jiangnan* were not merely beauties suffering unhappy fates; they played their parts in its prosperous economy, and were also blamed for its misfortune.

The royal court is just as unchanging as the North Star. When the Han people ruled the Central Plain, *jiangnan*, represented by the Qinhuai, could only be an auxiliary center of Chinese culture— responsible for collecting tax, paying tribute, and revitalizing the economy—sending an endless supply of gold and silver to the faraway north. Save for its economic prosperity, the north could not excessively tolerate *jiangnan* amassing too much strength. In other words, *jiangnan* could have status economically, but not politically. When the Han people suffered setbacks on the Central Plain, or the Yellow River was invaded by foreigners, after the landowners of the north had fled south, the center of Chinese culture was passively shifted to *jiangnan*. At this time, *jiangnan* had become a center of Han culture, and the last bastion of Chinese civilization. Historically, the Six Dynasties were a golden age for Nanjing. Why? Because, at that time, the base of Han culture had shifted to Nanjing.

Ultimately, the story of the Qinhuai River is the best way to understand China's great history. *Jiangnan* was not innately weak, and the Qinhuai River had not been degraded since ancient times. All of its faults, in a sense, came from the arrival of the defeated north. The Western Jin moved eastward and the Northern Song crossed southward. This was not the fault of *jiangnan*; it was not a debt to be paid by its people. Such movement brought about a great many problems. Peach Blossom Fan looks back on the Southern Ming, and the debauchery that could be found along the Qinhuai was never exclusive to *jiangnan*. The Qinhuai magnanimously accepted the defeated dynasty of the Central Plain and had no choice but to bear its shame. Many years ago, a shadow of defeat and disgrace enveloped the Qinhuai. This was a birthplace of last emperors, a byword for the downfall of empires. The waters of the Qinhuai flow on endlessly, carrying with them the lifebreath of Chinese culture, unspeakable tenderness and pain, and indescribable decline and despair. After victory in 1945, a number of Guomindang elders insisted that the capital be moved to Beijing. Their reasoning was that the air of national defeat hung heavy in Nanjing, and that it was corrupt and degenerate. Although Sun Yat-sen had a preference for the place, however, it was not suitable as a national capital.

Historical decisions have always had their own rationale. In truth, in the *jiangnan* region, the Qinhuai has become less and less important; its prominence has long since been a thing of the past. Nowadays, the undisputed ruler of the *jiangnan* region is Shanghai. In the eyes of many young Shanghainese, there is doubt as to whether old Nanjing, with its glory derived from the Qinhuai River, can be considered part of *jiangnan* at all.

Hexi, 8 February 2007.

Tianxia Wenshu ("The Literary Center of All-Under-Heaven")

One

One cannot speak of Nanjing without speaking of the Qinhuai River. One cannot speak of the Qinhuai River without speaking of the Confucius Temple.

Ancient Rome wasn't built in a day, and neither was the Confucius Temple. The Confucius Temple has slowly evolved, finally reaching its current form. It has slowly developed, flowing unhurriedly like the waters of the Qinhuai. The temple has always been in a state of flux, and it shall continue to change.

At the heart of the Confucius Temple stands the Temple of Literature.

There is nothing extraordinary about the Temple of Literature. In ancient China, any city that played host to scholars would have a temple of literature for those wishing to pay tribute to Confucius. The Temple of Literature in Nanjing has moved a number of times. At one point, it was in the south of the city, and then in the north. The Temple of Literature was nowhere near the Qinhuai, where the splendor of the Six Dynasties filled the air. It was most probably on the spot where the Nanjing City Government chambers now stand. If you go inside today, you can still see a number of traces suggesting this very thing.

For modern Nanjing, this is ancient history, requiring far too much complicated research, and no one feels the inclination to figure out the truth.

In short, the Temple of Literature moved next to the Qinhuai River, and in the eyes of the common people, the atmosphere was immediately changed. It was no longer called the "Temple of Literature" (wenmiao), but the "Temple of Confucius" (kongmiao), and offhandedly called fuzimiao ("the Master's Temple").

Such a solemn appellation, in the mouths of the common people, was immediately profaned.

In front of the Confucius Temple, there is a sign with four imposing characters on it: Tianxia Wenshu ("The Literary Center of All-Under-Heaven").

Since it is the literary center, there are arches in various eye-catching places—with inscriptions such as "Virtue may join Heaven and earth" and "Revere both the ancient and the modern." These phrases were inscribed by Zeng Guofan, the luminary of China's pre-modern society, and they are most appropriate.

Other places have their own temples of literature, upon which Tianxia Wenshu is also inscribed, but only the Nanjing Confucius Temple is worthy of such an inscription. Only the Nanjing Confucius Temple could make such a joke.

Nanjing's Confucius Temple is not famous solely for the temple itself. The area's prosperity cannot be considered without thinking of the legacy of the imperial exams. In other words, people came not to worship Confucius, but in the hope of achieving scholarly honor. The buildings in the Confucius Temple were, frankly, built in the name of Confucius, but for the purpose of the imperial exams. Everything was built around the exams. All of the concepts behind the buildings were related in some way to study.

The buildings in the Confucius Temple can be divided into three groups.

The first group is that of temples: temples to Confucius and other buildings related to the design of the temples in some way. The most eye-catching is the Great Hall, with six pillars and five rooms dedicated to Confucius, as well as his disciples Yan Hui, Zengzi, Mencius, and Zisi. The side rooms of the Great Hall are dedicated to the 72 sages of Confucianism. In ancient times, scholars would come here to kneel and kowtow, offering tribute one after another.

Once one passes through the Great Hall, there is a small doorway going through to the Palace of Learning (xuegong) out the back. The Palace of Learning is part of the second group of buildings. It is called the "Primary Place of Learning in the Southeast" (dongnan diyixue) and was originally a site for Confucian study. Most of the scholars in the past, having paid tribute to Confucius and his disciples, would come here to breathe a sigh of relief, rest their feet, and drink a cup of tea. Every nook and cranny is filled with a dense scholarly air. In the Hall of Virtue, the Pavilion of Revered Scripture, the Clear Sky House, or the Shrine of Esteemed Sages, one could teach and attend lectures. In every pavilion and every kiosk, the Four Books and Five Classics filled the air. All of the study rooms also had bookish names such as "The Path of Aspiration", "Accordance to Virtue", "Compliance with Humanity", and "Immersion in Art".

But do not be mistaken: the stellar reputation of the Nanjing Confucius Temple came from the reputation of the temple and its name as a seat of great learning. In truth, the "temple" part of its name was not seen as important by many persons. The Confucius Temple was a product of the exam system, a model for the imperial examinations. The "temple" was merely a pretense, the Palace of Learning a mere display. The temple and the Palace of Learning were both beautiful repositories for the hoarding of treasures, and the Jiangnan Tribute Hall, which acted as the imperial exam room, was the jewel in the crown.

So, if you come to the Confucius Temple, you need not pay tribute to the Master, nor sample tea in the Palace of Learning, but you must take a look at the Jiangnan Tribute Hall.

The Jiangnan Tribute Hall is in the third group of buildings, and though it may be last, it is certainly not least, and it is most certainly worth a visit.

The Jiangnan Tribute Hall and the Beijing Shuntian Tribute Hall are equally famous, widely known as the "Southern Gateway" and the "Northern Gateway" (nanwei and beiwei), respectively. The character wei ("palace gate") and the phrase gongxian ("tribute") are both other names for the exam hall. In ancient society, scholarship was the most noble of all endeavors. To study was noble, but if you could not pass the imperial exams, then it was all for naught.

Ten years of strenuous study for the chance to gain a name for oneself in an instant. Every scholar hoped for his chance to pass through the exam hall victorious.

For exam candidates, the Jiangnan Tribute Hall was a battleground of life and death. It was the only road to an official career—a long and winding road of vital importance, and a difficult path to tread into the unknown.

Everything here is deeply connected to the imperial exams. Every doorway, every corridor, and every threshold were seen as the "gates of hell".

Having tasted bitterness for so many years, hopeful scholars could finally look forward to sweetness. Under inscriptions which read "choosing scholars from those who know the scriptures" and "seeking the worthy for the sake of the nation", they charged through the gates of hell, hoping to take flight like mythical birds and to see their names upon the roll of honor, to leap like the mythical carp which becomes a dragon upon reaching the "Dragon Gate".

For the scholars, their Dragon Gate was Mingyuan House.

Mingyuan House is the most important part of the Jiangnan Tribute Hall. The name mingyuan has literary origins, coming from two characters in the phrase shen zhong zhui yuan, ming de gui hou ("Let there be a careful attention to performing the funeral rites to parents, and let them be followed when long done with the ceremonies of sacrifice—then the virtue of the people will resume its proper excellence"). The building was built in the Ming dynasty during the reign of the Yongle Emperor, and it was rebuilt in the Qing dynasty during the reign of the Guangxu Emperor. At the time, Mingyuan House sat at the center of the Jiangnan Tribute Hall, square-shaped and towering. At the top, one could look out over a great distance, and those responsible for invigilating the exams would stand here to look at the scenery. They could see whether exam candidates were cheating as they wrote their "eight-legged essays", and whether the guards were doing their jobs. They could see the moon rise in the east, and the sun set in the west.

The imperial exams were of fundamental significance. "In the daylight, banners flew as a warning; at night, lamps were hoisted high in search of aid." Here, any incident could result in losing one's head. It was like facing a powerful army on the battlefield. Scholars would live or die upon the results of their exams. Entire futures were determined in the exam hall. Exam candidates had to accomplish their task at one stroke; victory and defeat were determined within those walls.

The exam hall was filled with densely packed cells, 100 to a row, with rows on rows totaling 20,644 cells.

Such a huge place filled with such tiny spaces! The tens of thousands of candidates would eat, drink, relieve themselves, and sleep all in the same place. The exam period lasted nine days and eight nights. For novice scholars and the grey-haired seasoned candidates alike, this was the site of success or failure, the entrance to heaven or to hell.

Two

The prosperity of the Confucius Temple comes from the imperial exams; so does its lascivious air.

The exams are both a source of success and of failure.

In Chen Duxiu's autobiography, there is one particularly moving passage which records the scene of the period of decline in the imperial examinations. In the year 1897, during a hot Indian summer in Nanjing, 18-year-old Chen Duxiu sat the exams for the first time. His cell was close to the toilets, and the stench was overwhelming. As a result, his head swam, and he could not calm himself. He looked around casually and saw another student who had come from Xuzhou. He was quite the tub of lard, wore a long gown, and was completely naked. He had a pair of worn-out shoes on his feet and clutched his examination paper, muttering proudly out loud to himself: "Very well, very well, today I shall pass, today I shall pass."

A number of talented scholars came out of the Jiangnan Tribute Hall.

Quite a surprising number of candidates who achieved the title of zhuangyuan, the top scorer in the exams, were those from the Jiangnan Tribute Hall.

Undoubtedly, the imperial examinations can still be considered to be a good and effective system for selecting talented individuals. However, after the decline of feudal society, the imperial exams could, ultimately, only reach their limit.

The Confucius Temple was a cultural and economic powerhouse. The culture of the Confucius Temple was that of the imperial exams; the economy was one of hospitality and leisure.

The important buildings of the Confucius Temple are all those of the bureaucracy: built with government money spent from the public purse. It was a center of the culture of officials, but its economy was that of the common people. Without official support, the people would not have been able to indulge in such leisure; without the cooperation of the people, this seat of officialdom would have been built in vain. The most significant characteristic of the buildings of the Confucius Temple is the organic integration of official and popular buildings, each symbiotic with the others.

The story of the Confucius Temple is the story of *The Scholars* and of Peach Blossom Fan. Clearly, without the imperial exam system, many stories of the Confucius Temple would not exist. Without the exams, there would be no prosperity. Without the exams, there would be none of the joys and sorrows that transpired there. The imperial exams determined the cultural atmosphere of the Confucius Temple, brought in great economic benefit to the area surrounding it, and had a clear effect on the prosperity of the temple's surroundings.

Let us move on to the initial days of the imperial exams. As the triennial provincial exams approached, a sailboat with a flag on its mast—reading "By imperial decree, the imperial exams of *Jiangnan*"—would sail along the river. The carnival, a prologue to the exams, would begin around the Confucius Temple. Students would come, as would examiners as well as various hangers-on looking to freeload. The inns of the Confucius Temple area were immediately filled. The sons of wealthy men and penniless scholars alike would all find places to stay and eat. The wealthy would stay at the more illustrious establishments, the poor at the cheap inns. Hotels of every grade took advantage of the opportunity, their proprietors each smiling wry smiles, wishing that every day could be exam day.

Every businessman beamed from ear to ear. Stationery merchants, book merchants, art merchants, grocery merchants, fortune-tellers, pawnbrokers, clothes merchants, people smugglers, and matchmakers… they all waited in anticipation of the coming of the students and their money. The imperial exams provided for quite a large amount of people, and a huge economy sprang up to serve them, emerging like bamboo after the spring rain.

On the cobbled streets, stores opened their doors; the coming of the students was like rays of spring sunshine for the merchants of the Confucius Temple area. In fact, the students' arrival turned the Confucius Temple area into a haven for merchants. The buildings by the jetty were garlanded with flowers in their windows. The residents near the Confucius Temple changed in many different ways around exam time.

For the triennial exams, many students would take up residence in the surrounding area—even a year in advance. There were those who stayed for longer after having failed their previous attempt, studying long and hard for the next time they could sit the exams three years later. If they failed, then they would stay another three years, take the exams again, and fail once more.

The more students stayed along the Qinhuai, the better business was for the merchants. The more students who failed and decided to stay, the happier the merchants were. The stores were full of happy proprietors, and the brothels even more so.

After they had spent long enough upon the Qinhuai, scholars would produce tales of romance. For every talented scholar, there is naturally a beautiful woman. When the two met, stories may be made. In Peach Blossom Fan's look back on the previous dynasty, the Confucius Temple area is the residence of Li Xiangjun, and the place where Liu Rushi and Ma Xianglan come to work. The brothels of the Confucius Temple area were the favorite stomping grounds of failed exam candidates. The beautiful girls were there to soothe their heavy hearts, ensuring that they could not free themselves from the debauchery of the Qinhuai waterfront.

The Confucius Temple became known as "the mystic capital of earthly desires, a paradise of peace." With such a reputation, the cultural aspect of the Confucius Temple was rather diminished. The imperial exams were done for, as their grand stage could no longer be restored to prominence, and the Confucius Temple was still as bustling as before. The Jiangnan Tribute Hall declined while, across the river, the "Old Hall" was still thriving, its grandeur unbounded.

With its beaded door-curtains and decorated pleasure boats moored along the river, the Qinhuai River no doubt offered a charming scene. Standing on Wende Bridge, people would wait for dusk to fall. Lanterns would be lit on either side of the Qinhuai, with beautifully painted ladies leaving their establishments to be chosen by clients for carousing until daybreak. A painted pleasure boat would sail past with its engraved railings and painted balustrades, its windows beautifully adorned with silk. Carried on the wind would be the scent of wine and roasted meat, as well as the sound of birdsong.

Bringing up the dazzling Confucius Temple area and the Qinhuai naturally evokes those melancholy lines: "The singing women do not know the regret of the vanquished nation; across the river they still sing Flowers of the Jade Tree Hall."

However, in discussing the buildings of the Confucius Temple, we cannot overlook the houses of the surrounding area. The houses of the Confucius Temple are an important part of the overall building complex and are valuable remnants of *Jiangnan* culture. Of the buildings built by the people of the area, alongside the stores of various sizes were houses and riverboats which were characteristic of the Qinhuai River.

The river houses and the painted boats are the most vital symbols of the Confucius Temple, dotted along the flowing river. These houses and boats came about, developed, and expanded as a result of the exams, but they did not fall alongside the collapse of the exam system. It was thanks to these houses and boats that when the exams collapsed, in fact, the Confucius Temple remained as full of vitality as before.

Since ancient times, the Confucius Temple has suffered repeated damage, being destroyed and rebuilt time and time again.

Its constant reconstruction reflects Nanjing's unyielding spirit.

After all, this place is the greatest witness to Nanjing's history.

To appreciate the Confucius Temple is to appreciate Nanjing's past, to have your finger on the pulse of history, and to relive those glory days once more.

Hexi, 3 August 2003

Excursions on Donkeyback

In the autumn of 1907, a fourth-rank capital official came to Nanjing. At the time, the Viceroy of Liangjiang, Duanfang, ceremoniously offered the man his hospitality. The Viceroy of Liangjiang was a major regional government post during the Qing dynasty. Normally, he would have been completely justified in paying absolutely no attention to a fourth-rank official. However, this official had been dispatched by His Majesty himself, and so the viceroy had to entertain him. The official was a playful fellow, and when he came to Nanjing, he suddenly decided he wanted to see the Ming tombs. Thus, it was obediently arranged for him to be personally accompanied by the viceroy. Riding high on horseback, they trotted along, occasionally taking photographs.

I have seen a number of historical tourist photographs of the eastern outskirts of Nanjing, and what is interesting is that they are very different from those taken by the official on horseback. The people in the photographs are instead riding donkeys. There are both Chinese and foreigners in these photographs, wearing a traditional Chinese skullcap. Of course, there are many more foreigners, because at the time, foreigners were initially the only ones who owned cameras. Some of the foreigners are too tall, presenting an amusing sight as they ride upon their donkeys. Most of the Chinese in the photographs are tour guides, but sometimes one catches sight of a donkey's master standing casually to the side, caught in the shot by accident. How long these donkeyback excursions went on for is hard to say. In any case, they were still ongoing in the 1930s, and were mentioned in essays by Zhang Hengshui.

Discussing travel and culture in the same breath is a recent phenomenon. In the past, people did not speak thus. If they wanted to enjoy themselves, they did so in an idle and carefree manner. This is unlike nowadays, where it has become unspeakably vulgar to do something so simple as putting on the clothing of a different culture. Peasants at the time were fairly simple folk. They would raise a few donkeys while waiting idly for tourists to come along, at which point they would be satisfied to squeeze a few coins out of them. Now, one must invest highly and work to the utmost in order to redouble one's investment. Earning money was one thing, but most worrying was the prospect of destroying a perfectly good scenic area in search of profit. There are countless examples of this which I shall not speak here.

The Nanjingers of *The Scholars* would often head into the southern outskirts of the city in search of leisure. The reason is simple: although the novel was written in the Qing dynasty, it was a reflection on the Ming. Due to the presence of the tomb of Emperor Taizu of Ming, the eastern outskirts were off-limits. Anyone who blindly wandered in would be beheaded, and the common people did not want to go asking for trouble. After the fall of the Ming, the Qing dynasty had a very ambiguous approach to the Ming tombs. From historical photographs, we can see that the eastern outskirts of Nanjing were already in heavy decline by the end of the Qing dynasty. People of high status would generally not bother visiting the Ming tombs for fear of being taken to court, accused of harboring sympathies for the previous dynasty and stripped of their official positions. Only those of lofty ideals, such as Gu Yanwu, would visit the tombs in order to indicate their displeasure with the Qing. When Sun Yat-sen was elected provisional president, he ceremoniously made his way to the Ming tombs in order to offer sacrifice.

When Lu Xun was studying in Nanjing, he liked to ride horses in the ruins of the former Ming imperial palace. At the time, he was an angry young youth and would not have wanted to go on donkeyback excursions. The Manchu soldiers stationed there at the time would not have looked kindly upon the students, and would not only scold them, but also throw stones. It is said that Lu Xun had no fear at all and brazenly mocked the Manchu soldiers, even trying to challenge them in horsemanship. Lu Xun's earliest place of study was the

Jiangnan Naval Academy. The most talented graduates would likely have gone on to be naval officers. Additionally, the outskirts of Nanjing at the time were not located just outside of the city gates. Nanjing was too large of a city, and outside its residential areas were countless lands devoted to agriculture and wasteland. The Ming palace, located near Zhongshanmen, would have been completely overgrown.

Hexi, 25 August 2000

The Streets that Lu Xun Walked

Zhang Pinzhen once said that he wanted to write an essay on the streets that Lu Xun would have walked in his days as a student in Nanjing. This probably would be quite an interesting essay, and I hope that he will write it soon for the benefit of readers. Obviously, it would not be easy to verify which streets Lu Xun walked. From existing writing, we can see that neither the city nor his studies at a new-style college had much of an impression on Lu Xun. However, one cannot believe everything one reads. The resentment that Lu Xun showed was resentment toward his contemporary society. His brother Zhou Zuoren followed in his footsteps, also coming to Naning to study. From this development, we can see that, at the very least, he considered it an opportunity for advancement.

It is from Zhou Zuoren's writing that we can gather numerous records of the city at the time. In 1901, the first step on a journey from Zhejiang to Nanjing would have been going to Shanghai and then taking a boat upstream on the Yangtze. Starting from the Wusong docks in Shanghai, it would be a bumpy, day-and-a-half ride to the Xiaguan docks in Nanjing. The Shanghai-Nanjing Railway was only completed in 1908, and so the brothers would have had no choice but to take the slow boat ride to Nanjing. At the time, however, it would have been the quickest option because such a journey was taken on a large imported steamship.

Lu Xun spent four years in Nanjing, and Zhou Zuoren five. Both brothers spent the formative years of their youth in the city. After graduating in Nanjing, they both received top marks and went abroad to study. By coincidence, Ba Jin also went to middle school in Nanjing. Lu Xun did not spend much time at the Jiangnan Naval Academy, though. Placed in the engineering class, he spent all of his time deep within the boats themselves, never getting the chance to get on deck, and so he changed schools, going to the Mining and Railway College.

Zhou Zuoren, more well-behaved than his brother, spent five years in engineering at the Jiangnan Naval Academy, only changing course once he arrived in Japan. The Zhou brothers did not make direct use of their studies, however. Normally, considering that the state had invested so much in their development, with free education in China as well as abroad, it would be only right that they pay back the Qing government in kind. Yet, this did not prove to be the case.

Most of the new colleges initially built in Nanjing were in the north of the city because it was more desolate at the time. Nowadays, the Drum Tower is considered the heart of the city, but in the early twentieth century, it was in the less populated northern outskirts. In Zhou Zuoren's writings, he often speaks of how they would go into the city for leisure while engaging in their studies. Because the school was in what is now the Yijiangmen district, the students had to walk to the Drum Tower, then take rickshaws to the Confucius Temple, where they would drink tea and eat snacks while listening to music. Having whiled away most of the day, they would then make their way back, stopping at Beimen Bridge to buy some chicken or perhaps salted duck before taking a rickshaw back to the school. At the time, the drivers did not care that the north of the city was desolate and lacked any return passengers; they were simply happy to get the work.

The route that Zhou Zuoren took was the same one that Lu Xun took. At the time, new students would have worn a rather ostentatious uniform. The old students were just the opposite, wearing long Chinese gowns, and because the school uniform showed their status, there would have been all kinds of inconveniences—particularly in the teeming pleasure dome of the Confucius Temple. Students represent the future, and the young signify hope. If you presume that the youth are full of high aims, however, you are gravely mistaken. Students with truly high prospects are usually in the minority. The Zhou brothers would go on to future success, which had much to do with their hatred of things as they existed at the time. They were angry young men who refused to go along with the crowd.

Hexi, 27 August 2000

Zhu Xie

In the summer of 1932, after Zhu Ziqing had spent a year studying abroad in England, he boarded a ship home. It was a long journey, but he was able to find ways to alleviate the boredom. For example, the boat stopped off in both France and Germany, as well as Venice, Egypt, Mumbai, and Singapore. At the time, it was fashionable to travel by steamship, passing through various places of interest; as long as a place was worth a look, it would be added to the itinerary. It was during this trip home that Zhu Ziqing made the acquaintance of Zhu Xie, who had recently achieved his doctorate. The two men both enjoyed classical poetry, and thus they set to composing poems on the subject of the beauty of Venice. Zhu Xie was only 25, but his skill in composing classical-style verse was exceptional. He was a red-blooded youth, and Zhu Ziqing said of their collaboration: "Zhu was more agile in coming up with phrases than myself, and in composing poetry, we were evenly matched."

After Zhu Xie returned to China, he immediately became a professor in the economics department at National Central University. His generous salary made him an object of envy. With his high income, his days were carefree. It is not difficult to imagine the scene at the time; the young and promising foreign-educated professor in a highly popular economics department would have been quite imposing, indeed.

The period before the outbreak of war with Japan was a golden age for construction in Nanjing. The whole city was one giant construction site, with bulldozers toppling buildings left and right, and large-scale construction going on all over the city. With the rapid progress of the new Nanjing, the destruction of sites of historical interest got worse and worse under the banner of building the "new capital". Many people did not bother to take such damage seriously—after all, without destruction, there can be no construction, and if the old doesn't go, the new will not come.

Although Zhu Xie was a foreign-taught modernizer with a background in economics, he was concerned with preserving the old. Along with a love for composing classical poetry, he mourned the barbarous destruction of Nanjing's historical sites. There are some things that cannot be prevented. Considering how future generations would no longer lay eyes upon such sites, Zhu Xie took up his German camera and rushed about the city, observing and photographing one building after another. In a three-year period, he took over 2,000 photos. Many of the photos of old Nanjing that we see today have been chosen from his collection.

There are very few people who know of Zhu Xie nowadays. Following the popularization of classical photography, some people may find themselves sighing in wonder at these images, but few wonders exactly who took them and how. Usually, this is a specialty of foreigners. It seems that they are the only ones who like to stick their noses in other people's business, and who understand the significance behind preserving historical sites and relics. Of those conservative-minded Chinese who consciously took photographs of cities, in my opinion, Zhu comes out on the top. There are few documents that provide records of him. From what I can tell, Zhu remained a professor in Nanjing, becoming the chairman of the department and never applying his studies outside of academia. Because of the war against Japan, there was no scope for his abilities over the long period of economic construction.

Zhu Xie was from Haiyan in Zhejiang. The photographs he took of Nanjing were once compiled into publications, of which the most famous is *Jinling Guji Mingsheng Yingji* (Collected Photographs of Historic Nanjing), which was published in 1935, a year before the outbreak of war. It consists of 317 photographs paired with descriptions in Chinese and English. The composition of these photographs is quite good. There is a classically artistic flavor to them, and they are as good as those which any professional photographer could take.

Hexi, 18 December 2000

Remembering Tiger Bridge Prison

Everyone should strive to educate themselves, and if one gets the opportunity to look around a prison, it's not a bad idea. I remember touring a space in St. Petersburg, in which stood a prison cell that Maxim Gorky once passed through. It had a very high profile and tourists filed past, wishing to cast a reverent glance as they went on their pilgrimage.

I could not help but recall Nanjing's Tiger Bridge Prison. Some years ago, a newspaper noted that Tiger Bridge Prison had been demolished. By the time everyone found out about this decision, it was already rubble. You might feel it a shame, but there are many other shameful things nowadays. Thousand-year-old tombs are excavated or demolished; at not yet ninety years old, Tiger Bridge Prison stood no chance. To the decision-makers' credit, this was a place that held criminals—one cannot simply hang the banner of "historical significance" on whatever building one pleases.

Tiger Bridge Prison held a number of criminals, worthy of historical note. In that sense, it would be no bad thing to have left it behind for the education of future generations. My daughter's university had a field trip on which they engaged in a visit to a new-style prison. On their return, the students were deeply moved. Nowadays, students are still children. They were interviewing a bureau-level party cadre who was serving a prison sentence. His crime was only corruption, but his tone of voice as he spoke still made it sound like he was making a speech. Because of this, I was even more convinced that I should visit a prison. Prisons can not only reform criminals, but they can change us, too.

Tiger Bridge Prison was a product of the late Qing and was once considered a model prison of the *jiangnan* region. There are some essays that say that it was the earliest prison of China's modern era, built by the Qing government with the use of concepts of western judicial theory to gradually reform the prison system. Later on, it became the "capital prison" governed directly by the Ministry of Justice of the Republic of China. Nanjing is utterly swimming in history and culture. Wherever you look, you will find both. A number of famous people passed through Tiger Bridge Prison, including countless revolutionaries and members of the Communist Party. These included Chen Duxiu, the first general secretary of the Communist Party. In our middle school politics lessons during the Cultural Revolution, there was not a single student who did not know of Chen Duxiu. But there was confusion as to his significance—not only among students, but even among the teachers. When the Japanese bombed Nanjing in 1937, Tiger Bridge Prison was one of their targets. Chen Duxiu found himself buried beneath the rubble, and almost lost his life.

Zhou Zuoren found himself imprisoned there for treason. He was initially sentenced to 14 years in prison, which he felt was far too long. This sentence was later reduced to ten years. By the time his sentence had come to an end, his body had nearly wasted away. After the Communists took Nanjing, acting president Li Zongren issued him a pardon. Zhou Zuoren's works are beloved by many, but he was not a man of particularly good moral character. He was without doubt a collaborator with the Japanese, and yet he detested his imprisonment by the Nationalist government, calling Chiang Kai-shek a "bald idiot". Reading such words, I couldn't help but laugh. When we were young, we watched a film in which Chiang Kai-shek was only called "Baldy Chiang"; looking back on it now, Zhou's description seems much more vivid.

I am not in favor of the demolition of Tiger Bridge Prison. The footprints of history are all over Nanjing, and they are erased with each building that is torn down. If it still existed, then my daughter's university could have held a visit there instead. It could have been the site of their efforts to recover the old and support the new, to fight corruption and advocate for public decency. Some say that prisons are unsuitable for a city center, but in the middle of Hong Kong's most bustling district, there stands a large graveyard. Do not forget that graveyards are also a part of history.

Hexi, 1 September 2005

The Ballad of Nanjing

When I was young, I saw a film in which Chiang Kai-shek was portrayed not as a ferocious warrior, but as a disgraceful villain. As a ferocious warrior, he would curse like a sailor, but as a disgraceful villain, he was the subject of tricks played by his old adversary, the Communist Party. Later, during my studies, I discovered something more of a comic element in him—such as his frequent announcements of his resignation.

A few days after Nanjing became the capital of the Republic, its residents could see first-hand the farce of the Guomindang's key figures leaving their positions. If we say that the Guomindang at the time still retained some level of democracy, having its major figures leave office practically every other day can be considered part of that. At the time, newspapers across the nation were abuzz with fervent speeches sent via impassioned telegram. Such speeches were usually quite elegant and erudite, with telegrams being sent upon someone taking office and then again once they left. The best way of retreating while appearing to move forward was to overtly announce one's illness. "Comrade Zhan Tang has high blood pressure." "Wang Jingwei has diabetes." These were all pretexts and excuses, and each message became a superb subject of gossip for the common people.

Chiang Kai-shek's resignation was the most dramatic of all as a result of his stature and authority. Every move he made was an earthquake, astonishing all levels of society. In 1927, Nanjing was declared the capital, and before he could even sit down, Chiang had to regrettably renounce his resignation. Luckily, this resignation had a happy conclusion: he married the beautiful and talented Soong Mei-ling. He never stayed out of office for long, however. There was a common saying in descriptive writing of the past: xing san shen bu san ("disordered in form but not in spirit"). Chiang's resignation was essentially this: though he had resigned in appearance, he was not really considered to have done so, and not long after, he would return as if it had all been some kind of a joke. This back-and-forth showed that the contradictions of the past had not been resolved. Not only that, but in some cases, the chaos made them worse.

The Mukden Incident of 1931 was the biggest problem that the Nanjing government had yet faced. The Republic had only just begun to come into its own when the drums of war began to beat. Chiang could neither advance nor retreat, and he could only look on helplessly as the three provinces of northeast China were lost. Zhang Xueliang has passed away, and in his declassified autobiography, he said that there was no secret order designed to prevent resistance to this. But the central government, with Chiang as its head, had lost territory in a humiliating situation, and it was impossible for them to avoid public criticism from all sides. The Mukden Incident caused heavy and serious argument among the civil and military officials. Things were already chaotic enough as they stood, and so the First Plenum of the Fourth National Congress of the Guomindang descended into quarrels—with its usually-refined meetings turned into a place of insults and threats. "The officials laugh, doubting Yue Fei, while the military men call Qin Hui a traitor" (Lu Xun, Song of the Good Sort). Chiang had always considered himself to be like Yue Fei, the patriotic Song dynasty general, but others did not see him that way. If he could not be Yue Fei, however, he could still brand Wang Jingwei as a traitor. Wang's image as a Japanese collaborator is widely known, and Chiang was in no way wrong to liken him to Qin Hui, the general who had betrayed Yue Fei.

Left badly bruised by the criticism he received, Chiang resigned his post, offering his apology to the nation. His resignation was, of course, false—just more of the same. The army and government were still under his control, and not long after this, he once again took office. The common people of Nanjing have always enjoyed a good spectacle, and this was quite the eye-opening one. Looking upon this farce, Lu Xun wrote The Ballad of Nanjing, a poem satirizing the affair:

They all pay homage at the tomb,
where robbers dress like honest men.
They stand ten minutes in silence,
each man wanting to fight the other.

Hexi, 14 September 2005

Remembering the Dead

Since time immemorial, Nanjing has seen countless disasters and massacres. The massacre in December of 1937 shocked the world. Now, on December 13th every year, the city sounds its alarms to commemorate the victims.

The common people could never even have dreamed that 1937 would become an annus horribilis for the government of the Republic. That year had been the 10-year anniversary of the proclamation claiming Nanjing as the capital of the Republic. Chinese people are fond of round numbers, and the city celebrated it with great fanfare, holding all kinds of exhibitions. On April 29th, the Office of Population Statistics announced that the population of the capital was 945,544 people. In order to obtain this figure, the relevant personnel had worked for three months and five days straight, and a month beforehand, a survey of the rickshaw industry in the capital had shown that there were over 2,000 rickshaw businesses in the city, with 12,000 rickshaw drivers.

For a city to have a population of nearly a million in the 1930s was quite spectacular. For the nation, disaster was imminent, but Nanjing was in the midst of a golden age. Spring came, and the Municipal Bureau of Health advised residents of an outbreak of meningitis, recommending immediate vaccination. Chiang Kai-shek was willing to set aside his arrogance, and he "personally ordered Mayor Ma [Chaojun]" to "keep the appearance of the capital city in order." Thus, "The Bureau of Works drew up a detailed plan and conscientiously put it into action." Investigation teams immediately hit the streets, "forbidding the dumping of refuse into ponds."

On July 7th of 1937, the Marco Polo Bridge Incident occurred. The people of Nanjing did not see it as being any more severe than previous incidents. After the Mukden Incident, China had seen the Shanghai Incident of 1932, the Defense of the Great Wall in 1933, and the signing of the He-Umuzu Agreement in 1935. As citizens of the capital city, Nanjingers had marched and protested accordingly before finally becoming used to this state of affairs, or perhaps numbed by it. Even if Japanese planes had dropped bombs on top of them, the Nankinese wouldn't have considered it much of a big deal. On September 29th, the Xinmin News posted an announcement titled *A Reflection by Wang Xianglan, Wife of Liu Xiangzhi*:

Liu Xiangzhi was injured when 15 enemy planes struck on the 25th. He is currently in Central Hospital. His injuries are light, and visitors are welcome.

This surprising announcement's calm and serene tone is typical of the attitude of true Nanjingers. The people of Nanjing did not know the true catastrophe that was soon to befall them. Even if they had known, however, they would have had nowhere to hide. The common people have always been as they are. I have no way of saying for certain how many people perished in December of that year; the figures are up for debate, which is best left to the experts. There is one point that cannot be doubted: many lives were cruelly taken, and the Japanese invaders must bear the responsibility for this.

I cannot accept any criticism of the lack of resistance shown by the dead toward their killers. This would be to speak in defense of murderers, and to show disrespect toward the murdered. Their white bones piled up in mountains: what was the people's crime? We are lucky to live in the modern day, but our good fortune should not allow us to forget the past.

Nanjing is currently in the midst of building a subway system, and the city government has come to a decision: if, during the excavation process, remnants of the Nanjing Massacre are found—for example, mass graves—the course of the metro is to be changed. This is clearly a wise decision, because only with respect to the dead can we reflect upon our past, and upon the significance of life.

Hexi, 27 September 2005

Old Buildings Lost

There is a clear difference between the four-sided siheyuan courtyard houses of the north and the old buildings of the *jiangnan* region. The siheyuan better embody ancient Chinese culture while the old houses of the well-off people of *jiangnan* are of a somewhat more modern flavor. I once visited Mao Dun's hometown, and I also visited the old residences of Xu Zhimo and Yu Dafu. Mao Dun's residence was a typical southern merchant's house, with a reception area and a storeroom. At the same time, it had an air of culture, and it felt like a place of both business and literature. Xu Zhimo's house later became the location of a county bank. Seeing its opulence, one can immediately tell that his family was more well-off than that of Mao Dun. Yu Dafu had two residences. The first is in Fuyang, and is not particularly large, having the air of a small scholar's house. The other is in Hangzhou and is the famous "Cottage of Wind and Rain"; it has long been the site of the local police station.

When it comes to the former residences of writers, we can glean some knowledge from the writings of those writers or of others even if we have not personally laid eyes upon them. The more famous a writer is, the more likely their former residence will be made into some kind of cultural artifact. A generation of literary luminaries were born in these houses, and their reputations have spurred the preservation of these buildings. Literary figures born at the end of the nineteenth century were, for the most part, from more comfortable economic backgrounds. Although they were not all necessarily rich, there were very few who came from genuine poverty. Writers are fond of bewailing their poverty, and they like to speak sorrowfully of revolution. If we had the opportunity to see their former residences, however, we would understand that, sometimes, these words were sometimes not entirely true. For example, Yu Dafu's "Cottage of Wind and Rain" cannot be understood from its name alone. It is a thoroughly beautiful house with something of a Japanese style to it, and in no way inferior to the modern-day governor's house.

Following changes in the old urban districts, old houses are quickly becoming history. With the fading away of these buildings, old stories become more and more confusing. Save for those old buildings preserved as cultural artifacts, many old city districts have been razed to the ground—with one new-build, matchbox-like house after another springing up in their place. The few remaining great old houses have become living fossils, historical records of the distant past. If you wish to know someone's history, or to look back on previous eras, the opportunity to explore old houses grants us the ability to walk directly into the past and back again. Unfortunately, the majority of old houses have not been preserved, and there is no need for them to be. After all, we live in the real world. We cannot be without history, but if we would place realism and history upon the same set of scales, then realism will naturally come out on top. We recall such old buildings fondly, but we still long to live in modern houses.

Due to their special geographical location, the old houses of Nanjing are neither completely northern nor completely southern. Although they are located in *jiangnan*, on the border of Jiangsu and Zhejiang, they are also something entirely different. The old houses of Nanjing do not have their own set style. Many people with money and fame have settled here. Historically, the famous people of Nanjing have not included many of those born and bred in the city.

For a long time, Nanjing has suffered invasion and destruction. Various foreign cultures have easily put down roots in the city's earth. A friend of mine is of Hui nationality. Some centuries ago, his ancestors settled in Nanjing in what we now know as the residential areas in the south of the city. Of all the friends I know, there are perhaps none who have the claim to be an old Nanjinger quite like he does.

In past centuries, Nanjing has gone through quite a number of disasters. First, the Taiping armies came, and then Zeng Guofan invaded. He is considered a leading light of imperial China, and yet he was known as "Shaved-Head Zeng" at the time. During the Second Revolution, Zhang Xun was driven out of Nanjing. He came back even stronger, and the city saw three days of fighting. And then there were the shocking events of the Nanjing Massacre committed by the Japanese. The old Nanjingers are no strangers to the tragedy of slaughter. For Nanjing's old houses to have survived through such disaster is no mean feat. The seat of Hong Xiuquan's Heavenly Kingdom was destroyed in a sea of fire, in fact. Fire has likewise claimed the Confucius Temple on more than one occasion. The once flourishing Taiping Road was also destroyed by the Japanese, and it took decades for it to reclaim its former glory.

One man called Donkey Jiang was said to be in charge of raising donkeys especially for the Heavenly Kingdom. After the Taiping Kingdom fell, Donkey Jiang was unsure what to do. He had made a little bit of money that had allowed him to not only hide from the slaughter, but also to get him one rather nice house. The size of this house is enough to make one gasp nowadays. Compared to the bureaucrats, Donkey Jiang was nothing, but some years ago, his old house had become the residence of a regional theatre troupe—with over a hundred people and their families all living under one roof.

My earliest memory was made in this very house. I have never understood why, many years ago, Donkey Jiang built such a large house, which is so large that one could practically call it a manor. There is no real way for us to calculate the sizes and quantity of these old houses. I only spent a short time in Donkey Jiang's old house, but when my memories became clearer, my family moved to a small foreign-style house nearby. It was there that I started elementary school, experienced the turbulence of the Cultural Revolution, and started middle school, but Donkey Jiang's house was always where I went to play. Almost all of my childhood friends lived there, and it was there that we would play soldiers, tell stories, and do all of the things that kids are fond of doing.

In this house, when it was over a century old, there were at least ten children of my age alone, including myself. There were dozens of children of all ages. During my school years, because studying had never been very important, having so many kids to play with together in that old house was quite a wonderful thing. With so many kids there, trouble broke out on a regular basis, as we pointedly ignored each other, then made up, and then fought again, making an awful racket the whole time. Someone's younger brother would get beaten up, so we would return home for back-up, asking our older brothers to come back with us. From what I remember, the adults rarely bothered to get involved in children's affairs—probably because they were all at the same work unit and knew each other, so it wasn't worth losing face for something your kid did.

There was no toilet in the house. Each family had a chamber pot, and in the middle of the day, chamber pots both new and old would be left in the doorway. I remember letting off firecrackers for the New Year, and one mischievous child broke up his string of firecrackers, lit them, threw each one inside a drying chamber pot, and then put the lids on top. This game started off with laughter but ended up with a severe scolding. Also, as a result of the lack of toilets, as the kids played, they would pee wherever they liked. So, every corner in the old house stank of urine.

There was a large courtyard in the house, and that was where the stage stood, along with a decent-sized patch of grass that the children would often roll in. After the Sino-Soviet border conflict broke out, building an air shelter became a top priority. The grass patch became a rudimentary shelter. This shelter became quite the plaything for the children, however, who tried to sneak inside any way they could. That was until the tunnel was eventually filled with the egg-smell of condoms, after which no one dared venture inside again.

There weren't too many secrets inside the old house. Neighbors' spats and couples' squabbles were almost always out in the open. It was a single-story house with low windows and thin walls. Almost everything could be heard from outside. One time, the police came to arrest someone and, as they made their way in, everyone rushed out to watch them take an old woman away, saying she was a counterrevolutionary.

It was also a terrifying event when someone died in the house. The sound of wailing could be heard from far away, and the children could not bear to see such scenes. Even if it didn't affect them at the time, the scene would enter their nightmares later that night.

Among the kids who grew up in the house, there weren't any stories of romance. In my childhood and adolescence, there was a sense of hostility between boys and girls. In school, the boys and girls wouldn't talk to each other, and inside the house, it was as if they didn't even know each other. Unknowingly, we grew up with the girls developing first and starting to understand how to dress well. The boys would hide away somewhere together to swap vulgarities, talking about whose breasts were biggest.

Eventually, one boy let his side of the gender divide down, causing a scandal when, seemingly possessed, he held a neighbor girl close in the public kitchen and pecked her on the cheek. The girl was older than the boy, and she wasn't much to look at, either. Such a thing was really not allowed. At the time, there was no television, and kissing was truly a scandal. The girl was stunned, as if she had been electrocuted, and she immediately began to cry like she had been recently orphaned. In the end, that boy got a sound beating from his parents. The incident became huge news throughout the house. The boys all thought it was rather funny, while also understanding how shameful it was. The girls, meanwhile, thought it all terribly wrong—such loutish behavior!

The Season for Love Songs

I was once discussing the music of Hong Kong and Taiwan with an author from Taiwan. He said that the content of their lyrics rarely strayed from "I love you; I love you deep down to my bones," and so on. He didn't mean it in a derogatory sense; he just seemed not to care for such ridiculous language. Old-fashioned love songs would just address their subjects with the familiar terms a mei and a ge ("sister" and "brother"), unlike nowadays, where everything is all about ardent passion, loving someone to death, and smothering them with your love.

I have an innate enmity toward karaoke, and particularly dislike those who would sing at the dinner table—whether they are a singer employed especially by the restaurant, or those who would make noise regardless of their talent or of the effect they have on others, picking up a microphone and belting out songs. This sort of thing is enough to drive one to distraction. Mealtimes should be reserved for eating, not for indulging in something so gaudy. I remember that, once, while eating dinner on Hainan Island, people would toss coins to some crooner, an effeminate-looking fellow who stroked his hair and sang coquettishly, stopping only to say something into the microphone and then carrying on. People were reaching the end of their patience, and Wang Zengqi, who was there at the time, said something rather interesting. He wondered if he could pay the singer not to sing.

Really, even if he had been singing well, he shouldn't have done it while we were eating. There are some people who find it pleasurable, it's true—a kind of norm, in that it makes one feel as if one is in the proximity of the wealthy.

Nowadays, there's not a single song that's not about love. Pleasant songs about oaths of eternal love are out of step with the times, though, and thus have changed: now it seems that it's entirely about flirting. There are some very pretty girls who will stand and sing in restaurants, probably for a little bit of money. These days, people have no choice but to do almost anything for money, but I can never stop myself from feeling a sense of distress. People usually mind their own business when they eat. Because they've spent their own money, they can completely ignore these singing girls—or perhaps stare at them lecherously, ostentatiously demanding any song they please, confidently and impulsively offering them flowers. I often wonder what these girls' parents must think. These girls are grown, so nobody can interfere with their choices. I think their parents must feel an unspeakable sorrow. If you enter a loud textile factory, you will catch sight of those female workers who are almost swallowed up by the noise. If you see the young women who stand on the streets selling vegetables on a winter's day, with their bare hands and frozen looks, perhaps you might think that singing in a fancy restaurant for money might be a good choice.

The inundation of love songs has made us all rather numb to them. Such baseless, boring entertainment adds to the dullness of city life. The sound of the balladeer's voice never stops, with the singer and her audience both utterly indifferent to love itself. Love is an easy word to say; it is unconcealed and does not require extravagance. No one need pay a price for it. It seems to always be close at hand. But when we truly reach out, we discover that true love does not exist at an honest price. Love becomes a game, frivolous, a plaything... the opposite of love itself. I gamble my youth on tomorrow; you exchange the truth for this life. These are pretty words, and nowadays they seem as empty as the political slogans of the Cultural Revolution.

In the past, all love songs were described as mimizhiyin—decadent or obscene music. The dictionary describes the phrase mimi as "decadent, lascivious, vulgar delights". The stories of 20 years ago, for today's youth, are like a total fantasy. When I was in middle school, love songs were called huangge ("pornographic songs"). The youth of the time were not only unable to hum love songs, but even the older generation who could sing them kept them unsung out of fear. To sing love songs was to sing pornography, to be a criminal. This kind of extremely simple reasoning made everyone feel that love itself was a crime. My contemporaries all grew up in the same atmosphere of sexual repression. Many of us first understood sex by sneakily reading Feng Deying's novel *Bitter Herbs* and its descriptions of the rape of Chinese women by Japanese soldiers. As we grew older, our male classmates would swap vulgarities that only bad students would dare speak out loud.

I remember that, at that time, the only foreign movies we had access to were the Soviet-made films *Lenin in October* and *Lenin in 1918*, and a few Romanian movies. There was one Romanian children's film called Michael the Brave, which included a scene with a group of children swimming in a lake. There was a young girl wearing only a bra and panties; this brief scene had quite an effect on us. In the dark, we couldn't see who was shouting, and thus there was a constant chatter. *Lenin in 1918* featured a section from Swan Lake. There were a few people who bought tickets to see it multiple times, and once the half-hour Swan Lake section had finished, they would immediately walk out, making no attempt to hide their exit. After the Cultural Revolution, singing pornographic songs had already become a specialty of the more mischievous children. These so-called pornographic songs were a few of the love songs from the 1950s, such as the famous "Moscow Nights".

In the year I graduated high school, we were sent down to the countryside to work. Almost all of the boys were humming the tune under their breath. We had a classmate who could play the harmonica, and when the teacher wasn't about, he would play it over and over again. I hear that puppy love is widespread among the middle-schoolers of today, but when I was in middle school, boys and girls looked upon each other as foes—to the point that they barely spoke. If anyone accidentally brought up a girl's name, he would immediately be shunned by the other boys. There was no shame in casting an occasional glance at the girls, but boys mostly used their attitude of contempt to show their interest in the opposite sex. At the time when I was working in the countryside, and perhaps just as I was about to graduate, two very good-looking female classmates walked past us. One rather brazen classmate of ours with a bad reputation pointed at one of them and couldn't stop himself from blurting out: "I'd die for her!"

This was the first time we'd ever heard someone express fondness for girls so openly, and we were so shocked that none of us could even speak. Everyone was used to expressing their enmity toward girls. We gave them nicknames and spread all kinds of false rumors about them. We called well-dressed girls "immoral", and paired them up with boys in our imaginations. To consider boys and girls equal, at the time, was a thing of extraordinary shame. So, to have someone so nakedly express their love stunned us all into silence right then and there. Perhaps all of the boys were secretly in love with the same girl; perhaps this one girl reminded us of other girls. Whether or not middle-schoolers should be in love is a different topic of discussion, but one cannot deny that all boys have one girl or another on their minds. Everyone has a love song in their heart that they would dearly love to sing, but no one ever dares to do so.

Two months later, we were about to graduate, and it seemed as if everyone suddenly grew up. Many people went into town and bought the cheapest cigarettes they could find, and they would smoke them while looking at the sky and pondering their worries. One boy indifferently sang "Moscow Nights" in front of a female teacher.

> My beloved, sitting by my side,
> You look quietly at me, saying not a word.
> I want to say something to him, but I dare not.

The teacher heard this and became angry. "What song is that you're singing?" she asked.

"It's a revolutionary song," he replied.

"That's no revolutionary song", she said. "That's pornography."

The boy disagreed, saying that it wasn't pornographic at all. The teacher would not accept his denial, and the boy became anxious.

"How do you know it's a pornographic song?" he quibbled. "That is, unless you know it, too."

"You're the one singing it," said the teacher. "I've never sung it before."

Of course, the teacher knew this song. She'd been a university student before the Cultural Revolution, skilled in both sport and singing, and with a temperament as vivacious as any boy. But time, place, and status had all changed for her, and she could only issue her student such a stern rebuke.

Of our classmates, there were many who studied for ten years together, but none of them became husband and wife. After graduating high school, even though we lived in the same city, we became like strangers passing each other on the street. Nowadays, one hears these mournful love songs all over the place, but for those of our generation, the season for love songs has long passed. Those years of romance passed as if they were nothing, and thinking back on them, one cannot help but feel somewhat pained. A year ago, we all met up for a low-key elementary school reunion party. Men and women sat together and began talking of the past and the present. The traces of our childhood remained on our faces. We were young no longer, and thinking back on that time where we'd refused to even speak to each other, we all found it secretly amusing.

A year ago, at the Shennongjia Writing Competition, one of Chi Li's enthusiastic readers sighed: "Oh, you've changed—you weren't like this ten years ago!" Chi Li found herself unsure whether to laugh or cry, completely lost for words. This impassioned sigh also caused Fan Xiaoqing, another female writer at the same conference, to sigh and ask how a woman is supposed to withstand the passing of a decade. For a stone, a decade will see no change at all. For metal, one might see a slight layer of rust. But for people—and women, in particular— it is quite a harrowing thought. Going back to our elementary school reunion… the time that had passed was not 10 years, but 20. Those delicate young girls had become women, and though there was a beauty in their maturity, no one can resist the passing of the years.

We say that beautiful women cannot withstand the passing of time, but in truth, it is just as hard for average-looking women to escape misfortune. The girls, whom those boys once yearned after, belong to the distant past. The season for love songs is long gone, never to return.

Remembering the Willow

In the place where I live now, it is quite difficult to catch sight of a willow tree. In the public square nearby, among the granite and the lawns, they removed a mid-sized willow. Every time I see it swaying in the wind, I feel a sort of familiarity that I have not felt in a long while. The spring wind blows through the tree's myriad branches, bright as gold and soft as silk. It is a pity the poor thing looks so lonely, so out of step with its surroundings. At the very least, it isn't quite conventional enough, because the willow is more suited to being placed by the waterside.

Historically, Nanjing has been the home of many willow trees. Even in my youth, I remember willows being everywhere, like a scene from Tang and Song poetry. Most ruthless are the willows of Taicheng. No matter what changes occurred in this city, no matter what hardships it underwent, the willows remained. Alongside the Qinhuai River, there are all sorts of pools and stretches of empty wilderness where the weeping willows droop. Willows are a natural representation of great change. In all the bleakness after the chaos of war, the one thing that can inadvertently grow to be full of vitality once more is the desolate willow. Willows have witnessed all of the joys and sorrows of humanity; they are the best witnesses to history. I feel that the willow's nature represents the traditions of this city. Although it has been through much hardship, it continues to survive.

One friend of mine, a painter, once used the word gudian ("classical") to describe the willow. He compared its posture to the plane tree, pointing out the contrary directions in which their branches grew; one drooped downward, and the other stuck upward. A century ago, one would not have seen any of the plane trees that are so prevalent in Nanjing today. The plane trees that we see nowadays, in fact, came from France, the saplings having been purchased for a huge sum taken from the French Concession of Shanghai during the construction of the Sun Yat-sen Mausoleum in the late 1920s. The plane trees changed the atmosphere of Nanjing. In the midst of the pathos of tradition, they added Republican splendor. In the ancient city, these trees with their upward-pointing branches caused a sudden and fundamental change. Nowadays, the plane trees are more representative of this city than the willows.

In a city, green is extremely important. It is not necessarily a bad thing for trees to be diversified by species from abroad. From the perspective of the city residents who benefit from the change, it was clearly a good move to exchange the willows for plane trees. Beneath the scorching sun, cyclists can seek shade beneath them, cooling off from the heat. In any case, I still look back on the willows with utter fondness. They not only remind me of my childhood but put me in mind of the history that I never lived through. Nowadays, grass lawns are quite popular in this city, and compared to the willows and the plane trees, their green grass is richer. Whether or not this is a good thing is hard to say. They feel too decorative, and we are not allowed to get close to them. Often, we can only use them as background for photographs, and someone must always be there to stand guard, to pull up the weeds, and to water them. Perhaps there are many of us who do not cherish such labor, but lawns are somewhat a case of style over substance.

Willows are an important element of the work of Feng Zikai, though. Without willows, perhaps we would not have his works. As I recall, his residence was named "Small Willow House". Willows are not unique to Nanjing, or to the *jiangnan* region. They will tenaciously survive in any place that has humidity. Among the traditional trees of China, the most common are the willow, the pine, the cypress, and bamboo, as well as peach and plum trees. In Liu Yuxi's *The Willow Branch*, there is a line: "In the city, the peach and plum disappear in an instant; only the willow trees remain forever." The red of the peach, the white of the plum, and all the abundance of spring can disappear with the wind. Great flowers bloom but rarely, but the willow tree is even more worthy of contemplation.

Hexi, 15 August 2000

Seeing the Willow Through the Mists

Eighty years ago, when the Republican government designated Nanjing as its capital, the Yangtze was still under the control of the Beiyang Army. No one imagined that the revolutionary situation would develop so quickly. There was no need for a protracted war. Historically, the southerners had never been a match for the northerners, but the Northern Expedition crossed the Yangtze with irrefutable force, and within a year of the fighting's start, the fractured nation was united once more.

The newly inaugurated Nanjing government set to work, spiritedly building their new capital. They invited luminaries from both home and abroad, and a year later, they came out with The Capital Plan. There was a fundamental train of thought that ran through the plan: accepting Western methods of city planning on the macro level while employing traditional Chinese style on the micro level. Since it was only a "plan", however, it was hard to avoid it being bogged down in idle theorizing, and the years during which they could work flat-out to achieve it were few. Not long after the plan was created, there came the Mukden Incident, and then the Shanghai Incident, and as war with Japan inched ever closer, the building plan found itself bound hand and foot. After that came eight years of war, this to be followed by the Chinese Civil War. For the ambitious city planners, there just wasn't enough time to do a lot of things.

But even so, the results were astounding. The Capital Plan brought an abundance of capital to Nanjing, and some years later, when tourists would come to Nanjing, they would be startled by its rapid progress. Alongside the vast improvement represented by the official residences of the Republican era, almost everyone speaks in praise of the greening of the city, and of its wide avenues lined with towering plane trees. These plane trees were the best product of the Republican era, completely overturning its ancient historical image.

Historically, Nanjing has been filled with willow trees, as the Tang poem says: "Most ruthless are the willows of Taicheng, which as before envelop the ten-mile dike like fog." In the ending of Peach Blossom Fan, there is a mournful line: "In that place where no man lives but many willows stand." Willows seem to be both ruthless and full of feeling, and they are most appropriate to representing grief. In appearance, the plane trees rise upward, stretched out like a halo, high-spirited and imposingly official. The willow droops downward, subdued—revealing a history of great changes.

Nanjing is not only suited to plane trees; it is even more suited to the willow. The proverb *shui xing yang hua* ("as mutable as water, as dainty as the willow") is used to describe a fickle woman. One only needs a little bit of water for life to sprout forth. "The lush willows are shrouded in mist, stirring gently in the wind, the countless branches sweeping away the setting sun." A few days ago, I accompanied an out-of-towner friend on a visit to the Stone City Park. We passed the willows on the outer banks of the Qinhuai River, and on a number of occasions, my visiting friend was quite moved, saying that he had not realized there were so many beautiful willows alongside the city's plane trees. He did not know that the willows had been abundant since antiquity, nor that these ones had been newly planted, nor that these new willows were old dreams from before the 1980s.

The pre-80s Capital Plan had a section specifically devoted to the governance of the Qinhuai River. The specific program laid out was that, besides the current Confucius Temple area, the city would continue to retain the original style of the waterfront. Other houses had to be moved far away from the course of the river, where city developers would then plant willows along the embankment, building a wide road to keep the waterfront and the buildings effectively separated. If things had gone according to plan, the plane trees that line the roadsides of the modern-day city would not stand alone; all of the inner Qinhuai River, including its tributaries, would be turned into a boundless strip of green thanks to the willows planted along the riverside.

Unfortunately, this plan could only be carried out along the outer Qinhuai, and not until after the 1980s.

12 April 2007

The 480 Temples of the Southern Dynasties

For the common people, China's ancient temples have long been a topic of discussion. In some of the more lewd stories, innocent monks and nuns have become the main characters. When people are alive and go out to enjoy nature, temples are an important scenic spot; when they die, monks are asked to perform the necessary rites. Nowadays, when we speak of Western civilization, we mean Europe and America. However, in China's history of cultural exchange, the first ray of sunlight that pierced China from the West was that of the large-scale arrival of Buddhism. Its influence is wide-ranging and deep, and in no way inferior to the influence of Europe and America.

When I was young, I often heard adults talk about monasteries and nunneries. When I grew older, I understood a little bit more, but I couldn't understand why Jiming Temple was made up only of nuns, whereas the Confucius Temple had neither monks nor nuns. Then the Cultural Revolution came. A temple on Changjiang Road had its possessions confiscated and put on display. Many small children came, running all over the place and then coming home covered in sweat. I never personally saw the monks being dragged out and paraded through the streets; I only ever saw pictures of the scene. In the early 80s, a classmate and I cycled to Doushuai Temple in Jiangpu, staying there overnight and chatting with the monks. I asked how they'd fared through the Cultural Revolution, and one old monk very calmly said that, at the time, they weren't allowed to practice Buddhism and could only work in a factory, silently thinking of the Buddha. I remember that the amiable-faced monk consistantly tried to convince me to follow the path of Buddhism; he felt I had the seed of some intelligence in me, and that I could accomplish much if I committed myself to Buddhism. I think he encouraged everyone he met to do so, because if I truly had had some sort of particular intelligence, I would have had the sudden realization that staying there might mean I would never leave.

The figure of 480 temples being built during the Southern Dynasties period is, of course, only an approximation. I am not a Buddhist, but like many other ordinary people, I like to go to temples to join in the scene, burn some incense, and bow reverently. Perhaps it is because I like that look of serenity upon the faces of the monks and nuns, or because my real life is far too chaotic, but every time I set foot inside a monastery, I get the sudden feeling that I am in some way vulgar or unworthy.

There are many temples in Nanjing, and I don't know which ones are most worth visiting. Friends who come from out of town go to the Sun Yat-sen Mausoleum, Xuanwu Lake, and the Confucius Temple, and then, seemingly having exhausted Nanjing, they lazily ask me where else might be worth going. I tell them to consider visiting Yangshan Quarry, the Two Mausolea of the Southern Tang, Niushoushan, and the Tomb of Zheng He, which are all worth a visit. Other than those, if you've got time, there are a number of temples you can visit, such as the Jiming Temple and the Xixia Temple, but these are very well-known already, and if you don't go then it's no great matter. There are also a number of small temples that nobody knows about which you might end up enjoying.

One such example is Doushuai Temple in Jiangpu, where there is an old and definitely eminent monk. A number of very famous temples have invited him to take up a position as head monk there, and he has politely refused them all because, being tourist attractions, none of them are quiet enough for him. There is also Longquan Temple on the southern outskirts of the city, which few people will have heard of. It is actually not far from the Gate of China and can be reached by bicycle. Longquan Temple was first built in the Tang dynasty and is surrounded by mountains on three sides. There is a spring at the summit that flows constantly, forming a pool just in front of the monastery. If you want to look upon this beauty, your only option for entrance is a small, minor road. Perhaps it is due to this small, twisting path that people have rarely visited the temple for many a year. The Guomindang elder Zou Lu once resided there, and you can still see the inscription he left behind. There are a number of scenic spots on the southern outskirts that can be easily overlooked. For the modern generation, if you can't get a plane or a train there, then it is too far and must be considered tourism.

Hexi, 25 August 2000

Autumn Cool and Summer Heat

Nanjing's summers are formidable, especially in my memories. Nowadays, every house has air conditioning, and our memories of the intense heat have already become fuzzy. True heat is no longer anything to fear; all you need to do is turn on the AC. What are hard to bear are those days where it's not quite too hot, where you could get by without turning on the AC, but then when you get in bed, you suddenly find that there's not even the slightest breeze to be found. Thus, husbands and wives will have a difference of opinion: one will say it's hot, the other will say it's fine, and after a brief misunderstanding, they will begin to bicker.

I had a classmate from the north who said he absolutely despised Nanjing's summers. Back in the day, as he was studying and the summer holidays approached, he would roll up his woven mat every evening and roam across campus to find somewhere cool to sleep. The heat can make people lose all of their senses. There were so many mosquitoes on campus, but my classmate was so stubborn that he preferred to be bitten to death by mosquitoes rather than be stifled by the intense heat. When I think about it, this was probably a symptom of heatstroke. The first chapter Jin Shengtan's On Happiness says this about the difficulties of bearing such heat:

"In summer, the seventh month, the summer sun sits in the sky, and there is neither wind nor cloud. The front and rear courtyards are as hot as a furnace, and even the birds do not dare to fly. Sweat covers the body, crisscrossing in streams. When food is placed before me, I cannot eat it. I call for my mat, wishing to sleep, but the floor is moist as ointment. Houseflies land upon my neck and my nose, and I cannot shoo them away. There is none who can tolerate such a situation. Suddenly the sky darkens, and the carriage axels are slick with timely rain, with its sound like thousands of coins dropping, falling from the eves like a waterfall. The sweat on my body temporarily dissipates, the ground is dry as if it had been swept, the houseflies have disappeared, and my appetite returns: ah, is this not happiness?"

This is quite a wonderful passage: not only does it speak of the heat, but also the delight felt when it dissipates. Only when one has borne such sweltering heat can one appreciate the cool autumn weather. It is like looking back on a dark past from a happy present. Without bitterness, one cannot enjoy sweetness. Twenty years ago, for ordinary city residents, there weren't even any electric fans to speak of, let alone air conditioning. In the mid-80s, the most overbearing advertisements on television were for "Great Wall Electric Fans" and "Camel Electric Fans". To turn one of those on before you slept in the evening was once an unimaginable pleasure. As evening comes to Nanjing, the air pressure lowers, and it becomes even sultrier. As night falls, the air seems to congeal. I remember how people could once be found cooling off in the shade until the dead of night. Kids didn't fear the heat; they fell asleep in a daze. The next day, they woke up and heard people saying, "Oh, last night, it was so hot that I couldn't sleep."

Nowadays, a phrase like that sounds strange to the ears of the younger generation. But without the ritual of cooling off, the way that many imperceptible little lessons are learned has changed. Much of the knowledge that our generation acquired, from major principles to sexual knowledge, was learnt while we were cooling off in the shade. In the past, there was no television. After we had eaten and taken a shower, talking rubbish was typically the only thing left to do. Whether one had the gift of the gab or sat silently listening to others, that was enough for one to happily while the evening away. It is by no means unbearable to look back on those olden days of Nanjing summers, where we would listen to people chat, lying back and looking at the stars. That beautiful past will never return, and it remains only in the memories of a generation.

Not long ago, I was on the phone to one of my classmates, who had just returned to the north. He was recalling his memories of the

Nanjing heat, but he was nowhere near as angry about it as he had been back then. There has been a sudden change in this world: the north has also become a furnace. In the past, Beijingers would never sleep on straw mats, or use electric fans or air conditioning, but in the past few years, it has all been turned upside down. "Damn," grumbled my classmate, "Beijing's even hotter than Nanjing." He spoke calmly of the difficulties of living in Nanjing when we'd been classmates, but at the same time, he sounded like someone who was pleased with himself, sounding just like an old soldier who had survived the Long March. Back then, he would complain frequently about Nanjing. Nowadays, Beijing is the target of his complaints.

Hexi, 26 August 2000

Cycling in Nanjing

When I was young, there weren't many people who cycled in Nanjing. In the past, cycling was considered a kind of skill—something that not everybody could do. For example, my father rode a bike before I was born, but it wasn't until I was 19 years old that I actually saw him ride a bike in the street. That was when we went to Xiaolingwei to see a performance by a cutting-edge theater troupe. Nanjingers all remember the steep slope there: cycling up it wasn't easy and going down was even harder. At that point, my father was already 60 years old, and everyone was rather worried for him. He said it was nothing to worry about; once you've learnt how to ride a bike, you never forget it.

In the past, there weren't many bikes on the streets. One major reason for that was that they weren't something which could be bought by just anybody, and even if you had the money, you still needed a coupon for one. Nowadays, youngsters don't know what it was like to have money but no coupons. Middle-schoolers can own fancy new bikes. The phrase "kingdom of bicycles" appears on the pages of newspapers with a tone of pride. Foreigners also praise cycling as a form of exercise and as a way to protect the environment. Perhaps I'm approaching it with the wrong attitude, but for some reason, when I see bicycles flooding the streets, I feel a sense of dismay. I can't stop myself from wondering… if someone who hasn't ridden a bike in over a decade takes to the street, they might find themselves in an accident at the first intersection they pass through. If you don't believe me, get one of those old bureaucrats who drive to work to cycle alongside the rest of the commuters at rush hour. There's no way he'd get home without a scratch.

I don't think there's any need to feel proud of our kingdom of bicycles. We are always unclear on the boundaries between self-assurance and pride. Physical exercise and environmental protection are only single aspects of the subject, a last resort. Statistics show that one American consumes as much energy as two Europeans, 40 Indians, or over 400 Zimbabweans. In China, most people don't cycle because they want to exercise or protect the environment. All the commuters care about is the most effective use of their time. If you can still consider cycling to be a pleasure after being stuck behind countless red lights and scorched by the blazing sun thanks to the cutting down of trees along the boulevards, all while inhaling the exhaust fumes of the cars ahead of you even on a day when the pollution index has reached new limits, then you must be some kind of saint.

Putting people first and making it easier to go outside is the issue that any city must consider first and foremost. Pride and self-assurance are of no use. When a city develops rapidly, the way in which one travels to work becomes much more important and much more difficult. Too many bicycles, excessively long routes, and filthy air: under these circumstances, riding a bike is clearly not the best way to get to work. After all, commuters are not the same as day-trippers. My daughter cycles for half an hour every day. Whenever she passes over a bridge, it is clear that its design makes it a real struggle for cyclists like her to surmount it. There's nothing wonderful about this struggle. People persist in cycling because taking a car would be even less convenient.

Hexi, 31 December 2000

A Gathering at Anleyuan

In the winter of 1937, Nanjing was under heavy fire as the Japanese armies encircled the city. One young officer, who had just graduated from the Whampoa Military Academy, had ordered the artillery to successfully shoot down an enemy plane, and he was happily heading to headquarters to receive a commendation. At that moment, headquarters took stock of the larger situation and issued the order to retreat from the siege.

Over eight years of war against Japan, young officers were hardened by battle, and they rose through the works to the rank of general on the basis of their outstanding service. After reading this hero's memoirs, I always wanted to write a biographical novel about him. Any life as glorious as his was worthy of such effort. The heroes of the War of Resistance have long since become grey-haired old men. The years passed, and now the son of one of these old men, long past the age at which his father performed such feats of bravery, is the manager of Anleyuan Restaurant in Nanjing. Just as impressive as his father, this descendent of a war veteran has his father's natural stubbornness. He speaks to me in a voice that suggests some kind of challenge. "You've gotten to know a lot of people these days. At the moment, of all the Hui restaurants in Nanjing, mine is the best. Do you believe it? If you don't, then get a few experts to come and try our food."

Of course, I wasn't convinced—every restaurateur believes his own establishment to be the best. There are so many Hui restaurants in Nanjing, how could he say for sure that his was the best? When it comes to eating, I am a layman; inevitably, I pretend to understand things I don't. Thus, I invited a number of Nanjing's finest gourmands for a gathering at Anleyuan. When people are boastful, there's no harm in frightening them to teach them a lesson.

Of the younger generation, when it comes to gourmet culture, Nanjing writer Huang Tienan is an undeniable expert. His work,

King of the Kitchen—serialized in the Yangtse Evening Post—garnered high praise from readers; alongside this accomplishment, he has the formidable title of Secretary-General of the China Cuisine Association. I told the manager of Anleyuan that, of all of us gathered there that day, apart from myself, Huang Tienan was the least knowledgeable about food. The manager was somewhat stunned, and with a nervous laugh, he said, "Very well, it's a rare opportunity to receive advice."

Li Bai wrote this of Caishiji in Anhui Province: "We came here only to drink wine; sir, let us not recite poetry here." It's not that I wished to scare him wantonly. There will always be someone out there more talented than yourself, and the day had allowed me to convene some of Nanjing's finest. Among such culinary experts, someone like me can only sit in silence. Even Huang Tienan didn't dare be presumptuous, and he was so modest that he seemed to have changed into a different person entirely, sitting in silent respect of his elders. In attendance was Wu Botao, a professor in his 80s. Wu was born to an upper-class family, and when it came to food, he was even more knowledgeable than the gourmand of Lu Wenfu's novel *Gourmet*. There was also Hou Minggao, a member of the Chinese People's Political Consultative Conference. His work *On Delicacies* is soon to be published, and part of his illustrious career has included choosing the menus for dinner parties held by Chiang Kai-shek and Soong Mei-ling. There was also the famous painter Ma De, and the writers Zhang Pinzhen and Gao Xiaosheng, both of whom have written essays on the topic and remain as knowledgeable and eloquent as they have ever been in their long careers. Getting guidance from such a crew of experts is no mean feat.

Zhang Pinzhen reminded me that, since we were appraising this cuisine, the quantities should not be too large. Sure enough, the dishes were small, dainty, and exquisite, like the lamb skewers roasted on toothpicks or the Jinling duck neck, which was bundled into a kind of sausage made from duck neck-skin, and then stuffed with shrimp and pine nuts. Only those who have eaten it can know how wonderful it tastes. This was an Anleyuan innovation, and for the expert gluttons present, it was a top-quality dish. The best-looking dish was the feicui yazhang ("jadeite duck feet"), with the boneless snow-white claws placed atop a dish of green vegetables. The most unusual dish was the stir-fried fish with banana, which was tender and smooth. Eating it, you wouldn't believe that you'd just consumed either banana or fish. Each wonderful dish placed before us was like an assault by an enemy on the battlefield. I was left dumbstruck; all of the dishes were amazing. Then came the stir-fried duck, which was clearly nothing out of the ordinary. But just as I had put it in my mouth, and was about to say as much, Wu smacked his lips and made the final decision, saying that this was clearly an authentic and skillfully made Hui dish. I blushed, took up my chopsticks alongside everyone else, and reached for more. Finally, there came some steamed dumplings made with mandarin fish as the skin. I was stunned, but I heard Hou fussily say that "If the skin were thinner, it would be better."

After we had finished eating, the red-faced manager came up to us and asked our opinion.

"Wonderful, truly wonderful," said the old fellows.

"There's not many restaurants about nowadays that are as authentic as yours," said someone else with a smile.

The manager was deeply moved; the experts had met another expert, and it was like running into an old friend in a foreign land. Everyone was thoroughly content. Talking loudly the whole way, he showed the gentlemen to the door. As the Chinese saying goes, food is the god of the people. Eating together, we can gain much more knowledge and experience. In life, one may die well or live wretchedly. There are heroes both among the living and the dead. Some accomplishments are easy, and some are much more difficult. Eating is not something that can be done by just anyone.

Nanjing in Culture

Nanjing leaves a strong impression on people. Many people are convinced of this before they even set foot here. For example, according to Shi Zhecun's research, the Tang dynasty poet Shi Yuxi did not come here as a traveler, but it is not right to say that he had no right to speak of it as a result. For this great poet, even though this ancient capital of the Six Dynasties existed only on paper for him, he was so jealous of the verse written about Jinling by others that he just had to write five poems about it himself, all in one go. Of these, there are two seven-character verses which have become a trademark of the city, beloved by calligraphers and painters both famous and nameless, and hung upon the walls of every hotel and restaurant in the city to be admired by visitors. "The mountains surround the ancient capital, and the waves beat against its lonely walls" speaks of the city's stone walls. "Once sparrows nested before the hall of Wang and Xie, now the common people fly in" is a contrast and a lament for the present and the past.

In the poetry of the Tang and Song era, Nanjing is filled with culture. There was an air of melancholy to this culture, as well as an element of finding one's own entertainment. Men of culture rarely enjoy success, and having failed, they could use Nanjing's long history as an excuse to drink and complain, looking upon the past and comparing it to the present. "The wind blows through the willow catkins, and the women of Wu exhort their patrons to drink." Li Bai came, free and at ease, and drank heartily, one cup after another, before he happily wrote these verses, looking over the sons of Jinling who had come to send him off. "My lord, ask this of the waters running east: will they last longer than our thoughts of parting?" There is no way to compare these two things—thoughts of parting are formless, and the running waters have form. Literature and poetry are the act of comparing the impossible.

The floating clouds cover the sun, and the capital is hard to see. Because Nanjing is so rich in history, it is easy for those researching it to find themselves lost in it. When cultured outsiders come to Nanjing, they rely on what they know of the poetry of the Tang and the Song dynasties, and they ask after the Taicheng spoken of in "the most ruthless are the willows of Taicheng," or the island of white herons of "the water split in two by an island of white herons." These place names are shown on tourist maps, but if you truly believe in them, you will only be deceived.

Also from the Tang dynasty is Du Mu's "the singing women do not know the sorrow of defeat, and across the river they still sing Flowers of the Jade Tree Hall," which vividly connects Nanjing to national disgrace. The city is famous as the birthplace of last emperors. The great Sun Quan may have been a hero, but his descendants wished to shackle themselves to the rolling waters of the Yangtze. Following on this personage, Chen Houzhu and Li Houzhu were even worse, with each much more interested in women than in heroism. They were all hopeless emperors; the city never stood a chance and neither did the nation. Chen Yinke carried out an analysis of the poetry of Du Mu and came to a categorical conclusion. He believed that the singing women (shangnü—an archaic term, with shang meaning "trade or commerce" and nü meaning "women") who did not know the sorrow of defeat were actually the "singing women of Yangzhou and the boat merchants of the Qinhuai." He felt that our understanding of the line was "vague and derivative, and to proclaim it the peak of poetic perfection was quite laughable."

I am a Nanjinger, born and bred, and I have always had the utmost respect for Mr. Chen, so I can only kindly accept this unique opinion. I appreciate the good intentions of those who wish to free Nanjing from the shame of national defeat, but I fear that the majority of readers and people of culture will not let it go so easily. On one hand, Nanjing is bathed completely in the light of culture; on the other, it is bound by its chains. History and culture cannot arise without good cause. If we take the verse of old as the criterion for judgment, then no matter whether it's by quantity or quality, Nanjing ranks among the best. From this understanding, to conclude that Nanjing is the most historical and most cultured city would also not be far from the mark. And this so-called history and culture cannot be separated from the city's wretchedness.

Nanjing's cultural halo is embodied not only in the poetry of the Tang and the Song, but also in everyday contemporary life. Tolstoy said that every happy family is alike, while each unhappy family is unhappy in its own way. In order to stress the awareness of tragedy, he looked upon happiness as being simple. In fact, there are many different kinds of happiness.

There is no harm in making a cultural observation of happiness. Nanjingers have always had a sophisticated ability to feel happiness. Those who have read *The Scholars* will recall those scholars who, having drunk their fill, sat in a scenic spot ruminating on the present and on the past. They caught sight of two fellows hauling dung buckets who were then resting in the shade. One clapped the other on the shoulder and said:

"Brother, we've sold our wares for the day. Let us go to Yongning Temple and drink tea there, then we shall return to Yuhuatai and watch the sunset."

These words left the drunken scholars dumbfounded, only able to say that even the lowliest of manual workers in the city had the vapor of the Six Dynasties. Vapor and smoke are similar things, but poetically, smoke represents vulgarity while vapor represents elegance. Likewise, yanzhi and jinfen ("rouge" and "gold powder") have roughly the same connotations, but to speak of liu chao jinfen ("the gold powder of the Six Dynasties") is to speak of an entirely different grandeur. Nanjingers are used to finding happiness in the small things while not caring too much about the big things. Different places have a different index for happiness. Beijingers base happiness on whether they have an official position; Shanghainese on whether they are making money. Nanjingers are not really suited for either pursuit and so they do not care much for either.

When friends of mine speak of those who have climbed the ranks and made money, there is no envy in their eyes, but instead schadenfreude. The saying in these parts is that only diaoren ("damned wretches") have become officials or gotten rich. As well as apathy, there is also a sense of disdain. A favorite saying of Nanjingers has always been duo da de shi ("is it a big deal?"). In a Nanjing accent, this is said in a descending tone of voice, full of indifference and completely unconcerned. Not using measures of success or failure to decide who is a hero is a major strong point for the city. Here, you don't need to worry that you have no future. Getting along fine or not so fine is all the same. When Nanjingers summon up their ambition, they suddenly realize that they have suffered a long time in silence, and they vow to leave town. In the 80s, it was fashionable to move to Shenzhen, which seemed like a city full of opportunity. Now things have changed, and the destination is Shanghai, where the streets are apparently paved with gold.

Nanjing once wanted to build an international metropolis. At the end of the 1920s, such construction was the watchword; by the 1990s, it had returned once more. Though it might have excited its advocates, no one else really cared. Anybody can talk big, but nobody needs take such talk seriously. Happiness has never depended on the size of a city or how tall its buildings are, nor its income or how many bureaucrats it has, nor the square footage of its buildings. That doesn't mean these things are meaningless, but it's not right to rely on them entirely, either.

Happiness requires a little culture from time to time. In other words, people have to feed themselves spiritually, too. Nanjing has never been short on culture, but to simply have culture is not enough; one must enjoy it, too. I am not saying that other places do not know how to appreciate such things. I am simply saying that true Nanjingers seem to know how to appreciate them a little better.

Hexi, 1 February 2007

Nanjing's Character and its Authors

How can one become an author? What kind of city is most conducive to the birth of writers? These questions have been debated for a long time. Every answer has its own merit, and we can discuss these things for our own amusement, but when it comes to actually arriving at the truth, nobody is quite sure, and nobody really understands the issue. I have always held Shen Congwen's words in high regard. He thought there was nothing dangerous about being a writer: as long as there was nothing wrong with you mentally, and you could put effort into writing, then the more you wrote, the better your writing would get, and thus you would naturally become a writer. There is nothing strange about writing better with the more one writes, but to get worse the more one writes is rather strange.

Nowadays, one often hears that certain places are most conducive to producing writers: in Jiangsu, Nanjing is given as an example. This is an interesting viewpoint. As the saying goes, three men may make a tiger, and falsities can come to be considered truth. One may see countless newspaper reports about the thriving literary community of Nanjing. The authors of this city seem to be touted as an outstanding local specialty; such a label arouses the interest of young editors, who will frequently rush to Nanjing to gather up manuscripts. The importance of public opinion should not be overlooked, after all. In the Ming and Qing dynasties, Suning and Hejian in Hebei Province specialized in producing palace eunuchs. Their task was to serve only one man. Not far from Nanjing, the city of Yangzhou specialized in producing what were termed shouma ("skinny horses")—poor young girls who were trained in the arts of singing, dancing, music, and calligraphy, then sold off as concubines or to drinking establishments. Their task was to serve many men. Nowadays, thanks to countless portrayals in film and TV, readers are familiar with how eunuchs were bought and sold, but they are less familiar with shouma. To put it bluntly, shouma were mistresses, trained especially to become such.

It is obviously rather lacking in sincerity to discuss writers in the same breath as eunuchs and shouma. Speaking loftily, one may call writers engineers of the soul. But facts are facts. Facts will inevitably cause dispute, and facts cannot be suppressed. Whether for better or worse, the fact that Nanjing has produced quite a number of authors is irrefutable. There are many Nankinese authors throughout history; in our modern age, this phenomenon seems only more obvious. In the literary scene of modern China, there are many authors from Jiangsu, and of those who have made it, most of them are from Nanjing. Many university students give up on the greater opportunities offered by Beijing or Shanghai after they graduate, and they choose instead to stay in Nanjing, hoping to become writers.

Previously, my view was that the thriving literature scene of Nanjing was a result of the fact that the city is slightly behind everywhere else. Though Nanjingers might talk themselves up, feeling that the city in which they live is some international metropolis—in that it has a population of millions and a large number of skyscrapers—it cannot compare to the larger cities of Beijing and Shanghai. It ranks well among the other provincial capitals, but to tell the truth, Nanjing has always been a village among cities. To say that Nanjingers are rustic folk, and perhaps a little behind, wouldn't be entirely wrong. When you compare Nanjing to the overbearingly advanced cities of Beijing and Shanghai, though, falling behind might have its own benefits. For example, in Beijing, you can't help but think about your own position on the bureaucratic ladder, and how, living in the shadow of the empire, the lure of the bureaucracy is strongest. In Shanghai, you can't help but think about how much money you have. It is China's biggest financial city, and those who can rampage along the Bund are undoubtedly millionaires.

It's better in Nanjing. Perhaps you want to be a bureaucrat or a rich man, but here, there are fewer opportunities and less pressure by comparison. Nobody cares if you've made it into the bureaucracy; nobody cares if you've made your fortune. I feel that Nanjingers aren't cut out for the world of bureaucracy or of business, and so many feel they have no other choice but to write. Thinking about it now, this is still somewhat boastful, taking it for granted and guessing at the causes according to the results. When one is speaking, it is hard to avoid generalizations, to deludedly focus on one small part of something as an attempt to see the whole picture. It seems that reasoning like this should be thought through carefully, as it might not entirely make sense. Anywhere you go, you will find places that are a little behind, with people who make for neither bureaucrats nor businessmen. Wherever you go, the common people and the poor will make up the majority. So then, why have other places not become hives of literature as Nanjing has?

Among the armies of writers in Nanjing, there are not many authentic Nankinese. From this, we may reach two conclusions. The first: Since being a writer has little to do with one's native place, the view of Nanjing as the birthplace of authors collapses. There is no such thing as a free lunch; the notion that the soil of Nanjing is somehow superior for raising writers is a bubble to be popped. The second conclusion: so many people have become writers in Nanjing after all, like everyone active in the lively literary circle of today. They are the core of Nanjing's writers, and their numbers and their achievements far surpass those of indigenous Nankinese writers.

In either case, both conclusions have merit, and neither is that outlandish. As an old saying goes, the tangerines of the south may become bitter oranges when transplanted to the north. Regardless, you still need a tangerine tree in the first place. Clearly, the great number of Nankinese writers has come about as a result of everyone's efforts. And as Shen Congwen said, the more one writes, the better a writer one will become. Write more, and then even more still. Everyone knows that, in the history of Chinese literature, Tang poetry is greatest. Why? Because so many people were poets back then. With so many poets, the standard is bound to rise. Take Shakespeare's plays, for example. Nowadays, we consider them to be stellar works. Researchers tell us how he could reach such a high artistic standard:

in Shakespeare's time, there were a great number of brilliant dramatists about, and a great number of brilliant theater audiences. Shakespeare's birth was by no means an isolated event.

The character of a city may not necessarily have a definite relation to its writers. Following the development of society, differences between cities have become less and less pronounced. We always like to imagine and presume a number of elements that are extremely conducive to producing writers—emphasizing, for example, the character of Nanjing, its literary abundance, and its long and sad history. All of these extrinsic factors can have an active effect on the work and thought of writers. The character of a city can be an interesting topic of debate. It has given us a great many fine excuses; at the same time, it can lead to substantial errors in judgment. Is the city of Nanjing truly as cultured as we presume it to be? The answer is, clearly, that it is not: in a time where culture is commonly lacking, any such self-belief can be proven to be utterly laughable.

Nanjing is a very tolerant city—one that has never been xenophobic. Not only is it not xenophobic, but it is more than willing to hand over the reins of authority to outsiders. As Wang Jun's ships leave the State of Yi, Jinling's royal splendor is suddenly lost. It seems that the atmosphere of this city is quickly taken over by others. Nanjingers do not really care if they are being led. When they show up in front of the TV camera lens, officials of all ranks will often have a strong out-of-town accent. In Nanjing, it's not only easy to be a writer, but it's easy to do almost anything. Nanjingers don't care if others behave atrociously in their city. They even feel a sense of admiration for outsiders. Take food and drink as an example. For many years, Nanjingers have been extremely excited about the opportunity to taste the cuisines of other places. Nanjingers will heartily devour all sorts of different foods.

The benefits of such tolerance are easy to see when it comes to creative work. Tolerance is of the greatest assistance to the literary world, and it is at the root of all literature. The tree of literature sometimes does not care too much about what nutrients are offered to its growth. It does not care for pay, or rank, and sometimes, all it needs to grow heartily is free, fresh air, sunlight, and rain. Literary creation has always been thoroughly individualized. It has always needed unique things; it is individualist and not collectivist. It can appear quite laughable to hope that everyone will flock around you, and that your vast fame and power will move the masses; as a result, you will be attempting the impossible. To commit misdeeds in order to provide for good literature can turn out to be doing the wrong thing for the right reasons; spoiling things through excessive enthusiasm will often lead to the opposite result to what one intended.

Tolerance means giving creators enough free space, not interfering with their work, not coddling them, and allowing them to emerge or perish on their own. For a number of years, the biggest torment that literature has suffered is that of excessive interference. Whether it comes from outside or from within the author's own heart, it can be fatal. Literary creation doesn't need many additional conditions. Many people who are preparing to write will often fall into a vicious circle, thinking "If I do such-and-such, then I will become a brilliant writer." "If you give me time, if you let me write, if you guarantee that I will be published, if policies permit me, if leaders care about me, if I have a beautiful woman by my side, if the media is promoting me, if I do this, if I have that, then I will become a great writer, and then I shall write the next Dream of the Red Chamber." Literature and art have never believed much in "ifs". If someone wishes to become a writer, a tolerant city like Nanjing wouldn't be a bad choice. However, if you choose this city, then that choice is, at most, only your first step. If you truly believe that coming to Nanjing and sleeping in the cradle of literature will bring you fame and fortune, then you are sorely mistaken.

The question is a very simple one. The experience of those who came before us has proven that there are no "ifs" when it comes to becoming a writer. if the writers of Nanjing had not worked so hard, sitting down to write each day, then all this talk of "Nanjing producing writers so easily" would be absolute bunk.. Literature is the easiest way to fool people. Many writers appear in Nanjing's past and in its present, but that does not mean that they will continue to do so in the future. It is merely coincidence; there is nothing certain about it. In truth, whether it is the splendor of the past or the prosperity of the present, there is still something gravely lacking. There are still doubts to be raised. Literature is currently in a slump. Although that does not mean it has deteriorated, anyone can see that it is not as prosperous as it once was. On the national stage, perhaps this is because literature is no longer thriving quite so much, or because authors are no longer paid so much attention as they were given before, and people are no longer striving to outdo one another in this field. In Nanjing, a few still persevere. This has led to a few achievements, but to be honest, these small achievements are not enough to proclaim that literature thrives once more.

Nanshan, 18 June 2007

Drinking Tea at the Vanguard Bookstore

When Qian Xiaohua was studying at Nanjing University, he was a frequent guest at my house. We were schoolmates in a sense; he was young and polite, and I was senior and less so. When things happened, he liked to discuss them, saying he was seeking my guidance—when, in fact, he had already made his plans. For example, he said he wanted to set up a bookstore, and asked me all sorts of questions. I couldn't offer him any ideas, but I didn't want to temper his enthusiasm. There were already plenty of bookstores on the street, and experience would suggest that managing a bookstore was not the path to riches. Luckily, he was still young and capable of anything, able to take a knock and keep going. He was a man of culture, and if he was going to dip a toe into the muddy waters of business, what else could he do but open a bookstore?

The result went beyond expectations. It started off as just a small shopfront in the south of the city, having little in the way of influence. But then it got busier and moved to a spot by the gates of Nanjing University. The shopfront was still small, but its unassuming entrance led to a sumptuous hall.

When it comes to elegance, variety, and tasteful decor, of all of Nanjing's bookshops, the Vanguard Bookstore would probably come out on top. Though I'm ignorant and inexperienced in such things, I've seen quite a number of out-of-town bookstores; few could reach such a level as this.

Drinking tea at the Vanguard Bookstore means tasting the pioneering work of Qian Xiaohua. He grew up at the foot of Mount Mao in Jiangsu Province and has a passion for the art of tea. Using his own tastes as a guide, he guesses what others might like. Choosing a book at a bookstore can be quite a romantic process. There's something sentimental about poring over books with a good cup of tea. I remember when he started the bookstore, Qian Xiaohua once very proudly said that he knew more about books than other people. He knew what kind of books cultured people liked because he was a thoroughly cultured man himself. Only a bookworm could say such a thing... and it turned out to be quite right, too.

The bookstore is a gathering place for literati, and historically, there is a reason for this. In the 1920s and 1930s, Japanese national Kanzō Uchiyama opened a bookstore in Shanghai. Anyone who was anyone in the literati was practically obliged to stop by. The Vanguard Bookstore has had quite far-reaching influence on Nanjing's literary scene. Among its patrons, most are university students, who need only walk a few paces from the gates of the university. Booklovers who cannot find the objects of their desires elsewhere also like to try their luck at the Vanguard, often returning home after a pleasant surprise. It is quite normal for old friends to bump into each other and for classmates to spend a good while there in conversation. Sampling tea and discussing literature can often feel like the preserve of the stuffy literati, but since there is money everywhere, there's nothing wrong with letting the penniless scholars do it, too.

Drinking tea at the Vanguard Bookstore doesn't cost money, and it's a place for bookworms like Qian Xiaohua. It's not right to open a bookstore without expecting to turn a profit, and it's also unsustainable. Qian Xiaohua has his ways. Since he doesn't mind if you go to the store, drink tea, look through a few books, and leave without buying anything, the most important thing is whether you can live with yourself for doing so.

Hexi, 15 October 1999

Repairing the City Walls

The city in which I live is home to the world's longest city wall. This is quite a unique scenic spot. As I recall, the Ming city wall is badly damaged, covered in weeds, and surrounded by tall trees. I have climbed the wall with friends on a number of occasions, exploring in all directions. The Nanjing city wall is not only damaged, but actually has gaps in places. Taking the risk to try to climb over these gaps is quite a fun game. When I was young, I never understood why they needed to build only parts of a wall. We were often warned that we could fall and break a leg, or even die. The reason behind the gaps was to stop us from playing on top of the wall, but for children, the places you want to play in most are the ones you're not allowed to go.

For historical reasons, the Nanjing city wall had long been split up into partitions. In the mid-1950s, Zhu Xie rushed about everywhere trying to fight against attempts to tear apart the wall. As a result, he was branded a rightist. Zhu Xie was the son of Zhu Xizu, who was a follower of Zhang Taiyan, who was himself a schoolmate of Lu Xun. Zhu Xizu was the first dean of the Chinese department of Peking University, as well as of its history department. Following in his father's footsteps, Zhu Xie was a professor at Nanjing University, and dean of the economics department. After the communist revolution, he served as the deputy chief of the provincial Ministry of Culture. Many of the photos of old Nanjing we see today were taken by him. In the early 1930s, the Guomindang designated Nanjing as their capital, carrying out large-scale construction. Bulldozers filled the streets, and former famous scenic spots were torn down one by one. Zhu Xie arrived back after having received a doctorate from abroad; he knew the importance of preserving history. He could not stop the bulldozers, however. He could only take photographs all over the city, leaving behind these precious scenes for future generations.

One single scholar could not save Nanjing's city wall. In the face of power, there was nothing he could do but voice his objections. Nanjing is a historically famous city. One thing in its history which one may ruminate on is the fact that it is constantly being destroyed. "Most ruthless are the willows of Taicheng"—the helpless scholars, pushovers that they were, could only complain about the willows.

Six hundred years ago, Zhu Yuanzhang, the first emperor of the Ming dynasty, built the walls of Nanjing. He thought he was building a country that would last forever; he didn't expect that, under his son, the wall would become an object of ridicule. To be blunt, no matter how big the city wall was, it has no significance outside of the history books. Opposing the destruction of the wall was, in essence, opposing the destruction of history. History is a mirror, and with this mirror we may look at the past and also imagine the future. Tearing down the wall is, in itself, part of history. There is no need to cover it up; it should be faced head-on. The experience of history is worth noting. This was Chairman Mao's guidance, which everyone once pored over as if they were monks reading sacred scripture. Looking at Nanjing's current circumstances, we see that reconstructing the city wall would bring about destruction far worse than tearing it down. Although they tore quite a few holes in a perfectly good city wall back then, a complete revamp now would be a barbarous trampling of history, almost completely destroying the sense of great historical change that the wall represents.

Why are we always unable to change the shortcomings that brought about history? Six hundred years ago, it was built at great cost, then torn down, and then rebuilt. We are tired of such turbulence, and so is the ancient city herself.

Hexi, 30 November 2003

Inscriptions on the Bricks of the City Wall

People often become inured to the things they see around them every day. For example, the common people of Nanjing rarely pay any attention to the city wall that can be seen throughout the city. It was there when we were born—growing weeds and shrubs, dilapidated but not entirely broken. One part would be collapsed. Another part would have a huge gap in the middle. When I was young, we would climb up the wall to play, standing on top and looking out as far as the eye could see. We could see the whole city... the violet air of Purple Mountain, the meandering Qinhuai River, and the distant Yangtze. The white walls with black roof tiles, mixed in with a few Republic-era, foreign-style buildings. This was a few decades ago.

I rarely thought about how the wall was made of bricks, each one bearing an inscription. Many years ago, a friend of mine who was researching the wall brought up the subject of these inscriptions with me. I was confused. To prove it, he clasped a hand to his chest and said that he would take rubbings and present them to me as a gift. I was moved. Later on, I saw a thick volume entitled *The Inscriptions of the Nanjing City Wall*. When I flipped through its images, I was moved even more. I am not well-versed in calligraphy. I simply took it for granted that hanging such rubbings on the walls of my house would be like doing so with the work of a famous calligrapher. What's more, the works of famous calligraphers often come with a price tag which is far too high for someone as unversed as myself; I could not dare hang them upon the wall.

I hadn't expected that the inscriptions on the bricks could ultimately become a book like the Cihai dictionary, with 400 A4 pages and providing plenty of food for thought, twice as thick as any other book. Because I have this book, I can easily understand these inscriptions. You don't have to read them, but if you do, you will immediately expand your knowledge.

From a city planning perspective, there may well never have been a city in history quite as mad as Nanjing in this regard. Everyone knows that the construction of Nanjing's city wall was only semi-completed. When the Yongle Emperor moved the capital to Beijing, the great construction basically stopped. We can learn a lot from the records left upon the bricks, however: the scope of the city wall, and the effort expended in its manufacturing. At the same time, it also provides us with an accurate record of when the bricks were fired and the period in which they were laid. More importantly, the bricks help us to understand how the early years of the Ming dynasty evolved from its rural roots. These very common things make for important historical resources.

To a calligrapher, although the bricks are a product of officialdom, they reflect the best popular calligraphic styles. Whether in seal script, clerical script, regular script, or cursive script, they offer a part of the history of calligraphy that cannot be overlooked. Of course, what we remember most upon looking over them is the string of names of people who once lived. Some are connected to official titles. For example, there is the official Zhang Xu, the scribe Di Zhong, the magistrate Liu Zhijiang, and the chief Jiang Qiyan. Some are simple, straightforward, and common, like the kiln worker Tang Bing, or the brickmaker Yin Tingzhu. Among the names of the 20 kiln workers of Guangxin, about three quarters of them have names that end in numbers, such as Wang Youyi (one), Wang Zhen'er (two), Xu Yingsan (three), Mao Qingsi (four), Zheng Longwu (five), Fang Qianqi (seven), Yi Shaoba (eight), Zheng Congjiu (nine), and Yu Deshi (ten). They are only lacking a "six"; among the names of the Fuzhou kilns, you will find Zhou Renliu and Deng Zhengliu.

If one were writing a historical novel, these names would be quite useful. I can even sense their very breath.

Hexi, 30 July 2008

The Ineffable Xuanwu Lake

According to expert analysis, Nanjing's Xuanwu Lake Park has a hundred years of history. A round number like that is all which is needed to excite people, provoking both celebration and discussion. According to Chinese tradition, bainian ("century") is not a good word at all. It often has hidden connotations, but the excitement around it means we do not pay attention to them.

Experts carefully point out that the reasoning behind saying that Xuanwu Lake Park was the first in China's history is that, during the Qing dynasty, parks were owned by the emperor or by private individuals. The idea of a park that belonged to the common people was unthinkable. In 1909, the Nanyang Industrial Exposition was held in Nanjing. So that visitors could conveniently gaze upon Xuanwu Lake, the Viceroy of Liangjiang opened a passageway in the city wall named Fengrun, which would later become Xuanwu Gate, and thus Xuanwu Lake Park was born.

The word for "public park" in Chinese is gongyuan, with the first character gong meaning public, communal ownership. In a feudal society, such public ownership would be the herald of the future republic. Fortunately, having attended the celebrations, I went home and searched online, discovering that Longsha Park in Qiqihar was in fact older—having been established in either 1904 or 1907, depending on how one defines it. Experts point out that Longsha Park was actually the earliest public park built in the Qing dynasty. It is hard not to feel a little put out for Xuanwu Lake Park, as if it had narrowly missed out on a Guinness World Record.

Whether or not it was the first isn't all that important. What Nanjingers should be proud of are the records of the Capital Plan of 1929. Compared to the metropolises of Europe and America at that time, the amount of area devoted to public parks in Nanjing was clearly greater. With Xuanwu Lake Park and the Sun Yat-sen

Mausoleum Scenic Area, the number of "acres of parkland per capita" was greater than that of Washington, and comparable to New York, Berlin, London, and Paris. In other words, Nanjing was a leader in parkland per capita at the time.

Since I was taking part in the discussion forum, it was hard to escape making a speech. I summoned up the courage to make two points. The first was that I hoped Xuanwu Lake would never become industrial land. Over a decade ago, I ran into an old classmate who was performing a survey of the area. He was enormously proud of himself, having just received a commission from a foreign financial group that was planning to build a world-map themed World Park which would be covered with buildings of all styles, like Window of the World in Shenzhen. At the time, I thought that all had been decided upon, and that Xuanwu Lake would be lost forever. Thankfully, that was not the case.

My second point was that it should become the garden of Nanjing, truly belonging to the people—allowing residents to enjoy it to the full. It would be rather a tragedy for a large public park to be located in the middle of the city solely in order to attract out-of-town visitors, with all concerns only being for other people's money and not a single city resident in sight. It would be like having a great mansion and not living in it, leaving it empty in the hopes of one day charging rent.

Perhaps removing the entry fee would not be a bad idea. Experiences both home and abroad have shown this to be quite effective. The courtyard stands empty and spring passes; the pear blossoms cover the floor, and the door does not open. It is no good having a park with no personality. In the 1930s, during the most prosperous era of the Republic, with the arrival of summer, the gates of Xuanwu Park would be open, not charging for entry. It became a wonderful place to cool off during the summer, and the whole park was filled with the sounds of carousing all through the night. Such a scene makes old Nanjingers pause to think fondly on the city's past.

Hexi, 19 August 2009

Nanjing, Nanjing

Recollections on Prosperity and the Regal Aura of Jinling

Nanjing is the seat of the Jiangsu provincial government. Of all of the famous ancient capitals in the nation, whether we speak of the Four Great Ancient Capitals or the Six Great Ancient Capitals, it has always held pride of place. Jinling has been the seat of kings, the capital of ten dynasties, and has seen the rise and fall of a hundred generations. If you wish to understand Jiangsu and its famous cities, then Nanjing cannot be ignored.

Nanjing's existence owes itself to a number of coincidental factors. Cultural historians have many different theories regarding its birth. It is generally believed that Nanjing was founded during the turbulent Warring States period, in 472 BCE. Nanjing first belonged to the State of Wu, which was defeated by King Goujian of Yue. King Goujian then ordered his advisor Fan Li to build a castle named Yuecheng on land near the State of Chu in order to provide a base of operations from which to attack Chu. Their efforts failed, and not long afterward, the State of Chu defeated the State of Yue. In high spirits, King Wei of Chu arrived in Nanjing, and upon seeing the city's natural geographic advantages, surrounded by mountains and water—the so-called "coiling dragons and crouching tigers"—he couldn't help but feel a sense of dread. In order to suppress the city's regal air, taking the advice of feng shui experts, he buried gold on the rear face of Lion Mountain. Thus, Nanjing came to be known as Jinling—"golden hill".

Nanjing's prosperity has a direct relation to its establishment as the capital of Wu during the Three Kingdoms period. In the large area of the middle and lower reaches of the Yangtze, Nanjing is not the only place suitable for building a capital. Sun Quan did not choose Zhenjiang, where his father and older brother had made their mark in the military. He did not choose Wuchang, the city where he had been crowned emperor and which had stood as his capital for eight years.

A popular folk song at the time said, "I would rather eat the waters of Jianye than eat the fish of Wuchang / I would rather die in Jianye than live in Wuchang." "Jianye" here refers to Nanjing, and "Wuchang" signifies modern-day Ezhou in Hubei Province rather than Wuchang, part of modern-day Wuhan. Ultimately, following the people's will, Nanjing was made the capital of Wu. This decision was the material basis for its prosperity in the Six Dynasties era.

Nanjing's prosperity in the Six Dynasties era is discussed most enthusiastically. To find out what this prosperity actually entailed, we have only classical writings to look through. Since ancient times, countless tomes have been written on Nanjing; anyone looking for famous writings and aphorisms has a cornucopia of differing perspectives awaiting them. To summarize such sources, the majority of descriptions are nostalgic searches for times past, full of sentimentality. For example, Zuo Si's Wu Capital Rhapsody describes the prosperity of Nanjing at the time, saying that if the inhabitants of the city were to flick their sleeves, the dust would cover the sky, and that if they wiped away their sweat, the falling beads would turn the road to mud. The descriptions of literati always tend to be somewhat exaggerated, but they are mostly accurate; they all remember the glory of the past.

The flowers of the Palace of Wu are buried along a desolate path; the kings of Jin have long since been interred. Skimming over historical documents on Nanjing, we can see that there always seem to be gloomy recollections of the flourishing capital. Once sparrows flew before the hall of Wang and Xie, and now the common people shuffle past. This became the timbre of all songs of Nanjing. This clearly cannot be separated from Nanjing's unique history. To be honest, I don't think that you'll find another city in China that provides a clearer outline and framework for the development of Chinese history. Nanjing is an incredible history book. To read this city is to recall the history of China. Nanjing is particularly suitable for visits from men of culture. Traces of the past are everywhere, saturated in the flavor of culture. With every ruin one visits, one is taking part in a serious historical conversation. When it comes to scenery, the mountains and waters of Nanjing are beautiful enough to compete with any city in China. But Nanjing's great advantage is in its history and its culture.

Historically, Nanjing has gone by many different names. Jinling, Shicheng, Moling, Jianye, Jiankang, Jiangning, Baixia, Jiangzhou, Jiqing, Yingtian, Shangyuan, and Tianjing. Each name has countless stories behind it, and each name was changed for its own reasons. Those who bestow a new name upon a city are, naturally, conquerors. There are those who took their throne here and those who lost their empires here. With the changing of dynasties came the changing of names.

Describing the regal air of Jinling, the poet Li Bai put it most plainly: "The land is the residence of kings, and the mountains are crouching tigers and dragons." Such a place, thought Li Bai, must produce emperors. For those who wished to become accomplished in Nanjing, the regal aura of Jinling provided them with an excuse to have courage in their convictions. The subtext was that one had achieved the Mandate of Heaven. In other words: as this place has a regal aura, it means that I do not wish to rebel, but rather to claim the mantle of emperor here means that I am fulfilling the Will of Heaven which I dare not disobey. In the Three Kingdoms period, one important reason that Sun Quan was slow to claim the title of Emperor of Wu was that he felt that he himself was illegitimate. He waited patiently until Cao Pi and Liu Bei had both declared themselves emperor, and only when the time was right, did he establish the State of Wu, declaring himself an emperor, as well.

Compared to ruling the Central Plain, the so-called regal aura of Jinling announced an overt desire for separatism. In the history of China, the Yangtze River Basin has always been under the yoke of the Yellow River Basin, taking orders from the central government of the north. Jinling's regal aura suggests that the Yangtze should take pride in itself, that it should be on equal footing with the Yellow River. For the north, which has the Yellow River at its center, the regal aura of Nanjing is an implicit danger. It is a reminder and a warning.

Under usual circumstances, the northern central government cannot afford to be too lenient with this so-called royal air. Thankfully, in reality, the regal aura of Nanjing does not pose much of a threat to the northern power structure. Although Nanjing is known as the capital of ten dynasties, for most of them, it propped up forces that were on the retreat. It seems that only in the early Ming dynasty and during its short-lived time as the Republican capital could Nanjing give orders to the entire country, exercising its authority as the central government. More often, Nanjing could only govern half the country at most, serving as the site of a government-in-exile. As the Western Jin collapsed, it was the home of the retreating Eastern Jin; when the Ming dynasty fell, Nanjing played host to the short-lived Southern Ming.

Nanjing was the capital of both the Eastern Jin and the Southern Ming, and they were both invaded as the ethnic minorities of the north took control over the Central Plains. In these crucial times, Nanjing's royal aura did not just mean separatism, but the recovery of lost territory and of the nation of the Han people. In these times, Jinling's royal aura became a backbone of Han culture—the last bastion of the Han government. The confrontation between Yangtze culture and Yellow River culture was no more; the two cultures were forced to meld together, having no choice but to integrate. The royal aura of Jinling became the slogan for the unification of the Han people.

Since ancient times, Jinling's royal aura has always been called into question. There have been countless battles fought to defend Nanjing throughout history, and almost none of them have ended in victory for the defenders. This is what Li Shangyin, who spent a number of years in Nanjing, lamented: "Three hundred years have passed as if in a dream. Where are the dragons and tigers of Mount Zhong?" Ever since Sun Hao, the last emperor of Wu, saw his "banners lowered upon the stone walls," the city has been host to ruler after ruler of vanquished nations. Empires have fallen in other places, but no place is as famous as Nanjing for it. It was in Nanjing that Chen Houzhu jumped into a well with his concubine; it was in Nanjing that Li Houzhu wrote his poems. No city is quite as suitable as Nanjing for empires to fall, and no other city has been the site of so much discussion regarding the destruction of nations.

The aura of defeat surrounds the city even more so than its aura of regality. The golden age of the Six Dynasties and the splendor of the Qinhuai River went hand in hand with the downfall of empires. Thus, living in a trance became normal throughout Nanjing's history. In other words, living in the intoxicated dream that Nanjing provided was both a cause and a result of the nation's downfall.

The Ten-Li Qinhuai

The Qinhuai River has been a witness to the history of Nanjing—a living artifact of the legendary splendor of the Six Dynasties. The Qinhuai River is 110km long. It covers seven districts of the Nanjing area, and is divided into the inner and outer river. What we often call the Inner Qinhuai runs from Dongshui Pass through Bailu and Wende Bridges, snaking its way eastward, passing under Wuding and Zhenhuai Bridges, and finally reaching Xishui Pass over a journey of around ten *li* or five kilometers. This stretch of river has been the most prosperous part of Nanjing since antiquity. This scene of bustling prosperity along the ten-*li* Qinhuai has many different names from antiquity, such as the Taoye Ferry, the Wuyi Sunset, or the Changgan Li, but tourists visiting the Qinhuai pay no attention to these separate names. For the common people, these significant cultural symbols of old Nanjing are clearly unimportant. Does the river not carry significant cultural weight?

One cannot speak of Nanjing without speaking of the Qinhuai River, and one cannot speak of the Qinhuai River without speaking of the Confucius Temple. The Confucius Temple is the sole object of interest for many. Rome wasn't built in a day, and neither was the temple. The heart of the Confucius Temple is the Temple of Literature. The Temple of Literature itself is not particularly remarkable; in ancient China, any city that had a place for scholars to pay their respects to Confucius would have a temple of literature. Nanjing's old Temple of Literature was originally nowhere near the bustling Qinhuai with its Six Dynasties splendor; the moment it moved to the riverside, the people's attitude toward it suddenly changed. It was no longer the Temple of Literature (*wenmiao*), but the Temple of Confucius (*kongmiao*). By offhandedly calling it the Master's Temple (*fuzimiao*), its very solemn name was immediately cheapened by the common people.

Among the buildings of the Confucius Temple are the Palace of Learning and the Jiangnan Tribute Hall. The Palace of Learning is also called the Pangong or "School Palace". It was built in the Northern Song dynasty. The Jiangnan Tribute Hall was the largest exam hall in ancient China and was built during the Southern Song dynasty. The biggest feature of the Confucius Temple was its culture and its economy: its culture was that of the imperial exams, and its economy was that of drinking, feasting, and merry making. The story of the Confucius Temple is the story of The Scholars and of Peach Blossom Fan. Clearly, without the exam system, many stories about the Confucius Temple would not exist. Without the exams, there would be no splendor. Without the exams, there would not be the joys and sorrows of meeting and parting.

As the triennial exams approached, a banner would be hung from the mast of a boat that read "By imperial decree, the imperial exams of Jiangnan", and which would sail across the river. And thus, the merriment of the Confucius Temple area would commence. Exam candidates would arrive, examiners would arrive, and a great number of people whose living depended on the exams in some way would arrive along with them. The hospitality industry immediately flourished. Moneyed sons of the rich and penniless scholars would all find places to sleep, eat, and drink. Hotels and taverns of all ranks would rise to the occasion, happily doing business. Sellers of pens, paper, ink, inkstones, classical books, calligraphy, clothing, and assorted goods would come along with fortune tellers, pawnbrokers, people traffickers, and matchmakers: they would all vie for the business of the exam candidates. The exams provided for a great number of people, with a whole service industry springing up around them all at once. The storefronts of the cobbled streets would be open, and under the auspices of the imperial exams, the economy of the Confucius Temple area would bloom like flowers in spring.

The exams happened every three years, and many candidates would have already taken up residence in the surrounding area as early as a year beforehand. There were some who stayed even longer. Since they had failed the previous exams, they thought they might as well take up lodgings on the riverbank, study some more, and prepare for the next attempt. Fail, wait three years, fail again, and try again. The more scholars lined the riverbank, the happier the merchants became. As more of those scholars stayed behind, the merchants became happier still. Rows upon rows of merchants were thoroughly satisfied with the situation, and so were the proprietors of the brothels. The brothels that lined the streets of the Confucius Temple area were a favorite hangout of failed candidates. Beautiful women could soothe their broken hearts, drive them to despair, leave them entranced, and drag them so deep into debauchery that they might never escape.

The literary center of the Confucius Temple was known as "the mystic capital of earthly desires, a paradise of peace". With this sort of glorious reputation, culture was at an all-time low, and appreciation of culture also suffered. At the time, the doors with their beaded curtains and the pleasure boats sailing along the Qinhuai River, lined with beautiful women, would present quite a charming sight. Standing on Wende Bridge, people would meet after dusk, but both sides of the river would be brightly lit by lanterns. Beautifully painted women would come in and out, singing songs and choosing clients, carousing until daybreak. A decorated pleasure boat sails past with carved railings and painted balustrades, its windows covered by silk curtains. It is hard to imagine anything quite so beautiful. The wind blows, bringing the smell of wine, meat, and perfume, and the sound of prosperity and merriment. With scholars spending so long on the banks of the Qinhuai, it was inevitable that their thoughts would turn to romance. Every talented scholar needs a beautiful woman, and when the two meet stories arise. Peach Blossom Fan looks back on the dynasty before it, and thus we have Li Xiangjun's love nest, and also the places where Liu Rushi and Ma Fenglan did their work.

There are blue-green bricks and small roof tiles on the gables and flower-garlanded windows on the temple. All kinds of people lived in the Confucius Temple area. It is worth noting that the unique characteristics of the houses of the area should not be overlooked. Alongside the shops of varying sizes, the riverside houses and painted boats are also very representative of the culture of the Qinhuai River. They are vivid symbols of the Confucius Temple area, forming scenic lines that flow along the banks of the river. The river houses and painted boats came about as a result of the development and growth of the imperial exams, but they did not die alongside the exams. It is because we still have the river houses and painted boats that the Confucius Temple still remains lively despite the collapse of the exam system. Since ancient times, the Confucius Temple by the Qinhuai River has suffered repeated destruction and reconstruction.

Its constant renovation reflects the unyielding spirit of the Nankinese. After all, it is this place that serves as the best witness of the cultural history of Nanjing.

A Strategic Town in the Southeast

As the capital of Jiangsu Province, Nanjing cannot avoid a certain sense of disappointment. Historically, it has been the capital on more than one occasion. The feeling of a capital city is buried deep within the people's hearts. For a long time, Nanjing was the primary strategic town in the southeast, its position unassailable by other settlements. Closer to contemporary times, in the Ming and Qing era, Nanjing came second after the imperial city of Beijing. In the early Qing, Jiangnan was first among the provinces. Nanjing was the location of the governors of Jiangnan, Jiangxi, and Henan, and now acts as deputy for military affairs in the provinces of Jiangsu, Anhui, Jiangxi, and Henan. Moving further into history, it became the residence of the Viceroy of Liangjiang, who governed Jiangsu, Anhui, Jiangxi, and Shanghai, a major position in government of the time.

Jiangsu and Anhui were separated during the reign of the Kangxi Emperor, and the governor of Anhui was stationed in Nanjing for a long period of time. In other words, even though the provinces had been split in two, the officials of Anhui were unwilling to leave the city. It is hard to imagine that the officials in charge of the administration, finances, and affairs of Anhui Province would be allowed to stay in Nanjing for nearly a century, governing the province from afar, but this was the case until 1760, the twenty-fifth year of the reign of the Qianlong Emperor, when they finally moved to Anqing. We can see the huge influence that Nanjing had on Anhui. Many people from Anhui are accustomed to coming to Nanjing to go shopping or being treated in its hospitals, seeing it much in the way that people from Suzhou, Wuxi, and Changzhou would see Shanghai. The feelings of acknowledgement that history shapes are not formed within a day or two, and once they have formed, they do not easily change.

Nanjing's important position among the cities of China is not solely due to its position as the ancient capital of ten dynasties or even its regal aura. Emperor Wen of Sui once ordered the whole city razed to the ground, setting all of the buildings of the Six Dynasties to the torch. This was the most disastrous blow in all of Nanjing's history. There have been a number of similar massacres, but whatever wounds have been sustained, this city has always been able to recover within a short space of time. Nanjing's importance lies in the fact that, no matter in what era, no matter whether the country was divided or united, it has always been foremost among the strategic towns of the southeast. The provinces of the southeast have, historically, been the economic lifeblood of the northern central government. If you want a stable income, then stability and prosperity in the southeastern provinces is extremely important. It was the usual practice for the central government to send major officials to take up positions in Nanjing; through Nanjing, it would exercise its power over the southeastern provinces.

Compared to its position throughout history, Nanjing has seen a clear decline in the modern era. A major reason for this was the rapid development of Shanghai. If you look at a map, you will understand. Shanghai and Nanjing are too close together. Under normal circumstances, whether it is the provinces of the southeast, or the East China Region as people are more used to calling it nowadays, only one city can be representative. If one grows, the other must shrink. If one undergoes rapid development, the other must slow down. Over a century ago, the International Settlement was founded in Shanghai. At the time, it was merely a small county town under the jurisdiction of Songjiang in Jiangsu Province, nowhere near the level of Nanjing. Because Nanjing was the seat of the Viceroy of Liangjiang, the province-level government was moved entirely to Suzhou. What Shanghai did could not be controlled by the county magistrate. First, he invited the prefectural magistrate of Songjiang to step in; the prefectural magistrate's efforts were also futile. Above him was the provincial inspector general. None of these men could settle the matter. Eventually, they asked the viceroy.

Circumstances changed rapidly. The International Settlement meant the arrival of foreigners, and so Shanghai became westernized, with the Chinese government having no control over its affairs at any level. With Shanghai's surprisingly rapid development, it became a colossus, an undeniable international metropolis. By comparison, Nanjing, which was also undergoing rapid development, was left in the dust. Nowadays, the only control Nanjing has over Shanghai is as part of its PLA military region. This gives Nanjingers a measure of comfort. Nanjing, which has always thought so much of itself, has had no choice but to obediently surrender its throne to Shanghai as a strategic town of the southeast.

Nanjing is a very tolerant city. Nanjingers are polite, non-xenophobic, and used to accepting the commandments of fate. Now, Nanjing is still the biggest city in the southeast outside Shanghai. It has not been the location of the Jiangsu regional government for all that long. Before Nanjing was declared the capital of the Republic in 1927, the provincial capital had always been Suzhou, before moving on to Zhenjiang. After the People's Republic was established in 1949, Jiangsu was divided into two administrative offices, north and south. Nanjing was a municipality of the central people's government until 1953, when the two offices of north and south Jiangsu were merged. Nanjing was stripped of its title as a centrally administered municipality and became the capital of Jiangsu Province.

Echoes of the Republic

Even now, passing through the streets and alleys of Nanjing, you can still see traces of the Republic, completely inadvertently. People will tell you that this was the headquarters of the Guomindang and that the assassination attempt on Wang Jingwei was made here. It is a beautiful golden-colored building with a high bell tower. If we go further back in time, we find that it was the residence of Zhang Xun, the Braid General. When the Xinhai Revolution broke out, Zhang Xun escaped. It was here that representatives of the 18 provinces of the nation met to declare the establishment of the Republic of China, appointing Sun Yat-sen as provisional president. This is where the Republic of China was born, where the first page of modern Chinese history was turned. At the same time, this was also where the Senate of the Republic of China was provisionally established—it being the first democratic institution in Chinese history.

There are so many places in Nanjing where one could erect monuments. In insignificant city blocks, every street has a story, and every old building has something to say. Nanjing is like a living history museum. No matter where you go, you will bump into the incidents and legends of the past. Obviously, much of what you see is the legacy of the Republic. There are two reasons for this. The primary reason is that the Republic is closest in time to our own. Because the old buildings of the Six Dynasties, Ming, and Qing dynasties are so distant, the likelihood of them suffering from some disaster or another is high. Considering the countless disasters that have occurred in Nanjing, and the fact that many of the old buildings were made from wood, it is no surprise that many of the remnants of other ages no longer exist. The other reason is that a huge amount of construction went on during the Republican era. The old city was transformed, and many valuable old buildings were torn down, with many historical remains destroyed. As they say, a skinny camel is still bigger than a horse—and Nanjing still has more remnants from the Republican era than any other city in China.

Nanjing was the first city in China built according to international standards, using a comprehensive city zoning plan. In the 1930s, Nanjing was the location of the Nationalist government and the site of a large-scale construction project. Not only did it benefit Nanjing, but it also attracted vast amounts of investment. Many years ago, when it came to city planning, green spaces, and public works, Nanjing was a subject of much admiration. This was an extremely rare opportunity for urban development. With the great efforts of engineers and public works officials in the Nationalist government—who adopted American and European city design on the macro-level while retaining traditional Chinese style on the micro-level—Nanjing became "the most beautiful, tidy, and meticulously planned city in China," as Harvard University's Professor William C. Kirby wrote. Another American, Israel Epstein, praised Nanjing's city planning before the outbreak of the Second World War. He described Nanjing as a capital city with a Prussian flavor, on a level with the finest cities of Europe and America.

The echoes of the Republic that we see around us today are the remnants of a glorious history. Although it was seriously damaged by war, the damage sustained by Nanjing was comparable to that of London or Berlin. Compared to Tokyo, many more buildings survived intact. As a result of this, Nanjing still makes for a fine representation of the Republican era today. Of course, along with the old buildings of the Republic, it is worth mentioning the city's foliage. A great many trees were planted in the Republican era to be enjoyed by their descendants. For greenery, Nanjing is hard to beat. In our modern times, where skyscrapers are everywhere, the lush greenery and old Republican buildings are the most beautiful thing about Nanjing.

One Day's Touring is Not Enough

For tourists, a little preparation is in order before seeing the sights of Nanjing. Because it is so rich in tourist attractions, this is not a place where you can simply ride past the scenic sites. As well as the beautiful landscape of mountains and rivers, there are also the relics of the distant past. It is rare for a city to have both mountains and rivers; to interweave them so organically with history and culture as Nanjing does is rarer still. To tell the truth, even if you had plenty of time and you had prepared meticulously, and even if you had a fantastic tour guide, you would still only be able to scratch Nanjing's surface.

Nanjing's mountains are not particularly tall. The tallest of them is Purple Mountain (zijin shan), also called Mount Zhong (zhong shan or "Bell Mountain"). Mount Zhong is 448 meters high. It runs from east to west like a sword splitting Nanjing in two. The imposing Mount Zhong is its handle, with the pieces of its fractured blade stuck in the mud formed by a series of smaller foothills. These foothills have their own names, like Mount Fugui ("Riches and Honor"), Mount Jiuhua ("Nine Flowers"), Mount Jilong ("Chicken Cage"), Gulou Hill ("Drum Tower"), Mount Wutai ("Five Terraces"), and Mount Qingliang ("Cooling"). On the westernmost summit of Mount Qingliang is the famous City of Stone. Before the Tang dynasty, this faced the rolling waters of the Yangtze, a place where countless heroes would look out upon the landscape and sigh.

The small foothills are not to be overlooked. They are the backbone of Nanjing, each one famous in its own right, each with its own beautiful views. When people speak of the flourishing and distinguished cultural atmosphere of Nanjing, it is this place of which they speak. Nanjing is home to the world's longest and best-preserved

Two

The eventual success of the Xinhai Revolution went completely beyond all expectations. According to the revolutionaries' intentions, the revolution should have started on the distant periphery before making its way inward, finally reaching the Qing monarchy. But the facts prove that it is not enough to start an uprising on the periphery; it will easily be snuffed out. As everyone knows, the Wuchang Uprising was more like a minor incident that inadvertently started the entire revolution. Revolutionary partisans were left in the lurch, and they ultimately had no choice but to drag Li Yuanhong out from beneath his bed and crown him the leader of the revolution, ultimately to no end.

Thus, to some extent, the success of the Xinhai Revolution was not due to the strength of the revolutionaries, but to the weakness of the Qing regime. Cities fell like dominoes, and with the Qing empire fading on its deathbed, many had no choice but to hoist their banners, issue announcements, and post up leaflets. The moment they could circulate their announcements, it was settled: they were liberated. The provincial inspectors-general of the empire immediately became provincial governors of the republic, the highest authorities in their respective provinces. Banners went up along city walls and revolution became a lively game; liberation became fashion. But, fundamentally, the old remained. There were still bureaucrats, and the common people were still the common people. The county magistrates changed one character in the titles—going from zhixian to xianzhishi—and were essentially the same as before.

At the time, Nanjing took on a particular significance: the whole country was in chaos, the battlefield constantly shifting. Yuan Shikai sent a telegram to Zhang Xun, who was responsible for defending the city: "Our reign depends upon the southeast." His meaning was clear: As long as Nanjing stood, the partisans could not succeed in their revolution. As long as Nanjing stood, even though the cities along the Shanghai-Nanjing Railway had been taken and the other provinces had already declared independence, the Qing army could still recover. At that moment, the revolution could not be stopped, but Yuan Shikai had victory for the counter-revolution within his grasp. His Beiyang Army had their hands around the throat of the Revolutionary Army. They had Wuchang surrounded by their artillery; he needed only give the word for the three cities of Wuhan (Wuchang, Hankou, and Hanyang) to be retaken.

The revolutionaries also saw that the crux of the matter was clear: Wuchang, the center of the Xinhai Revolution, could not be defended. The fact was that the Revolutionary Army, headed by Huang Xing, was no match for the Beiyang Army. The only way to get Wuhan out of danger was to immediately take Nanjing: "If Nanjing does not fall within a day, Wuhan will be in danger. If Wuhan cannot stand, then the Yangtze region cannot be defended. The Manchu barbarians shall return to glory, and the fall of the motherland approaches!" For a moment, Nanjing became absolutely crucial. Thus, the Jiangsu-Zhejiang army was formed, and the strength of the revolution and the counter-revolution would be decided here.

Though it was a decisive battle, compared to the Warlord Era, the war against Japan, or the Civil War, the capture of Nanjing was not particularly large, and its casualties were also limited. In the end, it was still a decisive battle over the changing of dynasties. In one stroke, thousands of years of feudal rule over China were ended. The taking of Nanjing meant that fate, on the brink of changing, was once more on the side of the revolution. Clearly, the Wuchang Uprising had stunned the country, and the taking of Nanjing formally signaled the end of the Qing dynasty.

The laid-back Nankinese could not imagine such a result. They could not imagine that their city, in all of China's tumultuous history, could play such a crucial role. The Revolutionary Army attacked from multiple directions, and the Nankinese, always happy to watch a chaotic scene unfold, were spectators once more. Once the sound of artillery and sporadic gunfire had ceased, curious Nanjingers wandered the streets. Among the famous leaders of the revolution or any of its prominent figures, you will not find a single native Nankinese. When it comes to revolutionary history, the Nankinese can only feel somewhat ashamed.

Three

The Xinhai Revolution is a confusing concept. It can mean the Wuchang Uprising, and it can also refer to a series of violent incidents in the cities. Perhaps it was from that moment that "revolution" became a commonly used, positive word, and "counter-revolution" fundamentally became a term of abuse. The conclusion is usually very simple. The textbooks instill us with the standard answers to questions which appear endlessly in exams; as a result, students know the Xinhai Revolution inside and out. First, they overthrew thousands of years of feudal rule; next, Yuan Shikai seized control of the achievements of the revolution. All of my historical knowledge comes from light reading. From an expert perspective, this is rather unorthodox. For years, I have been a lover of unofficial history, reading history from unorthodox sources, understanding the past from the essays and notes of our forebears. Re-examining our understanding may bring up some new and differing viewpoints on what kind of place Nanjing was at the time of the Xinhai Revolution, however, and what the opinions of its people were at the time.

When Nanjing was finally liberated, its people began anew, happily cutting off each other's pigtails. Everyone suddenly discovered that there was nothing serious about cutting off the queue. It was as if fighting for revolution had a different price and a different conclusion at different stages. The pigtail that the Qing dynasty had imposed upon the Han people had come to be associated with the head. To cut off one's pigtail meant ending one's life. Then the situation had changed, and even Yuan Shikai kept up with the times. Cutting off one's pigtail was as simple as buying a pair of scissors. Times changed, and cutting off the pigtail was no longer an issue; keeping the pigtail became the issue.

Observers' writings suggest that the Nankinese were not sufficiently deferential at the time of the Xinhai Revolution, and perhaps that was true. Nanjing was the residence of the Viceroy of Liangjiang, who administered what was then the most prosperous area in the nation, controlling the economic lifeblood of the Qing government, which had always been seen as vitally important by the royal court. But Nanjingers didn't care about that at all. They didn't really care what type of political status their city had. They greeted the revolution with a thoroughly calm and realistic attitude. This was the attitude not only of the common people, but also of the rank-and-file officials. While Nanjing was under artillery fire, save for the few high-level officials who fled with their tails between their legs, the majority of officials simply watched the changes happen dispassionately. They did not plan to get directly involved with the revolution, and nor did they prepare to sacrifice their lives in loyalty to the Qing.

Li Ruiqing was headmaster of the Liangjiang Normal School at the time, which was Nanjing's highest educational establishment. Looking at the attitude of a cultured man such as Li Ruiqing can help us to get a picture of the city at the time. He was one of the earliest cultured officials to be involved in higher education in China, once visiting Japan to observe their educational system. After the Hundred Days Reform, modernizers found themselves at a disadvantage. The conservatives were very much in power, but after the end of the exam system, the abandonment of classical schooling, the rise of the new educational system, and the suspension of old-style private schooling, teacher training had become an unstoppable trend. University students at the time clearly weren't as radical as they are today, or even as politically conscious as the students of the later May Fourth movement. Although Li had students in the Revolutionary Army like Chen Zhongfan, who would later become a noted professor, he was only a mess cook, and they were so few in number that they were insignificant.

At the time, the radical students still only quietly cut off their pigtails. As the head of a school of a university, Li Ruiqing neither encouraged nor hindered his students; he let them do as they wished. While the Revolutionary Army fired their cannons, his only demand was that the students still show up to class on time. To be an earnest student while the country was in chaos is no mean feat. He was rather stubborn, and something of a bookworm, but what he did was not easy. Zhang Renjun, the Viceroy of Liangjiang at the time, was very moved, and he admired his calm, collected approach, considering him a rare talent, someone who "could be trusted with one's life." He was immediately promoted and appointed as a second-rank in the local government of Jiangning. This was quite a high-ranking post, equivalent to a deputy governor or a head of the provincial department of civil affairs nowadays.

Having benefited from the chaos, Li Ruiqing was unable to accomplish much. The situation could not be changed, and very soon afterward, Zhang Renjun fled, as did Zhang Xun, the "Braid General". American and Japanese consuls urged Li to hide away on foreign warships, but he was still a natural scholar. He refused to abscond with funds and run, and instead "shut the doors to the state provincial warehouse, where there was amassed huge amounts of gold," waiting calmly for the Revolutionary Army to arrive. On the day that Nanjing was taken, he was well-dressed and sat upright in his classroom, blankly watching the arrival of the Revolutionary Army.

The revolutionaries did not make things difficult for Li Ruiqing. Undoubtedly, this scholar was not a particularly high-profile target. Having relinquished his official position, he returned to school. News spread throughout the faculty, and he was welcomed back to be put in charge of the college. Unfortunately, Li did not want to cooperate with the new government. Ordered to make a list of school properties and hand it over to the bureaucracy, he wrote a letter to the governor and was dismissed from his post. Seeing his students impoverished and ragged, he was heartbroken. He sold his own horse and carriage, shared the proceeds among his students, and left, his hands clean.

Four

Due to the attack on Nanjing by the Jiangsu-Zhejiang army, anyone who came to govern the city soon became the topic of debate. Evaluation of such things can lead to stubborn disagreement. The revolution gave partisans the chance to be on equal footing. The young armed officers all thought themselves worthy of leadership for their deeds. The revolution had not yet achieved success, and its heroes began to fight and scheme amongst themselves, struggling for power. After Nanjing was taken, revolutionaries sprang up all over the place, and speculators also appeared promptly. Even though the revolution had not ended, and Wuchang was still in a state of emergency, Nanjing was already just like a bureaucracy. Wu Yuzhang—a member of the Tongmenghui who represented the military government in Sichuan—hurried to Nanjing, where the recently-established Provisional Government of the Republic of China had already handed out all its titles. There were no ministerial positions, nor deputy ministerial positions, and old friends could only apologize, offering him a position as a bureau chief.

From the moment of its liberation, Nanjing became a seat of power. Being unable to use someone as talented as Li Ruiqing was a great regret of the newly-formed Republican government. One could call it a result of Li's stubbornness or his virtue, or simply a result of the fact that the new government did not have the time to go searching for talents. The new government had much to do and many important discussions to undertake. Because of its unique position in Chinese history, Nanjing easily gained authority in the Xinhai Revolution. Just as Li Yuanhong had accidentally become a leader of the revolution, the fact that Nanjing—the ancient capital of the Six Dynasties, with its regal aura—became the seat of power for the Republican government was only to be expected, considering the pressure of the various powers it was under.

At the time of the Wuchang Uprising, the Revolutionary Army's banner was the 18-star flag. It still had something of an association with the Han people, for expelling the Manchus and restoring China. The 18 stars represented the 18 Han provinces. The national flag eventually settled on by the Nationalist government in Nanjing was the five-color flag representing the five races: Han, Manchu, Mongol, Hui, and Tibetan. This five-color flag should not be overlooked. Two months elapsed between the Wuchang Uprising and the taking of Shanghai, from Han independence to the peaceful coexistence of five races. The Xinhai Revolution had taken a big step forward. The notion of "China" at the time was that of former Qing territory. This was no longer a revolution of the Han people, but a revolution for all Chinese.

Nanjing quietly changed the character of the revolution. We can see from its conclusion that it still had a fundamental weakness, and it was this weakness that led to Yuan Shikai seizing the title of president. However, sometimes compromise is not a bad thing. Concession is also not without significance. Compromise and concession can allow us to reach a common understanding for the best conclusion. This conclusion was the abolition of the monarchy, opposition to racial separatism, and putting a stop to confrontation between the north and the south. From the moment it was free, Nanjing took on the duty of leadership and of mediation. The most important contribution of the Xinhai Revolution was that it satisfied the demands of many different powers, finding a point of equilibrium for the future and a plan for everyone. During the Xinhai Revolution, Nanjing was the site of the first democracy in Chinese history. It was disordered, full of shameful scheming and contemptuous trickery. But, in the end, it was still on the up. Although democracy at the time of the Xinhai Revolution was still in its early stages, it was one of the most beautiful periods in the history of modern China. In the years that followed, its methods of peaceful discussion and consideration of the popular will in order to lead the nation would be completely replaced by violent revolution.

On December 14, 1911, the National Assembly convened in Nanjing. After endless dispute over whether Huang Xing or Li Yuanhong should be appointed president, it was discovered that Yuan Shikai also approved of republicanism. Immediately, the elections were postponed, and the seat was reserved for Yuan Shikai for when he chose to switch sides. Obviously, Yuan Shikai, still in the enemy camp, was the first choice for president. Huang Xing believed this to be true, as did both Li Hongyuan and Sun Yat-sen. On December 25th, Sun Yat-sen returned to Shanghai from Marseilles, France. Due to his prestige, he received great support from revolutionary groups and achieved the approval of both the constitutionalists and the old guard. It was unanimously believed that he would make for the best interim president before Yuan Shikai finally switched sides. As a result, from that moment on, the word "interim" was appended to Sun Yat-sen's title as president.

In other words, Yuan Shikai's ultimate formal ascension to the role of president cannot be explained simply as a case of seizing power. Nor can it be described as a weakness of Nanjing, as the move represented popular sentiment at the time. In truth, whether Nanjing was right to ultimately choose Yuan Shikai during the Xinhai Revolution is irrelevant. It was, in the end, absolutely in respect for the popular will. The Duke of Zhou feared slander and gossip; Wang Mang was deferential before he usurped the throne. It was Yuan Shikai who let the public down; it was Yuan Shikai who spoiled everything. If he had died not long after his election, then perhaps he would be immortalized in history.